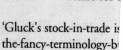 

About the Author

Malcolm Gluck is the busiest wine writer there is. He is wine correspondent of the *Guardian* where his weekly column, *Superplonk*, has run for six years in the newspaper's Saturday magazine. He writes a monthly column in the *Scottish Sunday Post*, has a weekly wine column in the *Sunday Express*, and is consultant wine editor of *Sainsbury's Magazine*, 1994's Magazine of the Year.

He is preparing for BBC 2 a series of TV programmes on wine to be broadcast during autumn 1996. He also finds time to deal with a voluminous post bag and to play with his two young children.

He dislikes oysters, neckties and stuffy, overbearing wine critics who 'put themselves above the interests of the readers they serve'.

Gluck on High 1996

Malcolm Gluck

CORONET BOOKS
Hodder and Stoughton

British Library Cataloguing in Publication Data

Gluck, Malcolm
Gluck on High. – 1996
I. Title
641.22

ISBN 0 340 65418 X

Typeset by Palimpsest Book Production Limited,
Polmont, Stirlingshire
Printed and bound in Great Britain by
Mackays of Chatham PLC, Chatham, Kent

Hodder and Stoughton
A division of Hodder Headline PLC
338 Euston Road
London NW1 3BH

To Bill Galley, who let me in

CONTENTS

INTRODUCTION

There have been many revolutions connected with the world of wine over the past twenty years but one of the most significant is the least appreciated. It is to do with women. Women in wine is unique among revolutions for surely it is the only one in history in which its supporters cry 'Down with it!' More and more drinkers in this country, whether they know it or not, are downing wines in which women have had a strong say. Women are a subject I know a little about. I am married to one.

To begin with, there is an increasing number of women who now buy wine professionally. These women work for the major high street wine retailers, the supermarkets and, increasingly, wine merchants. The number of women making wine has also increased dramatically over the past five years (though men, world-wide, dominate oenology). Added to this is the fact that women, through their enthusiastic devotion to white wine, last year for the first time in recorded history pushed beer off the top of the list of Britain's favourite alcoholic drinks. Women also, so my publisher tells me, buy more than their fair share of this book. Lastly, and very far from leastly, there is that spicy new addition to the world of wine, the 1990s female wine critic who, following the lead of Mrs Pamela Vandyke-Price in the 1970s, now occupies an unprecedented and influential position. Men used to be the unchallenged high priests of wine criticism. Even the early TV cook Fanny Craddock (now, sadly, late) deferred to her Johnnie on matters vinous, but with the new crew, the glam Ms Jilly Goolden and the glabrous Mr Oz Clarke, there is, amongst all that polish and no spit, a feeling that it is the woman who wears the trousers. And, in the right circumstances, sheds them – as Jancis Robinson has revealed. The publication of the frequency statistics of Ms Robinson's marital sex-life, in a respectable Sunday newspaper supplement, has now put the wine critic on a par with the pop star and the chat show host. Mr Hugh Johnson, that mould-breaker of the sixties, is, surely, no longer on top.

Women are not, of course, a complete novelty in the business. Several Victoria Wine shops were managed by women from the period around the First World War. A certain, and very saintly, Miss Butterfield worked at the Ealing Mall branch for forty-eight years and never once, so it is said, touched alcohol.

This is hardly the style of the modern woman in wine. At the annual South African wine tasting last year I saw Somerfield's Angela Mount put her lips to 300 different wines and judge them wheat or chaff. All in a day's sniff, swill and spit. She certainly calls the shots in her otherwise all-male department but has yet, as far as I know, to go as far as Ms Robinson and blab to the media. (The latter paragon, however, can surely be excused a few lapses of taste after spending five years leading the team which beavered away to compile the splendidly encyclopaedic *Oxford Companion to Wine* – £30 at all bookshops with reinforced shelves.)

Why are women going into wine? Natural talent. According to Ann-Marie Wasley, one of two women in charge of the wine-making operations at the big Renmano Winery in South Australia, women are 'more aware of taste and smell than men'. Richard Wheeler, of the Colchester wine merchants Lay & Wheeler, is happy to go along with this. 'My own wife,' he told me, 'has a perception of taste which sometimes puts me to shame.' Claire Gordon-Brown, who used to buy Sainsbury's champagnes (she now concentrates on product development for the department after producing two children with a third on the way), considers that the detail in a buyer's job is particularly well suited to a woman's temperament. 'There is such a mass of figures involved, sheer finicky detail, when you contemplate buying a wine, organising shipping, and getting it into 300 stores that many men find it daunting and, frankly, tedious. I think women are good at this sort of detail.' It is interesting here to consider these modern-day wine retailing logistics set beside the old boy way of dealing with suppliers which is at the heart of the male-dominated trade of wine merchanting. Men are appalling sentimentalists in their relationships with other men, which most suppliers are, and therefore much more likely to maintain such relationships in spite of the quality or value of the product in the bottle. Women are capable not only of greater objectivity than most men when it comes to judging a wine and to reviewing the integrity of that judgement over years, but of more resolutely responding to the duty they have to their customers when it conflicts with their feelings for their suppliers.

It is the supermarkets which sell the great majority of the wine sold in this country and they have led the wider recruitment of women as wine buyers. The high street wine chains are following suit. Wine retailers are female organisations, whatever the sex of their owners and highest management, because of their need to respond immediately to customers' needs. A willingness to listen is a feminine characteristic not a masculine one.

Liz Robertson (Safeway), Angela Mount (Somerfield), Liz Aked (Spar) and Arabella Woodrow (Co-op Wholesale Society) are all women running wine-buying departments. Between them they work with six buying colleagues and the only women are all Ms Robertson's – Sarah Kynoch, Piarina Hennessy, and Julie Marshall (who joined Safeway from Sainsbury's this past summer). The wine and spirits buying manager for the Co-op Retail Society is Christine Sandys. Kwik Save's most influential member is consultant Angela Muir. Marks & Spencer's Jane Kay is 50 per cent of the department and of Tesco's six buyers, under a male department head, five are women (Janet Lee, Anne-Marie Bostock, Judith Candy, Sara Marsay and Pippa Rogers). At Sainsbury's there are six wine buyers and one is a woman (Louise Perry). Waitrose, too, can muster just one woman, Dee Blackstock, in its five-strong department, but has

Jane Turner as managing director of its mail order subsidiary
Findlater Mackie Todd (albeit a non-buying role). Only Asda,
Budgens, Littlewoods and Morrisons are resolutely all-male.

Among wine shops Victoria Wine leads with three women
buyers (Rosemary Neal, Joanne Convert, Geraldine Jago) out
of a department of five. Thresher had, until earlier this year, Jo
Standen (from a department of four) but she is now a marketing
manager and no longer buying. Oddbins' four buyers are all
men although PR manager Katie MacAuley is buying some
wine for the new fine wine shops the chain has launched and
tells me that the company is 'trying to move towards a situation
where we have either a manager or an under-manager who is
female in every branch'. Booths, Unwins, Davisons and Fullers
employ only male wine buyers. Majestic has Debbie Worton
as marketing director and among its three buyers one, Nicky
Thompson, is a woman.

When it comes to wine merchants the revolution has been
slower to catch on but solid gains have been made. Men go into
wine merchanting for much the same reason they join the army
– to get away from women – so women buyers are not thick
on the ground. Lady Bute runs Bute Wines, and there is Helen
Verdcourt Wines, and there are several wine merchants and
importers with women employees in executive but non-buying
positions, but Yapp Sisters does not, yet, exist. Gabrielle Shaw,
who was buying director of Corney & Barrow for some years,
was a significant female presence but she is no longer at the
royal wine merchants. There is, however, Gillian Reynolds of
The Hermitage, Liz Berry of La Vigneronne, Margaret Harvey
of Fine Wines of New Zealand, Sarah Morphew of Barrel
Selection, Fiona Bacon and Melanie Daniel at Adnams, Jane
Skilton of Morris & Verdin, Pippa Wood of Lay & Wheeler,
Susan Anderson of Howells of Bristol and Fiona Roberts of
Forth Wines in Kinross who says that amongst all the men at
a trade tasting in Scotland she 'sticks out like a pork chop at a
Jewish wedding'. Ms Roberts also has no doubts of the merits
of women wine buyers. 'Women can be a lot more wily than

men in negotiating. Men have a game plan and they stick to it,' she told me, one of thirty women, out of a total of 189, who as a Master of Wine can append MW to her name. (Ms Roberts is the only MW I know who has corked ears. The first time I met her she was wearing earrings made from a pair.)

Master of Wine is a qualification women are studying to acquire in significant numbers. 'More and more women are coming on to our educational programmes than ever before,' says John Casson of the Institute of Masters of Wine. During the 1970s 3 women qualified for Mastership during the whole decade among 33 men. The eighties saw 11 women qualify and 26 men and during the 1990s 16 women and 47 men have qualified. On the basis of what one senior woman MW told me it is men who need educating more. 'Chilean, South African and Australian suppliers are appalling chauvinists,' she said. 'I once had to ask a male colleague to organise a meeting at which he repeated everything I had said the day before to a Cape wine-maker because the South African man simply couldn't accept a woman's word.'

Safeway's Liz Robertson points out that the women-in-wine phenomenon is a reflection of the way society has shifted. 'You'd find the same revolution in law, wouldn't you? Women are doing jobs they weren't doing thirty-five years ago,' she told me. 'I wouldn't pretend, however, that women can do better than men. We're certainly very different, though, to a traditional man in a traditional wine merchant's.'

Was this difference, whatever it is, the reason why Victoria Wine was partial to women managers all those years ago? No one is alive who can tell me. Which is a pity since it is thanks to William Winch Hughes and his founding of Victoria Wine in 1865 that the modern wine retailing revolution began. Hughes was the first to recognise that wine merchants did not cater for the man and woman in the street and he started the first wine shops which did.

If he was alive and sipping today he would be captivated to discover how far shops like Oddbins, Wine Rack, Bottoms Up and the new Victoria Wine Cellars have taken his ideas and he would, I am quite sure, scamper down the wine aisles of any supermarket with a delighted grin on his face. I don't suppose he would care one whit about the sex of the professional buyers of the bottles. He would be pleased enough to partake so cheaply of the fruits of their labours.

I cannot tell you how many of the wines in this book have been made by or bought by a woman. I have to confess I don't much care. Gender is not a consideration when I rate a wine or write about it – though having said that I was keen to interview Mandy Jones last year on the grounds that as an Australian woman making wine in so chauvinist and fuddy-duddy an area as the Premieres Cotes de Bordeaux, at the Norwegian-owned Chateau Carsin, she might provide some amusing insights. She did. 'Goodness,' said the locals when she first turned up at the vineyard. 'Do you know something about making wine? Do they have vines in Australia?' Having seen Ms Jones at work my impression is that her provenance was of such exotic fascination that it took precedence over her gender. It will, of course, only take one small mistake on her part for this order to be reversed; if she overfines her Bordeaux Blanc or messes with the wrong yeast they'll all say, the way we men do, 'Well, she's a woman – what do you expect?' not 'That's an Aussie for you '.

An interesting consideration here is whether there is any significance in the fact that the increase of women in wine is coincidental with the dramatic rise in the overall quality of wine over the past fifteen years along with a matching increase in its popularity (from a nation which consumed 288 million bottles of wine in 1979 we progressed to downing 816 million in 1993, and last year that figure was bigger but by how much I don't yet know). It was obvious many decades ago that at some point the intelligent woman would revolt at the male culture of the pub; hence the creation of the wine bar. But nowadays wine is a natural companion to food, not just gossip around a bar table, and this, surely, is the biggest reason that wine is now so popular in Britain and why we have so many wine shops, wine books, and wine and food commentators.

Where would I be without women? I drink to women every time I raise a glass. And I raise a glass many times a day.

How this Guide Works

Each retailer in this Guide is separately listed alphabetically. Each has its own introduction with the wines logically arranged by country of origin, red and white (including roses). Each wine's name is as printed on its label.

Each wine is rated on points out of 20. In practice, wines scoring less than 10 points are not included although sometimes, because a particular bottle has really got up my nostrils and scored so lamentably that I feel readers might be amused by its inclusion, I put in a low-pointer. Last year I wrote that over the past five years this miserable vinous underclass had assaulted my palate in steadily decreasing numbers and that the rise in the overall quality of wines was reflected in the rating figures. This year, I must make that six years. Higher ratings appear more frequently, but not necessarily higher prices. I have been forced, in the interests of fair ratings, to tack on a further half-point, such has been the increase in the general quality of fruit without the usual concomitant upping of prices.

I continue to be the only wine writer who genuinely rates wines on a value-for-money basis (the only one, in all likelihood, who even thinks in such terms). I expect expensive wines to be good but I do not always expect good wines to be expensive. Thus, a brilliant £10 bottle may not offer better value than a £3 wine because, although the pricier wine is more impressive it is not, in my eyes, anywhere near three times as impressive. I am increasingly disappointed by wines costing over £10 a bottle and this goes double for those costing over £20.

The full scoring system, from my initial tasting and scoring point of view, works as follows:

20 Is outstanding and faultless in all departments: smell, taste and finish in the throat. Worth the price, even if you have to take out a second mortgage.

19 A superb wine. Almost perfect.

18 An excellent wine of clear complexity but lacking the sublime finesse for the top, yet fabulously good value.

17 An exciting, well-made wine at an affordable price.

16 Very good wine indeed. Good enough for *any* dinner party. Not expensive.

15 For the money, a great mouthful with real style.

14 The top end of everyday drinking wine. Well-made and to be seriously recommended at the price.

13 Good wine, not badly made. Not great, but very drinkable.

12 Everyday drinking wine at a sensible price.

11 Drinkable, but not a wine to dwell on.

10 Average wine (at a low price), yet still a passable mouthful. Also, wines which are expensive and, though drinkable, do not justify their high price.

9 Cheap plonk. Acceptable for parties in dustbin-sized dispensers.

8 Rough stuff. Feeble value.

7 Good for pickling onions.

6 Hardly drinkable except to quench desperate thirsts on an icy night by a raging bonfire.

5 Wine with all its defects and mass manufacturing methods showing.

4 Not good at any price.

3 A palate polluter and barely drinkable.

2 Rat poison. Not to be recommended to anyone, even winos.

1 Beyond the pale. Awful. Even Lucretia Borgia wouldn't serve it.

From your viewpoint, the wine buyer's, the rating system can be compressed like this:

10, 11   Nothing nasty but equally nothing worth shouting from the rooftops. Drinkable but not exciting.

12, 13   Above average, interestingly made. A bargain taste.

14,15,16   This is the exceptional stuff, from the very good to the brilliant.

17, 18   Really terrific wine worthy of individual acclaim. The sort of wine you can decant and serve to ignorant snobs who'll think it famous even when it is no such thing. Often a bargain price.

19,20   Overwhelmingly marvellous. Wine which cannot be faulted, providing an experience never to be forgotten.

Prices

I cannot guarantee the price of any wine in this Guide for all the usual trite reasons: inflation, economic conditions overseas, the narrow margins on some wines making it difficult to maintain consistent prices for very long and, of course, the existence of those freebooters at the Exchequer who are liable to up taxes which the retailers cannot help but pass on to the consumer. To get around this problem a price banding code is assigned to each wine:

Price Band

1	2	3	4
A Under £2.50	B £2.50 – £3.50	C £3.50 – £5	D £5 – £7

5	6	7	8
E £7 – £10	F £10 – £13	G £13 – £20	H Over £20

This year, all wines costing under £5 (i.e. A–C) have their price band set against a black background.

STOP PRESS!

Although this is the most thoroughly researched and up-to-date wine guide available, some retailers introduce a few Christmas wines just as this book is going to press. It has always irritated me that these wines, in the past, have escaped my net. But no longer! Thanks to a bend-over-backwards publisher and a printer of equally untypical flexibility you will find a Stop Press section at the end of this book. Here are the last minute bottles – wines I tasted only after the bulk of this book was already printed.

Acknowledgements

I would like to acknowledge the fact that without the help of Linda Peskin I would be unable to put this book together; without Felicity Rubinstein and Sarah Lutyens I would be deprived of advice and encouragement; and without the continuous critical support of readers of Weekend Guardian *I would be lonely and adrift in an ocean of anodyne wavelessness.*

BOOTHS

In answer to my question 'Do you believe wine writers serve any useful social purpose and if so what?', this store replied, 'Yes. If you write in praise of a wine it walks out through the door.' To which I can only retort that I wish I could exit with such facility after tasting my way through the wines Booths sells. The range is vast (750 wines – more than Tesco's), sprawling and eccentric – though several outstanding bottles exist and several crazy ones. When, earlier this year, I was the only wine writer who could be bothered to make his way up from London, or from anywhere else in the country for that matter, to attend a Booths wine tasting in Knutsford (a town, appropriately in the circumstances, named after King Canute), I was confronted with things the normal supermarket would be horrified to stock. But then Booths, with its barely two dozen Lancashire and Cheshire branches (and one on its way in Cumbria), is not your normal supermarket. It is, quite simply, an extended grocery with checkouts.

Can you imagine being confronted with a £45 bottle of 1982 Bollinger? A £76 bottle of Echezeaux Domaine de la Romanee Conti 1990? Not to mention relative cheapies like £15 bottles of Cote Rotie, Vosne-Romanee Cacheux 1991, Sauternes, Doctor Vineyard riesling (from the most expensive patch of land in Germany), and decanters of vintage port? The conscientious taster is not only obliged to drink his way through these wines but is unable to resist the temptation to linger over the more remarkable ones (like the six-quid bottle of Cremant de Loire which is so much more enjoyable to drink, and buy, than the Bollinger). I lingered in the local brasserie at Knutsford where

11

the black pudding and kidney and oxtail pie went rather well with a mere £10.99 bottle of Mas de Daumas Gassac 1988 – a red with soft tannins delicious enough to suck through a straw. When I exclaimed to Mr Edwin Booth, master of ceremonies and so much else, that he must be addle-pated to open such pricey goodies for a self-avowed superplonker, he replied, 'I haven't opened them with you in mind. I opened them for me.'

Thus we are given a clue to much of the personal nature of this small supermarket/grocery/wine merchant chain. It is the Booth family personal fiefdom. They own 80 per cent of the shares with the remaining 20 per cent safely in the hands of valued employees. When I wondered (aloud) if Mr Booth might do a William Low one day (a Scottish supermarket which sold out to Tesco last year), he snorted in contempt.

However, the store's wine buyer, Alistair Morrell, did sell out; he's now at Asda. The new man, Christopher Dee, used to run his own three-branch chain of wine shops in Bradford and Leeds (under the name 'Vin Extraordinaire') and so he knows at first hand the competitive effects of retailers like Booths. With his guvnor, Mr Booth, taking such a passionate interest in wine, how will Mr Dee cope? When I toured the Knutsford branch and noticed old bottles of Rhine and Moselle riesling, some of it a decade old, one rarity priced at £27, I wondered if Cheshire might not be part of a newly independent European republic, like Andorra, where life is ordered differently. This impression was given added poignancy by a smartly dressed female customer examining these wine shelves; behind her, dressed in immaculate red and grey school uniforms, stood her two young sons, each with a trolley, ready to follow her anywhere she commanded. It was a most instructive exhibition.

And when I pointed out these phenomena to Mr Dee he told me he intends to get the bit between his teeth about the crazy wines which simply gather dust on the shelves but has no plans to reform the shopping styles of his customers. Mr Booth, then, may well find that some of his cherished pets, like the Yerra

Yerring Pinot Noir 1989 from Australia at £27 the bottle, bite the dust. We shall see.

Mr Booth also takes a great interest in food and his customers' tastes in same. The old style of northern grocering, where certain regular customers are known personally to the man at the top, still applies to Booths who think of wine and food in equal measure. This sets them apart from the pure wine merchant or wine chain in one single important regard. Wine is thought of as an adjunct to food at Booths, not simply as a range of alcoholic beverages which must attempt to meet all tastes, and so Booths wines very much meet the regular needs of the foodie rather than the momentary whims of the fashion-conscious wino. Mr Booth believes that 'style and individuality' are the factors which influence his buying pattern and only latterly value. In practice, this has meant a huge and unwieldy range which, although meeting the needs of the £3 shopper, can accommodate the lottery winner with £215 burning a hole in his pocket. The majority of the range is priced between £5 and £15.

The store's top half-dozen best-sellers reflect a broad customer base:

1. Booths Hock.
2. Bulgarian Cabernet/Merlot.
3. Abbaye St Hilaire rouge.
4. Merlot del Veneto.
5. Booths Claret.
6. Valdepenas tinto.

Five dry, fruity reds all pipped to the post by a sweet German white. Does that not suggest anything significant to your alert sociographic instincts, Watson? No? Well, let me suggest, then, that all those six wines are bought to satisfy the tastes of the male palate. Indeed, it may well be that men personally buy all those wines – the first one for their wives (busy elsewhere in the store stocking up on tins of foie gras and lobster in case anyone unexpected drops in over the weekend) and the remainder for themselves. Though it must be said that the soft fruitiness of the Venetian merlot might have some appeal as a unisex wine.

You are, of course, shocked that such behaviour is still tolerated in a Britain so close to the end of a millennium. The freedom women won (but only as recently as 1928, remember) to vote in elections on the same terms as men was quickly followed by the freedom to choose their mates' under- and neck-wear. But the decision about the wine is still largely a male preserve (hence the reason why the corkscrew, a twisted phallic symbol, is so important as an emblem of masculinity) and there is no doubt that Booths caters to these decision-makers splendidly. That woman customer I spotted training her two sons in trolley pushing was probably part of a counter plot which has only recently been hatched.

Booths is conservative. Unlike the big supermarket chains it is not opening new branches every other week. That new store at Ulverston in Cumbria, which should be open by the time this book goes to press, is the store group's sole expansionary move this year. The granting of a new alcohol licence for its store at Lytham in Lancashire was also a highlight. Though not so high, perhaps, as the winning of *Life* Magazine's Supermarket Wine Merchant of the Year award.

Booths, however, is not necessarily conservative when it comes to finding new sources of supply and, like all larger wine merchants nowadays, is looking very much to the so-called New World of wine for the future. When I asked Mr Booth which countries he expected to provide the most exciting additions to his range over the next few years the answer was Argentina, Chile, South Africa and France.

It is safe to say that five years ago France would have headed that list and the other countries would have come nowhere. Even at Booths, then, things aren't what they once were. And the evidence is liberally sprinkled amongst the wines which follow.

E H Booth & Co Limited
4-6 Fishergate
Preston
Lancashire
PR1 3LJ

Tel 01772 251701
Fax 01772 204316

ARGENTINIAN WINE RED

Syrah Luigi Bosca 1988   `13.5` `E`
Very flavoursome.

ARGENTINIAN WINE WHITE

Chardonnay Navarro Correas 1994   `13.5` `E`

AUSTRALIAN WINE RED

Brown Brothers Tarrango 1993   `15` `C`
Vivid, striking, softly smoky and rubbery and so gluggable
it's sinful.

Normans Chandlers Hill Shiraz 1993   `14` `D`

Penfolds Bin 407 Cabernet Sauvignon 1990   `16` `E`
Superb specimen. Soft fruit with blackcurrant flavour in solid
impressive form.

Penfolds Kalimna Bin 28 Shiraz 1991   `14.5` `D`

**Penfolds Rawson's Retreat Bin 35
Cabernet Sauvignon/Ruby Cabernet/Shiraz
1993**   `12` `C`
Soft and rather expressionless.

Rockford Grenache 1993 `16` `E`

Wonderful textured fruit – highly polished, impressively balanced.

Yaldara Shiraz 1993 `14` `C`

Good rich fruit, softly spoken.

Yarra Yerring Cabernet Sauvignon 1989 `11` `F`

Lovely fruit. Ugly price tag.

Yarra Yerring Pinot Noir 1989 `10` `H`

Aromatic, husky.

AUSTRALIAN WINE WHITE

Booth's Estate Semillon `12` `B`

Mooner Estate Chardonnay `13` `C`

Stylish, gentle.

Normans South Australia Chenin Blanc 1992 `14` `D`

Penfolds Bin 202 South Australian Riesling 1993 `14` `C`

Lovely acid backed up by a good finish.

Penfolds Bin 21 Rawsons Retreat Semillon/Chardonnay 1994 `15` `C`

Great clash of soft mango/melony fruit and pineapple acidity. Slightly exotic, generous, bold, delicious.

Peter Lehmann Semillon 1993 ····· 15 C

Ripe yet not floridly so. Lush and keen at the same time. A lovely bottle to enjoy by itself.

Rosemount Chardonnay 1994 ····· 13 D

Will develop over the next year to become a 15-pointer.

South East Australian Chardonnay 1994, Booths ····· 13.5 C

Elegant and stylish.

Wyndham Estate Hunter V Chardonnay, 1991 ····· 14 E

Flavour and style.

BULGARIAN WINE   RED

Bulgarian Cabernet Sauvignon 1989 ····· 15.5 B

Fantastic value!

Bulgarian Cabernet/Merlot 1993 ····· 15 B

Soft and ripe. Bargain.

CHILEAN WINE   RED

Cousino Macul Antiguas Reservas 1989 ····· 14 C

Santa Rita Reserva Merlot 1992 ····· 14 C

Stylish as ever.

CHILEAN WINE — WHITE

Santa Rita Sauvignon Blanc 1994 `14.5` `C`
Posh taste.

FRENCH WINE — RED

Abbaye St Hilaire, Coteaux Varois 1993 `14.5` `B`
Brilliant, dark, dry fruit.

Beaune Premier Cru, Chateau de Meursault 1990 `11` `F`

Bellefontaine Merlot, VdP d'Oc 1994 `15` `B`
Lovely, soft, rich velvet.

Bellefontaine Syrah VdP d'Oc 1992 `10` `B`

Bergerac Rouge (Booths) `12` `B`

Booths Claret `12` `B`

Booths Oak-Aged Claret `12` `C`

Booths Vin Rouge `12` `B`

Bourgogne Hautes-Cotes de Beaune Red 1990 `12` `D`

Bourgogne Pinot Noir 1993 `10` `D`

Cabernet Sauvignon VdP des Coteaux de Baronnies 1994 `14` `B`
Soft and juicy.

Cahors, Cotes d'Olt 1989　　15　B

Brilliant softness and yielding plummy fruit. Perfect maturity at a bargain price.

Chateau Grand Pontet St Emilion 1990　　14　F

Deep, impressive tannins.

Chateau Laval Costieres de Nimes 1992　　13　B

Sweet finish to fruit of some style.

Chateau Ollieux, Corbieres 1991　　14　C

Soft and cuddly.

Chateau Palmer 1983　　10　H

Silly price. Silly wine.

Chateau Pierrail Bordeaux 1992　　14　D

Real old-style dry claret.

Chateau Talbot 1986　　12　H

Lot of money. A lot.

Chateau Tourt Choilet, Graves 1990　　10　E

Chateauneuf-du-Pape Apotres 1991　　12　D

Some depth and flavour.

Cote Rotie La Garde 1987　　10　G

Cotes du Rhone 1993 (Booths)　　13　B

Dry and earthy.

Echezeaux, Domaine de la Romanee Conti 1990　　　　　10　H

Wonderful texture for the price of a suit. I'd rather have the suit.

Fleurie La Madone 1994　　　　　11.5　D

Ah! La Madone! What have you gone and done!?

La Vieille Ferme, Cotes du Ventoux 1992　　　15　C

Brilliant, soft, spicy fruit.

La Voliere Ollieux Corbieres 1991　　　14.5　C

Potent tannins.

Mas de Daumas Gassac Rouge 1988　　　16　F

Expensive but really big and bruisingly brilliant.

Mas de Daumas Gassac Rouge 1990　　　16　F

Very good wine now. Brilliant and possibly 18/19 points in 3/4 years.

St Emilion, Collection Pierre Jean 1992　　　11　D

St Maurice Cotes du Rhone Villages 1991　　　11　C

St Maurice Cotes du Rhone Villages 1992　　　14　C

Good fruit, good structure, good price.

Volnay Joseph Drouhin 1989　　　10　G

Vosne Romanee Cacheux 1991　　　10　G

FRENCH WINE   WHITE

Bergerac Blanc, Booths   `14` `B`

Fresh, flavoursome, bright. Very good value. Dry and stylish.

Booths Vin Blanc   `14` `B`

Terrific value for the genuineness of the fruit on offer.

Bordeaux Blanc, Booths   `11` `B`

Bordeaux Blanc Sec (Medium Dry)   `12` `B`

Bourgogne Aligote 1993   `11` `C`

Cave de Berticot Sauvignon Blanc 1994   `13.5` `C`

Sunny flavourfulness.

Chablis Premier Cru, Montmains 1992   `11` `E`

Chapelle de Cray Sauvignon Touraine 1994   `13.5` `C`

Better than the sancerre by a head of fruit.

Chateau de Meursault 1986   `10` `H`

Lousy value.

Chateau Menota Sauternes 1986   `12` `G`

Chateau Pierrail Rose 1994   `12` `C`

Dry beast.

Chateau Pierrail White 1994   `12` `C`

Cotes Bergerac Blanc (Booths)   `10` `B`

Gewurztraminer Turckheim 1994 `14` `D`

Got some guts!

James Herrick Chardonnay 1994 `14` `C`

Pleasantly flavoured and comforting but somehow not as exciting as it pretends. Rates well, can't deny it that.

La Vieille Ferme Blanc, Le Mont 1993 `11` `C`

Louis Chatel Sur Lie, VdP d'Oc 1994 `13` `B`

Good for fish pie.

Macon Villages Teissedre 1993 `12` `C`

Muscadet sur Lie Livraudier 1992 `11` `C`

Muscat Cuvee Jose Sala `15` `C`

Toffee-nosed and less than £4? Aristocratic sweetness never came so cheap.

Pinot Blanc Turckheim 1994 `13` `C`

Dry – fish friend.

Pouilly Fume H. Sequin 1992 `11` `E`

Sancerre Blanc M. Brock 1993 `10` `D`

GERMAN WINE WHITE

Berry Cateler Doctor Riesling Kabinett, H. Thanisch 1986 `14` `F`

Classic, yet better in 10 years.

23

Booths Hock $\boxed{13}$ $\boxed{A}$

As good as any Liebfraumilch on the market, at half the price.

Booths Liebfraumilch $\boxed{13}$ $\boxed{B}$

Good value here.

Gewurztraminer Beerenauslese Hammel 1992 (half bottle) $\boxed{12}$ $\boxed{C}$

Needs time.

Hochheim Riesling Kabinett Victoriaberg 1990 $\boxed{14}$ $\boxed{C}$

Put it down for 5 years.

L. Philipp Muller Thurgau $\boxed{11}$ $\boxed{C}$

Louis Guntrum Niersteiner Bildstock Kerner Beerenauslese 1985 $\boxed{13}$ $\boxed{G}$

Sybarite's aperitif.

Piesporter Michelsberg, Booths $\boxed{13.5}$ $\boxed{B}$

Aperitif.

HUNGARIAN WINE WHITE

Gyongyos Estate Chardonnay 1994 $\boxed{12}$ $\boxed{B}$

Not as lively as previous vintages.

Gyongyos Estate Sauvignon Blanc 1994 $\boxed{13.5}$ $\boxed{B}$

Feeblest vintage yet? Not as exciting as it once was, for sure.

ITALIAN WINE   RED

Barolo Villadoria 1991   `12` `E`

Cabreo Vigneto Il Borgo 1985   `13` `F`
Delicious.

Chianti Classico del Macia 1991   `13` `C`

Chianti Classico Motegiachi 1990   `13` `D`

Chianti Classico Riservadi Fizzano 1988   `13` `E`

Chianti Rialto   `11` `B`

Montepulciano d'Abruzzo Zonin 1993   `13` `B`
Soft and juicy.

Parrina Riserva 1990   `12` `D`
Very jammy.

Rosso di Montalcino, Argiano 1992   `13.5` `E`
Dark-centred. Tasty.

Teroldego Rotaliano 1992   `12` `C`

ITALIAN WINE   WHITE

Bianco di Custoza Rizzi   `12` `D`

Gravina Bianco 1993   `14` `C`
Dry, gravelly. Shellfish!

NEW ZEALAND WINE   WHITE

Villa Maria Chardonnay 1994   `14.5` `D`
Lots of dry, classy fruit here.

PORTUGUESE WINE   RED

Alta Mesa Estremadura 1994   `14` `B`
Simple, soft, ripe, very fruity, delicious chilled and poured over parched tongues.

Foral Duoro 1992   `14` `B`
Dry. Good casserole wine.

PORTUGUESE WINE   WHITE

Alta Mesa White Estremadura 1994   `10` `B`

SOUTH AFRICAN WINE   RED

Clear Mountain Pinotage   `13` `B`

SOUTH AFRICAN WINE   WHITE

Charles Gerard Reserve White 1991   `15` `C`
At its peak of quiet authority.

Clear Mountain Chenin Blanc `14` `B`
Layered fruit here, agreeably complex for the money.

Oak Village Chardonnay 1994 `13` `C`

Two Oceans White 1993 `10` `C`

SPANISH WINE RED

Cune Rioja Crianza 1990 `14` `C`

Cune Rioja Reserva 1987/88 `16` `D`

Ochoa Navarra Red Tinto 1993 `14` `C`
Soft. Good value.

Ochoa Tempranillo 1990 `16` `D`

Raimat Merlot 1990 `15` `D`
Such depth! Good flavour.

Vina Real Reserva 1981 `14` `D`
Bargain for the age.

Vinas de Gran Crianza Rioja `12` `C`

SPANISH WINE WHITE

Artadi Rioja Rosada 1994 `14` `C`
Terrific little rose.

27

Carraixet, Moscatel de Valencia   15 B
Soft marmalade fruit and quince jelly acidity. Great value.

Monopole Barrel Fermented 1993   14 C
White burgundy style.

URUGUAY WINE   RED

Castol Pujol Tannat 1991   14.5 C
Great value.

USA WINE   RED

Glen Ellen Merlot 1993   13 C
Very juicy vintage.

USA WINE   WHITE

Glen Ellen Chardonnay 1993   14 C
Drier than previous vintages. Still good fruit.

FORTIFIED WINE

Booths Amontillado Medium Sherry   14 C
Also available in litre bottles at £5.29.

Booths Crusted 1989 Bottled Port `16` `E`
Soft, rich, beautifully mannered – a real catch.

Booths Finest Reserve Port NV `15.5` `E`
Well-manicured, handsome, rich, smooth – the perfect lonely hearts partner for cheeses (not blue) and biscuits.

Booths Fino Sherry `15` `C`
Lovely dry fruit.

Booths Manzanilla Sherry `16` `C`
Camomile and saline nuts. Brilliant.

Hidalgo La Panesa Fino `13.5` `C`

Niepoort LBV 1987 Bottled Port `14` `F`
One of the more expensive LBVs but one of the most satisfying.

Niepoort Ruby Port `14` `D`
Lots of character for a ruby.

Quarles Harris 1977 `16` `G`
Just superb with cake and blue cheese. Really hits the spot.

Tizon Palo Cortado Sherry `17` `E`
The unique effect of real fruit undercut by an intense dryness. Like a cello chord struck and lingering for minutes before it dies.

SPARKLING WINE/CHAMPAGNE

Bairrada Aliaca 1991 | 12 | C |
Dry, lean.

Bollinger 1982 | 12 | H |

Booths Champagne Brut | 14 | F |
Classic stuff.

Brossault Rose | 14 | E |
Worth the roses.

Comte d'Eaubonne | 14.5 | F |
Nutty and classy.

Cray Cremant de Loire 1992 | 16 | D |
Soft elegance of real cool class.

Mont Marcal Gran Reserva 1987 | 13 | E |
Good with smoked salmon.

Mont Marcal Brut Reserva 1989 (Spain) | 11 | D |
Old style and earthy.

Mont Marcal Cava 1992 | 13 | D |

Piper Heidsieck Brut | 13 | G |

Piper Heidsieck Demi Sec | 11 | F |

Prosecco Zonin | 14 | C |
Fruity for dinner ends.

DAVISONS

My belief in my powers of analysis takes a hammering here. Davisons, the way I see things, has to be the typical male-orientated wine chain. In the words of square-chinned managing director Michael Davies the chain is 'unquestionably the best claret retailer, unquestionably the best vintage port retailer and is questionably the best red and white burgundy retailer'. Pausing only to admire the chutzpah inherent in the lack of the negative prefix in 'questionably', my belief remains unshaken. Indeed, it is surely confirmed. Who else but men drink claret, port, and red and white burgundy? But then we turn our attention to Mr Davies's top-selling wines and we find evidence which totally contradicts this notion. The masculine appeal of Davisons' 80 shops (21 in north, south and west London, 4 in Berkshire, 6 in Essex, 4 in Hertfordshire, 15 in Kent, 2 in Middlesex, 3 in Sussex and 15 catering to the refined tipplers of Surrey) can hardly be responsible for the following list which represents the chain's top-selling wines:

1. Liebfraumilch.
2. Lambrusco white.
3. Jacob's Creek Semillon Chardonnay.
4. Hardy's Nottage Hill Chardonnay.
5. Jacob's Creek red.

No other retailer has so many white wines in its top-sellers list and on this evidence alone women must flock to Davisons in their tens of thousands. It cannot be simply in the hope of catching a glimpse of the tanned, handsome, ski-instructor-fit

31

Mr Davies himself. It has to be the appeal of the wines. Or could it be that all those claret and port drinkers are doing the shopping on their wives' and lovers' behalves? It is a mystery. I do not know the answer. Mr Davies himself, if you ask him, merely says, 'We have a large number of City and professional customers who come to us for our range, our service and our knowledgeable staff.' Curiouser and curiouser. He then adds that 'It would be difficult to pick an average customer. The most enjoyable is the one with a few extra pence in his or her pocket and who is prepared to experiment.' And curiouser and curiouser.

Whatever the precise answer, there can be no doubt that Davisons' customers can enjoy, if they have the wherewithal, one of my favourite Australian reds: E & E Black Pepper Shiraz from the Barossa Valley. This is a heart-stoppingly wonderful wine and that E & E can only stand for Effusive and Extraordinary. The 1992 vintage of it is in the list which follows, rating 18 points, and it has tannin to keep it humming smoothly along for fifteen years or so. It is beautifully blackcurranty, stunningly well textured, and drinkable now. It costs an unbelievable £12.50. (Unbelievable because there are fatheads out there in the big wide world paying three times that for burgundies and bordeaux which aren't a quarter so concentrated and tasty.)

When I asked Mr Davies what was the most significant change in his business over the past year he told me that it was 'the slowing down of claret sales – making our wines even more mature and even better value! No other retailer could offer a wine such as the Chateau Cardaillan 1985 at £6.49. We must have been mad! Chateau Filhot 1985 at £9.95 was not badly priced either. And what about our Grahams 1980 vintage port at £14.95?' He's right about his prices. The Cardaillan was a snip at that price for it is perfectly mature and deliciously drinkable. The Filhot, a sweet wine, I haven't tasted but the vintage has reputedly produced wines which didn't take long to assert their depth of honeyed character and so maybe it's a bargain too. The port is certainly well priced.

Davisons has coped with the changes in the UK wine market in spite of the recession so deeply affecting drinkers' choices. The shops now put on regular Saturday morning tastings for customers and if you look at the areas from where Mr Davies expects to find his more interesting wines in the next few years, these undoubtedly go along with developing trends. These areas are South Africa, Chile, and Eastern Europe.

The chain is not given to gimmicks or to making impulsive kneejerk responses to market conditions. Over the past year there has been little expansion. 'We closed some shops,' Mr Davies told me, 'and we opened others. We also re-merchandised a large number of our shops and put in new ideas.'

Davisons is a survivor. And it has survived, I suspect, because it hasn't changed drastically the ways it presents itself to its customers; rather it has developed the ranges of wines drinkers now increasingly enjoy and are prepared to experiment with, and it has understood that it must expand these in order to stay in business in the same high streets which house Victoria Wine, Thresher and Oddbins. The inclusion of three Australian wines in the chain's list of bestsellers, all good value, all firmly fruity and well structured, means that a great many less well known Aussie wines (like the E & E Black Pepper incendiary device) will be purchased, in spite of their high prices, because the customers trust Davisons not to sell them a bummer. Old-established, multi-branched wine merchants like Davisons, many of whose customers find Oddbins intimidatingly off-the-wall and super-markets too noisy, have to fight to present themselves as viable and soothing alternatives to the rash of brash new wine shops opening up (particularly in the heartland of Davisons' territory) like the Wine Cellar people, Wine Rack and Bottoms Up and the new Victoria Wine Cellars shops.

That so many operations should opt to ally themselves to an old-fashioned word like 'cellar' with its association of cobwebbed bottles and rats scurrying between is evidence, perhaps, that the old ways are not entirely dead. (Though if you ask me, the use of the word cellar is more likely to be a result of the misreading of the findings of the extensive and expensive consumer research these firms commission before they launch or re-launch themselves.)

I prefer the word Davisons to Cellar any day of the week. And so, I suspect, do all those City and professional people allegedly forming the bulk of the company's customers.

Davisons Wine Merchants
7 Aberdeen Road
Croydon
Surrey
CR0 1EQ

Tel 0181 681 3222
Fax 0181 760 0390

AUSTRALIAN WINE   RED

Church Block McLaren Vale Wirra Wirra 1992

A good, solid, hearty glug of rich, deep, Oz fruit (brambly dry, with a striking finish) which goes straight to the boots and cheers the weary traveller who's reached the fireside at last.

Craigmoor Mudgee Cabernet Sauvignon 1990

This is now rather a £4.49 wine than a £6.79 one.

E & E Barossa Valley Black Pepper Shiraz 1992

One of Australia's most flavoursome wines. If they were to take me out and shoot me tomorrow it is a bottle of this I'd take with me – inside my stomach lining to ward off the incursion of hot lead to which the rich, spicy, warm, thick fruit of this lovely wine would be impervious. It will rate 20 points in 7 to 10 years' time, I fancy, but as a treat today with a dish like lamb in a pastry crust with wild mushrooms in a Madeira sauce, you will still find yourself in heaven.

Hardys Nottage Hill Cabernet Sauvignon/ Shiraz 1993

Controlled soft spice laid on smooth blackcurrant fruit. Delicious, firm, well-styled. Available in South East regional stores only.

Hardys Parrots Hill Cabernet Sauvignon, Barossa 1992

Delightful soft fruit with minty undertones. Firmly blackcurranty, it has oodles of flavour yet it is never so impactful as to numb the palate for further glasses.

35

Ironstone Cabernet/Shiraz 1992

Something interesting to get your teeth into for not a lot of money. Rich tannins, gravy-edged fruit, and a deep delivery of flavour.

Penfolds Bin 2 Shiraz/Mourvedre

Peter Lehmann Grenache, Barossa 1994 `15` `C`

Will develop well in bottle over the coming year (and beyond). But this wine is eminently suited, with its depth and flavour, to partner casseroles now.

AUSTRALIAN WINE WHITE

Craigmoor Mudgee Chardonnay 1991 `14` `D`

Hardys Nottage Hill Chardonnay 1994 `15` `C`

Hugely attractive soft fruit with a superb citric edge. Balanced, warm and sunny yet cool and classy, this is an attractive chardonnay. Available in South East regional stores only.

Ironstone Semillon Chardonnay,
W Australia 1994

What a wine to enjoy with Thai fish dishes – especially mussels with lemon grass.

Penfolds Koonunga Hill Chardonnay 1992 `14` `C`

Peter Lehmann Chenin Blanc, Barossa
1994 `15` `C`

Will develop well for a couple of years if it's not drunk by fish stew eaters.

AUSTRIAN WINE   WHITE

Servus, Burgenland 1994
The name doesn't help, either.

CHILEAN WINE   RED

Caliterra Cabernet Sauvignon 1993
Beginning to lose its beauty, this beauty. Though it's very far
from haggish yet.

CHILEAN WINE   WHITE

Caliterra Estate Chardonnay Reserve 1993
Plump and ripe in the mouth. The aroma and fruit are lovely
but it's getting on a bit, this wine, and the finish is beginning
just ever so slightly to fade.

Caliterra Sauvignon Blanc 1994
A 17-point wine until this last spring when its whistle-clean
potency of fruit began to lose its brilliance.

FRENCH WINE   RED

**Bourgogne Pinot Noir, Domaine
J. M. Morey 1989**
Not bad, but it's a lot of money for the level of fruit on offer.

FRENCH WINE

**Chambolle Musigny, Les Nazoines,
Domaine Machard de Gramont 1988** `11` `G`

**Chassagne Montrachet, Domaine
J. M. Morey 1988** `11` `F`

Simply not as exciting as an eleven-quid wine surely should be.

**Chateau Beaumont, Haut-Medoc Cru
Bourgeois 1989** `13` `E`

Full, soft, mature, highly drinkable.

Chateau Bel Orme Haut-Medoc 1986 `13` `E`

Chateau Cardaillan, Graves 1988 `12` `E`

So highly polished the fruit has lost its sheen.

**Chateau Coudert St Emilion Grand
Cru 1990** `13` `E`

But you could let it lie till the century's end and you'd have a higher-rating wine.

Chateau de Barbe, Cotes de Bourg 1990 `13` `D`

Almost 14 points, but not quite – quiet on the finish.

Chateau Maucaillou, Moulis 1986 `13` `F`

Chateau Mendoce, Cotes de Bourg 1990 `14` `D`

Highly attractive, soft in its tannins and blackcurrant fruit. Stylish. Good value.

**Chateau Roquetaillade La Grange,
Graves 1986** `14` `E`

A wine to enjoy with food for it has well-developed tannins now powerfully melded with the warm, rich fruit. It will come into its own with roasts and grills.

Chateau Villars, Fronsac 1986　　

Lovely. Blackcurrant fruit with typical suede edges to it. Classy, deep, flavourful.

Chateau Villars, Fronsac 1988　　

Chateauneuf-du-Pape Domaine Font de Michelle 1993　　

Cote de Brouilly Domaine de la Voute des Crozes 1993　　

Savoury, soft, plummy, pleasantly polished. One of the least offensive beaujolais I've tasted.

Domaine de Limbardie, VdP des Coteaux de Murviel 1993　　

The child of the union of Henri Boukardoura and Madeleine Hutin. And a delightful infant, full of dry, savoury fruit which will develop power and strength until AD 2000.

Domaine de Montpezat, Cabernet/Syrah VdP d'Oc 1993　　

Staggeringly smooth and smug. Slips down the throat like a ferret down a rabbit hole – almost doesn't seem to return with the rabbit.

Domaine Saint-Martin Cabernet/Merlot VdP des Cotes de Thongues 1993　　

Fruity, bold, soft, savoury-edged.

Gevrey Chambertin, Vieilles Vignes, Domaine Burguet 1989　　

Delicious. Rotten value but delicious. Has rich, savoury fruit of some decisiveness but lacks the complexity a £20 wine must have.

Gevrey Chambertin, Vieilles Vignes, Domaine Burguet 1990 `12` `G`

Gevrey Chambertin Vieilles Vignes, Domaine Burguet 1991 `10` `H`

Certainly better drunk in 5 to 7 years but whether it will repay its £20 outlay by then is unlikely. That said, it will be an interesting wine when it's older.

Julienas Domaine Buiron 1993 `12.5` `E`

Almost delicious! But not quite (especially at over £8).

Moulin a Vent, Domaine Tour de Bief Duboeuf `11` `E`

Moulin-a-Vent Domaine Degrange 1993 `11` `E`

Prieure Donnadieu, St Chinian 1993 `15.5` `C`

Gorgeous ripe tannin, brilliantly textured plum and black-currant fruit. Delicious food wine.

Santenay Le Chainey, Domaine J. M. Morey 1987 `11` `F`

Savigny-les-Beaune Domaine Aux Guettes, Pavelot 1991 `12` `F`

St Amour Le Clos des Guillons 1993 `12.5` `E`

Has an interesting hammy undertone.

Vacqueyras Chateau des Roques 1992 `13` `D`

Hint of sweet fruit on the finish of a nicely rustic wine with good tannins. Expensive.

FRENCH WINE WHITE

Bourgogne Aligote Bouzeron, Ancien Domaine Carnot 1994 `11` `D`

Chardonnay Gibalaux, VdP d'Oc 1994 `14.5` `D`

Impressive voluptuous ripeness on the edge of the fruit gives this wine real class and controlled litheness of style.

Chassagne Montrachet Premier Cru, Les Chaumees Domaine Morey 1990 `14` `H`

It is a superb white wine. But then at £25 it should be.

Chateau de la Janniere Muscadet de Sevre et Maine Sur Lie 1994 `10` `C`

Chateau de Sours Bordeaux Blanc 1993 `13` `D`

Chateau de Sours Bordeaux Blanc 1994 `14.5` `D`

Impressive elegance and style here.

Chateau de Sours, Bordeaux Rose 1994 `12.5` `D`

Chateau la Borderie Monbazillac, Cuvee Selectionee 1991 `13` `F`

Wonderfully honeyed, waxy fruit of vigour, bite and real deep class. But what a price! Will age for quarter of a century.

Domaine de Pierre Jacques Chardonnay, VdP d'Oc 1994 `14` `C`

Delicious, there is no other word or it. Simply delicious.

Domaine Gibalaux Gris de Gris 1993 `13.5` `C`

Interesting. Not the least bit grey.

James Herrick Chardonnay, VdP d'Oc 1994   `14` `C`

Full, rich, melony fruit in the mouth which turns lemonic in the throat.

Le Chardonnay de Gibalaux Oak Aged 1993   `14` `D`

Why does it cost so much less than a white burgundy which doesn't taste so bonny?

Macon Loche, Caves des Grands Crus 1994   `13` `D`

Has some old-style hauteur about it, I suppose.

Macon Vire, Andre Bonhomme 1993   `12` `E`

Meursault les Cloux, Domaine Javillier 1990   `13` `G`

Pouilly Blanc Fume AC Domaine Andre Chatelain 1992   `13` `E`

Pouilly Fuisse Domaine Seve 1992   `11` `F`

Eleven points, eleven quid. You work it out.

Sauvignon de Touraine AC Domaine des Sablons 1992   `15` `C`

Tight gooseberry fruit, grassy supports. Delicious shellfish wine.

Sauvignon Trois Moulins, VdP d'Oc 1992   `14` `C`

Excellent varietal character.

St Aubin, Les Charmois Premier Cru, Domaine J. M. Morey 1990   `13` `G`

St Romain, Clossou le Chateau Jean Germain 1991 | 15 | F |

An impressive minor white burgundy. It has maturity and balance, an old-fashioned style of fruit and is very sure of itself. All is not lost in Burgundy with minor appellations so classy but why must it cost over a tenner?

St Veran Domaine de l'Ermite de St Veran 1993 | 10 | E |

GERMAN WINE WHITE

Bernkasteler Lay Riesling Kabinett, Estate bottled SAPrum 1989 | 14 | E |

Brilliant sherbet lime aroma with racing acidic fruit laced with lemon. Classy aperitif.

Oppenheimer Sacktrager, Kabinett Halbtrocken, Guntrum 1992 | 12.5 | E |

Begins well (even wonderfully) but doesn't cross the line in the same shape.

ITALIAN WINE RED

Barbera d'Alba, Prunotto Pian Romualdo 1990 | 11 | E |

I was looking forward to experiencing this wine's full embrace and was merely kissed, politely, on the cheek.

Merlot del Veneto Via Nova 1993 | 11 | C |

Sweet cherries.

ITALIAN WINE   WHITE

Chardonnay del Friuli Villa del Borgo 1993

Stylish, clean, some attractive prickly acid to the gentle fruit.

Nuragus di Cagliari, Dolianova, Vino di Sardinia 1994

Not as assertive as it has been in the past, though still highly drinkable.

NEW ZEALAND WINE   WHITE

Nautilus Sauvignon Blanc, Marlborough 1994

Delicate finish to the herbaceous beginning makes this an elegant aperitif.

Nobilo Sauvignon Blanc, Marlborough 1994

Grassy but full and ripe on the finish. Must be drunk with oriental food, Thai particularly.

ROMANIAN WINE   RED

Romanian Cellars Pinot Noir/Merlot

ROMANIAN WINE WHITE

Romanian Cellars Muscat/Riesling Italico

A sweet wine for the honey-dentured Liebfraumilch lover.

SOUTH AFRICAN WINE WHITE

Cape Cellars Colombar 1994

Delicious thing to come back to after a day's slog. Fruity, fresh, modern, ripe.

Cape Cellars Sauvignon Blanc 1992

KWV Sauvignon Blanc 1995

Sauvignon Blanc Saxenburg Estate 1994

SPANISH WINE RED

Don Giulias Tinto

Soft, compelling fruit with tons of flavour and gently vanilla-like underneath. Plump ripe wine of terrific drinkability. Exceptional value.

Gandia Tempranillo

Delicious bright fruit with a light dusting of tannins. Excellent value and good with food.

Laturce Rioja 1992

Superb new-style rioja. Agreeable gentle berried fruit admirably structured. Good value.

Mauro, Bodegas Mauro Tudela de Duero 1984

Pere Ventura Cabernet Sauvignon 1989

An extremely comforting wine. Not a harsh edge anywhere. I almost wish it had – it's very soft and fruity, dry and smooth.

Valserrano Crianza Rioja Alavesa 1990

A deliciously soothing rioja of fine texture (merely a touch of chewiness), good fruit and firm balance.

Valserrano Reserva Rioja Alavesa 1987

The Valserrano riojas are part of the dowry Davisons received this autumn when it married with wine wholesaler Mayor Sworder. On the evidence of this example, a beautifully flavoured, unblowsy, elegant, velvety wine, Mr Michael Davies has married well and profitably.

SPANISH WINE WHITE

El Coto Blanco Rioja, Bodegas El Coto

Good fish stew wine.

Oak Aged Viura Valencia, Gandia

Good as a glug, fine as a food partner. Has a subtle rich edge to clean, fresh fruit. Very food price.

Valserrano Blanco Rioja Alavesa 1994   12.5   D

SPARKLING WINE/CHAMPAGNE

Bollinger Grande Annee 1988 `10` `H`

This is rich champagne, mature, compelling, complex; but at a price of such absurdity only nuts would buy it.

Cava Pere Ventura `14.5` `D`

One of the new-style cavas: elegant, subtly fruity, fresh and clean.

Champagne Charles Ellner 1986 `16` `G`

Delicious digestive-biscuit aroma. Touch of croissant richness on the fruit. But considering this level of complexity, not a lot of bread where it matters most.

Killawarra Brut, Bottle Fermented `15` `D`

Gorgeous delicate wine. So elegant! Such finesse! What a good price!

Killawarra Rose, Bottle Fermented `14.5` `D`

Lovely rose with decisive fruit.

FULLERS

The flying wine-maker, that peripatetic individual who jets into an old established vineyard area and does things the modern way for a particularly far-sighted winery, also manages to fly up the noses of certain wine critics. What these critics fear is that it leads to 'international wines' where all local character is lost. In my view, however, examples of brilliant flying wine-making from areas which have struggled to create wines of outstanding flavour at reasonable prices will lead, in the long run, not to the homogeneity of character and congruity of fruit feared by the stick-in-the-muds but a blossoming of interesting wines for export. Fullers wine shops have an utterly splendid example from a little known area of Spain which illustrates this point to perfection. It is Castillo de Montblanc Dry Red Wine 1994 from the recently demarcated wine region of Conca de Barbera in Tarragona. It is made from the local tempranillo grape plus cabernet sauvignon and merlot. It has been put together by a team of international wine-makers headed by Hugh Ryman. There is a subtle licorice edge to the blackcurrant fruit, which is soft, well balanced and smooth, and there is a smattering of tannin. It is ludicrously delicious and of sufficient heft and flavour to have climbed with aplomb a mountain of roast vegetables which overlooked a savoury pond of sauce made from a vegetable stock cube finished with a reduction of freshly squeezed orange juice. Was the consumer of this bean-cheap feast in heaven? You betcha. Castillo de Montblanc rates 16.5 points, costs £2.99, and I hope all those dimwitted bigots who pepper flying wine-makers with scorn choke on it – if, of course, they can bring themselves to consider it.

Fullers has much to recommend it to the lovers of bean-cheap feasts. Especially when it comes to liquid accompaniment. For it is the only wine retailer I write about who also brews the world's best bitter. It is my local brewery (as local as such things can get in a city the size of London) and a pint of London Pride in the Walmer Arms after a day spent dizzily slapping my tastebuds on the fruit of the vine goes down wonderfully, restoring the wits as it polishes the palate. It has been a byword for many years in the booze business that grain and the grape do not mix, but in Fullers' case they mix splendidly. Fullers wine shops, all sixty-odd of them, are in carefully chosen locations and sell, courtesy of the best efforts of wine buyer Roger Higgs, some carefully chosen wines – expensive mid-range bottles as well some terrific £3 and £4 bargains. There are 13 Fullers wine shops in London, 9 in Middlesex, 9 apiece in Berks and Bucks, just one in Hampshire, 5 in Herefordshire, 2 in Oxfordshire, 11 in Surrey and 2 in Beds (but not together).

Mr Higgs's top-selling wines are:

1. Le Gascony Blanc, Vin de Pays des Cotes de Gascogne.
2. Bulgarian Cabernet Sauvignon Suhindol.
3. Liebfraumilch Egbert.
4. Chardonnay Vin de Pays du Jardin de France Bahaud.
5. Lambrusco Bianco Zonin.
6. Nottage Hill Chardonnay.

On the basis of this list it is easy to agree with Mr Higgs when he says, in answer to the question 'Who buys wine at a Fullers shop?', that it is 'a whole cross-section of people but especially those with a high level of wine knowledge and appreciation'. Lieb. and Lam. for the cross-section, I suggest; Gasc. blanc and Bulg. cab. sauv. and the two chardonnays for the high levellers.

With the regular Saturday tastings Fuller puts on, it is encouraging to believe that members of the more cautious group receive active encouragement to become part of the more adventurous bunch. Both types of customer would have witnessed the most significant change in Fullers' way of looking at wine over the past year and that is a shift away from Germany and Eastern Europe and an increasing emphasis on Chile, South Africa, regional France and Spain. The chain is, in my view, particularly well placed to do very good business in the £4–£7 wines which come from these countries yet which, in spite of higher price tags than many people consider appropriate for New World, or new old-world, wines, offer some tremendous fruit and complexity. Mr Higgs is also increasing his spread of one-off parcels of wine, making regular visits to his or her local shop a necessary part of the bargain hunter's week. For a wine writer like me, these parcels are often one of the most infuriating yet, paradoxically, most satisfying aspects of a business like Fullers'. On the one hand I'm miffed because I can't write about such wines as often as I'd like due to them disappearing quickly from the shops as the small quantity purchased is soon exhausted; and I'm delighted to see such wines appearing for the sake of the customers. More than once, I can tell you, I have tasted a humdinger of a Fullers wine and scribbled away furiously, straining to find fresh and forceful adjectives to describe the fruit, and I'm suddenly told it'll probably be all gone by the end of the month and so unless I can get my article off to the *Guardian* within the hour (impossible with the two-week deadline I work to), there's no point in me mentioning it. This creates an added irritation. When I bump into an acquaintance or one of the parents of a schoolfriend of my children he may well say, triumphantly, to me, 'I'm surprised you didn't know about that Leasingham Shiraz at Fullers – it was staggeringly good – what a pity your column missed it' and through clenched teeth I explain that yes I do know the wine and think it fabulous and all the time I am wishing, since I do not on principle personally buy such limited quantity wines before they are made available widely, that if only there was some of the damned wonderful stuff left I could buy some, and I wish the clever fellow smirking at me – and it is almost invariably a chap we are dealing with here – would at least do the decent thing and invite me round to dinner to sample said wine with appropriate steamy cuisine.

You know, in spite of all this aggro, I like Fullers a lot.

Fuller Smith & Turner plc
Griffin Brewery
Chiswick Lane South
London
W4 2BQ

Tel 0181 996 2000
Fax 0181 995 0230

ARGENTINIAN WINE   RED

Alamos Ridge Cabernet Sauvignon 1993   14 C
Subtle exotic edge to the dry fruit.

Catena Agrelo Vineyard Cabernet Sauvignon 1992   13.5 E
Touch expensive for the quality (undoubtedly good and dry) of fruit on offer here.

ARGENTINIAN WINE   WHITE

Alamos Ridge Chardonnay 1993   14 C
A richly endowed food wine. Chicken casserole would be a faithful partner.

Catena Agrelo Vineyard Chardonnay 1993   13 E
Hints of a classical education but still manages to drop the odd aitch.

AUSTRALIAN WINE   RED

Berri Estates Cabernet Shiraz 1992   15 C
Sweet finish to the dry fruit. Balanced, full (yet not overblown), perfect style of fruit for all manner of grilled meats.

Chateau Reynella Basket Press Cabernet/ Merlot 1992   15 D
A treat of plums and blackcurrants all wrapped up in velvet.

Chateau Reynella Basket Press Shiraz 1992
16 | D

Spicy, deep and so full of flavour you wonder for a moment – could grapes really be squeezed to yield fruit so rich?

Hardys Nottage Hill Cabernet Sauvignon/ Shiraz 1993
16 | C

Ironstone Cabernet Shiraz 1992
16 | D

For a description of this wine see the entry under Wine Cellar.

Leasingham Classic Shiraz, Clare Valley 1992
17 | D

Brilliantly orchestrated fruit and tannins in rich voice together. Superb depth, complexity and flavour.

Leeton Downs Shiraz Grenache 1993
10 | C

Madfish Bay Pinot Noir, Western Australia 1994
12 | D

Has some pretensions to pinot of the Alsace variety.

Penfolds Bin 35 Shiraz Cabernet 1992
15 | C

Ripe, soft fruit with some development ahead of it. Attractive berry flavours, well-structured and balanced. Very drinkable now but a 17/18-pointer in 3/4 years.

Peter Lehmann Grenache, Barossa Valley 1994
15 | C

Rich, structured, deep, dry, flavoursome – terrific rich drinking for under £4.

Rockford Basket Press Shiraz, Barossa Valley 1991
14.5 | E

Expensive, but so is the fruit – it's thick enough to coat a gearbox.

Very savoury, meaty, deep and smooth, this is an impressive wine
to drink now or for ten years ahead.

Rockford Dry Country Grenache 1992 `13.5` `D`

Rothbury Estate Shiraz 1992 `12` `D`

Rouge Homme Coonawarra Cabernet
Shiraz 1991 `13.5` `C`

Savoury and ripe.

Wirra Wirra Original Blend `10` `E`

Dreadful depth of superficiality. This wine is so highly polished
it is all surface. The wine has been filtered and fined till it shines
– and no character, or tannin, is left.

Wirra Wirra R S W Shiraz 1992 `13` `E`

Expensively bought deliciousness which is not hugely complex
but is undeniably an enriching experience.

Wirra Wirra The Angelus 1992 `15` `E`

Expensive but impressive and you can take all day and all night
to drink it. Such is the power of the soft tannins.

AUSTRALIAN WINE WHITE

Devils Lair Chardonnay Margaret River
1994 `12` `E`

Rum stuff, this tenner's worth of chardonnay. Very question-
able.

Green Point Victoria Chardonnay 1993 `14` `E`

A fine, rich, elegant wine with lots of disciplined flavour
and style.

Hardys Nottage Hill Chardonnay 1994

Best vintage yet. Lovely textured, oily fruit, never overdone or blowsy and a buttery, melony finish of surefooted delivery. Terrific value for such classy drinking.

Ironstone Semillon Chardonnay, W Australia 1994

Keen on the nose, sparky and fresh. The fruit is muted but tasty, but it is not hugely impressive on the finish.

Leeton Downs Semillon 1994

The tastebuds need a thorough coating in fish soup, or somesuch, to appreciate this wine at its best.

Lindemans Cawarra Semillon/Chardonnay 1994

Good with chicken casserole – has the weight of fruit to cope.

Penfolds Bin 21 Semillon/Chardonnay 1993

Penfolds Rawson's Retreat Bin 21 Semillon/Chardonnay 1994

Great clash of soft mango/melony fruit and pineapple acidity. Slightly exotic, generous, bold, delicious.

Penfolds South Australia Chardonnay 1992

Lovely polished, lush, woody fruit with touches of lemon, beautifully balanced. Elegant – a real alternative, at a far lower price, to fine burgundy.

Peter Lehmann Chenin Blanc, Barossa Valley 1994

Delicious. Or should I say delishlush? After a bottle of this wine you may have no choice.

Rockford Eden Valley Riesling 1992 | 13 | E

Delicious aperitif. Expensive.

Rockford Local Growers Barossa Valley Semillon 1990 | 15 | E

Grilled chicken's perfect partner: rich, toasty, melony, suggestion of peach, ripe, dry, oily and gently exotic. Lush stuff.

Rothbury Estate Chardonnay, Hunter Valley 1993 | 15.5 | D

Butter, oil, honey, lemon – the perfect marinade for the parched tongue.

Rothbury Semillon Chardonnay S E Australia 1993 | 14 | C

Delicious clash of warm fruit and chilly acidity. Has exotic undertones yet remains firmly prim. A controlled performance with wild touches.

Rowan Chardonnay, Victoria 1993 | 15.5 | D

Good structure from aroma to finish. Rich flavour, good acidity, lingering fruit.

Tasmania Wine Company Chardonnay 1993 | 13.5 | E

Odd sort of chardonnay (mature yet citrusy) at a high price. It is very drinkable but it's very thinkable at eight and a half quid.

Wirra Wirra Chardonnay 1992 | 14 | E

Impressively pricey.

Wirra Wirra Church Block Dry White 1993 | 13 | D

Wynns Coonawarra Chardonnay 1992 | 14.5 | D

Gently chewy fruit of estimable maturity and depth of flavour.
Not cheap but then it does give of itself.

CHILEAN WINE   RED

Caliterra Cabernet Sauvignon 1993 | 14 | C

Light, fruity, elegant with only hints of the nasty bell-pepper
dryness the so-called wine buff admires.

Caliterra Estate Cabernet Sauvignon 1993 | 14 | C

The word 'Estate' adds a quid to the price but not to
the fruit.

Cono Sur Cabernet Sauvignon 1993 | 14 | C

Dry and richly edged with a chewy quality to the fruit.

Cono Sur Pinot Noir 1993 | 13 | C

Cono Sur Pinot Noir Reserve 1993 | 14 | D

Firm and fleshy without being fat and flashy – except price-wise.

Cono Sur Reserve Cabernet 1992 | 14 | D

Torconal Merlot | 15 | B

Finishes with a touch of chocolate. Superb value fruit.

CHILEAN WINE   WHITE

Caliterra Casablanca Chardonnay 1994 | 16.5 | C

Superb rich edge to the final thrust of the elegant fruit. Impressive
wine with gusto, flavour and real style.

Caliterra Reserve Chardonnay 1994 `14` `D`

Drink it early. No staying power here.

Cono Sur Chardonnay 1994 `14` `C`

Some engaging fruit here tending towards firmness and lushness but held in check by balancing acidity. The whole makes a quietly impressive wine.

FRENCH WINE RED

Bourgogne Hautes Cotes de Nuits 'Les Champs de Perdrix' 1993 `12` `D`

Cabernet Sauvignon Coteaux de Bessille, Jules Boyer 1993 `12` `B`

Cabernet/Syrah VdP D'Oc 1993 `14` `B`

Cabernet/Syrah VdP d'Oc les Limouxins 1994 `14` `B`

Casserole wine – savoury and dry-edged.

Cairanne Domaine de la Presidente, Cotes du Rhone Villages 1994 `12.5` `D`

Like seeing wallpaper in a potting shed, the rusticity of this wine has been sacrificed for a smoothness of deep superficiality.

Chateau Batailley, Pauillac 1986 `10` `G`

Silly price for such rudeness of fruit.

Chateau Caroline Listrac, Medoc 1990 `13` `D`

Serve this wine with roast beef and you have truly arrived as a deeply serious individual.

Chateau de Roquenagade, Corbieres 1991   14   C

Rich and well-balanced. Will improve over the next 2 years if cellared.

Chateau Gazin, Pomerol 1988   13   G

Chateau Talbot, St Julien 1986   12   G

Chateau Teyssier St Emilion Grand Cru 1990   13   E

Some attractive fruit but what a price. Can't hold a candle to the Rockford Shiraz at the same price.

Cotes du Rhone Jean Luc Colombo 1993   12   C

Very soupy.

Cotes Rotie Gilles Barge   10   G

Crozes-Hermitage Bernard Chave 1992   11   D

Domaine de Coupe Roses Minervois 1991   12   C

Better in its youth.

Domaine de Raissac Cuvee Select 1994   14   C

An interesting tempranillo/syrah marriage. Has a breezy edge to the brambly fruit.

Domaine de Raissac Merlot VdP de l'Aude 1994   13.5   B

A hairy merlot of rustic flavour and depth.

Domaine de Roquenagade Cabernet Sauvignon 1991   14   D

Deliciously dry, soft, well-balanced tannins still opening out. Blackcurrant fruit of some weight and style.

Domaine de Sours, Bordeaux 1990 `13` `D`

Domaine St Hilaire Cabernet Syrah Cuvee Prestige 1992 `14` `C`

This cab. sauv. and syrah blend is very attractive. Splendid depth of fruit. Perfect with savoury foods.

Fixin Philipe Naddef 1992 `10` `E`

Gevrey Chambertin Premier Cru Les Champeaux 1991 `11` `G`

Grenache, Fortant de France 1993 `15` `B`

Rustic richness of a near opulent variety. Very attractively balanced. Delicious to drink by itself. Hums with herby fruit.

Hautes Bages Monpelou Pauillac 1992 `13` `D`

Wonderful texture – quite wonderful – but the fruit is still evolving and has tannins restraining the blackcurrant. Keep for 5 years more.

L'Esprit de Teyssier Bordeaux 1993 `12` `C`

A little austere.

Macon Ige Les Roches 1994 `11` `C`

Would you wear a string vest and nothing else in mid-winter? This wine would.

Mas de Montel Syrah VdP d'Oc 1992 `13.5` `C`

Montagne Noire VdP D'Oc Syrah 1994 `15` `B`

Black mountain fruit indeed. Brambly rich, earthy, gentle tannins. This is rich and ready – for casseroles. Bolstered by a poignant acidic lift on the finish.

Nuits St Georges Caves des Hautes Cotes 1992 10 E

Vendange Cotes de Roussillon Villages 1991 13 D

Impressive. But so is the price.

Winter Hill VdP de l'Aude 1994 13.5 B

Earthy, dry, brilliant value.

FRENCH WINE WHITE

Bourgogne Chardonnay Joseph Bertrand 1994 15 C

What's going on at Fullers? *Two* highly drinkable, high rating white burgundies under a fiver?! (see Macon Ige.) Amazing. This one has more bite and a mite more complexity.

Cave de Berticot Sauvignon Blanc Cotes de Duras 1993 15 C

Gentle creaminess of fruit is evident under the brisk acidity and this makes for a balanced, delicious wine.

Chablis Premier Cru Montmains Vauroux 14.5 E

Chablis Vauroux 1992 15 D

Delicious grilled fish wine. Has elegant fruit under a mineral shroud which is kept in check by a flinty acidity.

Chardonnay VdP du Jardin de la France, Bahaud 1993 13 B

Domaine de Raissac Viognier VdP de l'Aude 1994

14   C

Not as peachy as some but Old World chardonnay lovers will like it.

J. F. Lurton Domaine des Salices Viognier, VdP d'Oc 1993

15   D

Classic perfume of the viognier grape, rich and reminiscent of peach and banana. Delicious fruit builds on this without coarseness or any lack of style.

J. F. Lurton, Sauvignon VdP d'Oc 1994

12.5   C

Subdued passionfruit edge fails to ignite the fruit in this particular firework. An 'if only' wine.

James Herrick Chardonnay VdP d'Oc 1994

14   C

Pleasantly flavoured and comforting but somehow not as exciting as it pretends. Rates well, can't deny it that.

La Serre Chardonnay VdP d'Oc 1994

14.5   C

Depth, breadth, weight, length – has an all-round impressiveness, this wine. No misshapen edges.

La Serre Sauvignon Blanc VdP d'Oc 1994

14   C

Smooth, rich edge to the fruit which is lightly finished with citrus. Lacks New World sauvignon vivacity but it's a wonderful fish wine.

Laperouse Blanc Val d'Orbieu & Penfolds, VdP d'Oc 1994

14   C

Rounded fruit flavours energetically supported by the elegance of the acids.

FRENCH WINE

Le Gascony Cotes de Gascogne 1993

Macon Davaye Domaine des Deux Roches 1993

Warmly mature and fruity. Good old-fashioned flavour.

Macon Ige Les Roches Blanc 1994

How warming it is to be complimentary about an old friend! A purposely prim, firmly balanced, well-priced specimen.

Macon Villages Charles Vienot 1993 14 C

Fuller (no pun intended) than the excellent Les Roches Macon, this has less compensating freshness of acidity and balance. Nevertheless, it is a good bottle.

Marsannay Blanc Philippe Naddef 1993 12 E

Montagny Premier Cru, Denis Philibert 1992 14.5 E

Not profoundly overoaked as some Montagnys can be, this example, though expensive, is refined, elegantly fruity and delicious. Aromatic, firm, well-made.

Pouilly Fume Jean Claude Chatelain 1993 13.5 D

Almost, but not quite, hinting at the mineral pouilly fume of yesteryear.

Puligny Montrachet Henri Clerc 1993 11 G

St Veran Domaine des Deux Roches 1993

Has a delicious fresh, nutty finish to the warmth of the fruit. Classic.

Vieux Manoir de Maransan, Cotes du Rhone 1994 16 C

Complex, delicious, firm – this has character, flavour and style. Rich edge of baked fruit, subtle nutty background, brilliant with all sorts of fish dishes.

Winter Hill VdP de l'Aude 1994 16 B

Fresh, young, lively, cheap.

ITALIAN WINE RED

Chianti Classico Villa Cafaggio 1992 14 D

Sweet fruit with a dry, refined, earthy edge. Good soft tannins, depth of flavour and comforting structure. Touch expensive for the style.

Chianti Riserva, Villa Antinori 1989 14 D

Chianti Riserva Villa Antinori 1990 13.5 D

Elegant, classy and too refined? You could always try bunging clods of earth in the bottle.

Gabbia d'Oro Rosso 1994 10 B

It's getting better! It used to be the most limp-wristed red in Italy.

Montepulciano d'Abruzzo Citra 1993 16 C

My vote as the house wine in Fullers' list. This wine is winningly good value, friendly without being too soft or soppy, and it is utterly delicious. Brilliant pasta partner.

Teroldego Rotaliano Donini 1992 13 C

ITALIAN WINE   WHITE

Chardonnay del Triveneto 1994   `13.5` `B`

Not many decent chardonnays under £3. This one is an exception.

Orvieto Classico Antinori 1993   `12` `C`

NEW ZEALAND WINE   WHITE

Dashwood Sauvignon 1994   `12` `E`

Very coarsely humoured, this sauvignon. No elegance and little wit. But with smoked eel it would be uproarious.

Grove Mill Marlborough Sauvignon 1992   `18` `E`

Grove Mill Sauvignon, Marlborough 1993   `14` `D`

Grass and asparagus in muted collision. A great shellfish wine.

Highfield Estate Chardonnay Marlborough 1992   `13` `C`

Breezy edge of fresh-cut rhododendrons to the fruit – only kidding but it does taste like some plant or other.

Highfield Estate Sauvignon Blanc Marlborough 1993   `14` `C`

Asparagus and spinach fruit of interest to anyone contemplating putting those two vegetables together in a salad.

Hunters Sauvignon Blanc 1994   `13.5` `E`

Demure, classy, pricey, not typical NZ sauvignon blanc.

Kumen River Chardonnay 1993 `13` `G`

Vavasour Reserve Chardonnay 1993 `12` `F`

PORTUGUESE WINE · RED

J.P. Tinto `15` `B`

Light but quite delicious and fruity without a trace of tannic harshness, oxidation or sourness. Has a plum quality to it. A true quaffing masterpiece.

PORTUGUESE WINE · WHITE

J.P. Branco `14` `B`

Terrific price for a terrific style of fruit. Lots of freshness and a fair dollop of flavour. Great fish wine.

Joao Pires Dry Moscato 1992 `15` `C`

I love this wine. It is aromatic, spicy and mixes hot pears with cool melon – edgily exotic; it is wonderful as an aperitif or brilliant with scallops with a pea and mint puree.

SOUTH AFRICAN WINE · RED

Dieu Donne Cabernet Sauvignon 1993 `15` `C`

Impressive in spite of the austerity of the edge on the fruit. A food wine.

Fairview Shiraz/Merlot 1993   `14.5` `C`

Not quite as spectacular as previous vintages but still a very
soundly made wine.

Saxenberg Merlot, Stellenbosch 1992   `12` `D`

Stellenzicht Cabernet/Malbec 1992   `16` `C`

Curious texture to this beast. almost feline, so the blackberry
and plum fruit (which has a lovely weight to it) is well able to
take care of itself with a variety of roast and grilled meat. A very
good price for an individual, classy, well turned out wine.

SOUTH AFRICAN WINE   WHITE

Bellingham Chardonnay, Franschhoek 1994   `12.5` `C`

Muddy fruit flaunting a clean fruit price tag.

Bellingham Sauvignon Blanc, Paarl 1994   `14.5` `C`

Fresh, frontal attack followed through by some fruit of the vague
melon and raspberry variety, finishing with a gentle citricity.

Bin 410 Chardonnay 1994   `13` `C`

**Bouchard Finlayson Chardonnay
Kaaimansgat Vineyard 1994**   `12` `E`

Fatness of edge to the gently fruit gives it an appealing softness.
But not a £9 wine.

Dieu Donne Chardonnay 1993   `15` `D`

Faint echoes of lemon to the woody fruit make this an appealing
bottle. Some classiness on show, and style, and with more bottle
age might become truly outstanding.

Fairview Crouchen/Chardonnay 1994 `13.5` `C`

Curious cosmetic edge to the fruit.

KWV Sauvignon Blanc 1995 `13.5` `C`

**Spes Bona Chardonnay Van Loveren,
Robertson 1994** `12` `C`

Getting expensive at a penny under a fiver. The fruit is not quite
rich or complex enough.

SPANISH WINE RED

Artadi Rioja 1994 `15` `C`

A 100 per cent garnacha rioja which isn't common – and neither
is the fruit. Must be drunk with food.

**Augustus Cabernet Sauvignon, Puig &
Roca 1991** `8` `D`

Berberana Tempranillo, Rioja 1992 `15.5` `C`

Soft, sweet vanilla and dry coconut (echoes only) adding a lovely
lilt to the rich plumminess of the fruit.

**Casa de la Vina Valdepenas, Carrascal
Vineyard 1993** `14` `B`

Soft and luscious with dry edges. Excellent fruit at an excellent price.

**Castillo de Montblanc, Conca de Barbera
1994** `16.5` `B`

For a description of this wine, see the introduction to this
section.

Charchello Monastrel Jumilla 1994 `15` `C`

Has considerable length of flavour, this wine, and continues to develop its dry. licorice, blackcurrant fruit some time after it has disappeared down the gullet.

Don Giulias Tinto de Mesa `15` `B`

Light, tasty, dry – and bargain-packed from nostril to throat.

Palacio de la Vega Tempranillo, Navarra 1991 `15.5` `D`

Aroma, fruit, richness, complexity, style – it has them in fair proportion.

Rioja Casa del Marques Sin Crianza 1993 `17` `B`

One of the best riojas for the money around. Lovely balanced style with the fruit taking the acidity firmly by the hand. Dry damson fruit with a hint of blackcurrant sweetness on the finish. Has a woodiness achieved, I believe, by the immersion of oak barrels in the steel vats.

Rioja d'Avalos Tempranillo 1993 `13` `B`

Rioja Faustino Rovero Ulecia Crianza 1990 `14` `C`

Senorio de Nava Ribera del Duero Crianza 1990 `13` `D`

SPANISH WINE WHITE

Augustus Chardonnay, DO Penedes 1994 `15` `E`

Expensive but classy and classic. Better than the Puligny-Montrachet on Fullers' list at £16.

Can Feixes, DO Penedes 1994

Smoked fish eaters, rejoice! This wine is for you.

Castillo de Montblanc Chardonnay, Conca de Barbera 1994

Tasty, very very tasty.

Castillo de Montblanc Dry White Wine, Conca de Barbera 1994

Dry, nothing ripe, gentle echo of earthiness – this is an Old World wine telling its New World wine-maker that this is the way it's going to be in spite of everything.

Rioja d'Avalos Viura 1993

White rioja in the frascati mould.

USA WINE   RED

Saintsbury Carneros Garnet Pinot Noir 1992

Gamy, raspberryish, light. Fun. Like a children's Mercurey.

St Supery Cabernet Sauvignon 1988

Agreeable teeth-coating blackcurrant fruit.

Thornhill Barbera NV

Juicy fruit juice.

Thornhill Pinot Noir NV

Pleasant but little varietal character.

Thornhill Reserve Syrah NV

Rich and Rhone-like but a touch expensive. Very attractive fruit, with a soft ripeness.

Thornhill Zinfandel NV `15` `C`

Good, balanced, leathery, soft, aromatic, rich, spicy, well-berried – typical. Alcoholic (14.5%) but not aggressive. A zin for Rhone fans.

USA WINE   WHITE

Crichton Hall Chardonnay 1991

Think of it as Puligny-Montrachet and the £10 price tag won't seem a high price at all.

Kah-nock-tie Konocti Chardonnay 1992 `13` `D`

Fun but I'm not sure it's a £6 wine.

Paul Thomas Columbia Valley White, Washington 1993

An inspired marriage of semillon and riesling. Elegant, fruity, bold, marginally exciting. Fun and flavour under £4.

Thornhill California Chardonnay `14` `C`

Delicious woody aroma which leads through to rich-edged fruit, nicely balanced. Not a rich finish but a sound one.

FORTIFIED WINE

Dow 1980 Port `13` `G`

FULLERS

Dow's '75 Vintage Port   12   H
Winey, sweet, raisiny and medicinal.

Graham 1983 Port   11   G

Taylor's 1983 Port   12   G

SPARKLING WINE/CHAMPAGNE

Bollinger Grande Annee 1988   10   H
This is rich champagne, mature, compelling, complex; but at a price of such absurdity only nuts would buy it.

Champagne Brossault Brut   15   E
Lovely, light bubbly with real class. Wonderful tastebud awakener.

Champagne Brossault Brut Rose   16   F
Delicious rose with outspoken flavour, freshness and style.

Green Point 1991 (Australia)   14   F

Torre del Gall Cava 1990   14   E
An elegant lemony cava of some style.

Yalumba Pinot Noir Chardonnay Cuvee 1   16   E
Superb elegance and refined purpose.

73

MAJESTIC

Beers & Wines at Warehouse Prices. Now there's a sublimely simple slogan for you. It's emblazoned on my local Majestic Wine Warehouse. True, it doesn't quite barnacle the brain like 'A Double Diamond Works Wonders' but this is, perhaps, because on the face of it that statement is nothing more than the pure and simple truth. How else could a wine warehouse sell its wines except at warehouse prices? However, what is implied here is that by selling wine by the whole or mixed case, to which Majestic's warehouse liquor licence originally compelled it but which is now merely the way the company prefers to do business, customers strike a bargain unobtainable in a shop. And thus we enter that fantastical Wildean land where the truth is rarely pure and never simple.

The fact is that Majestic, with its forty-odd southern-based branches plus three up in Birmingham with twigs in Northampton, Nottingham and Stockport, has some marvellous wines and hardly needs the dubiety of the advertising slogan to drum up business. In July it opened its fiftieth branch – opposite the railway station in Southampton. The business turns over around £35 million a year (pre-tax profit £728,000, thus demonstrating that it's not easy getting fat on wine retailing's thin margins). By itself, Majestic accounts for over 4 per cent of the nation's champagne sales. Nobody goes to the company to spend less (individual average spend is around eighty quid). They go because they can mostly park outside, browse without being crushed by wire trolleys festooned with bad-tempered infants, taste certain wines every day of the week (last year, 47,000 bottles were opened in store for customers to sample), and meet affable and extremely helpful assistants who have cooperative biceps and possess refined tastes in muzak. These customers, Majestic have revealed to me, are mostly thirty-five years old and read the *Sunday Times*. Make of this what you will.

Denied the delights of supermarket shopping, and its unbeatable prices, the Majestic customer can indulge in other riches. That these proliferate so consistently is due in great measure to the fact that Mr Tony Mason, Majestic's wine-buying chief, allocates as much as a fifth of his budget to snapping up bargains. Last year, this enabled him, in auction, to outbid several merchants for stock sold by the owner of a defunct Channel Islands wine company which ended up on Majestic shelves and contained such beauts as Chamberyzette, the alcoholic, strawberry-flavoured aperitif, at £1.99.

Mr Mason also managed to run up the first 20-point Superplonk in the high street, Vidal-Fleury's Vacqueyras of the magnificent 1990 vintage which produced some great wines in this area of the Rhone. By no stretch of the imagination was it sold at a 'warehouse' price but by every stretch of the imagination it was a consummate bargain at £6.59. It had a quite wondrous chocolate silkiness spiked with glorious tannins undercut by a baked herbiness to its cushy, concentrated fruit and it led to the only violent incident in my wine-writing career.

My wife, having been offered the last glass of a bottle I had myself started and into which I had made serious inroads, threatened me with the empty bottle, demanding an instant, full replacement. This was, however, at eleven at night, impossible. However, I do not see why I should hold Majestic's failure to stay open twenty-four hours a day against the wine. It had to rate 20 points, for it had an incomparable perfection of texture and flavour which I have never before encountered for the money and in terms of enjoyment it compared with the most satisfying wines I have ever drunk. It marked a great return to flavour of the house of Vidal-Fleury, bought ten years back by the Guigal company in the same Rhone town of Ampuis, following a mediocre period in the seventies and eighties.

Without doubt, the red wine drinker will still find great bargains at Majestic even if he cannot still uncork the 1990 Vacqueyras. Look at the two lists compiled earlier this year which follow. The first is the warehouse's top-selling six wines; the second list comprises the wines which provide most income.

1. Le St Cricq Blanc de Blancs.
2. Blanc de blancs Henri Lambert.
3. Le St Cricq rouge.
4. Pinot Grigio del Veneto.
5. Il Paesano Merlot del Veneto.
6. Cotes de Rhone Lys d'Or.

Customers buy more of the above than any other wines, but the wines below are the ones bringing home fatter rashers of bacon:

1. Laurent-Perrier champagne.
2. De Telmont Brut champagne.
3. Roland Bauchet champagne.
4. Moet et Chandon champagne.
5. Blanc de blancs Henri Lambert.
6. Les St Cricq Blanc de Blancs.

If nothing else, this demonstrates the money to be made from champagne. How many cases of Henri Lambert (at £2.79 the bottle – a wine not rated in this book) have to be sold to equal the profit received from selling one bottle of Moet et Chandon (at £18.99)? The champagne houses themselves have, it is worth my remarking in passing, a different numerical conundrum to unravel. They make 300 million of bottles of champagne in a year but can only sell 260 million. What is to be done as the stocks of unsold wines get older? Answer: do deals with British wine retailers and supermarkets.

Who, you may ask, is buying all this champagne at Majestic? All those managers who work for the ex-publicly owned utilities is the reply. The typical Majestic customer 'is male, aged thirty-five plus', says Sarah Wykes, the chain's public relations manager. It is a safe bet that these rich individuals live in Farnham, Worcester, Weybridge, Nottingham and Chester. These are where the new Majestic branches were opened up this year and on this basis we can safely say the recession is over.

Majestic, for me, has always been a litmus test of recessional swings. Unlike other retailers who will sell you a single bottle, the case-only policy at Majestic means that when things are tough economically they really feel the pinch. Buying a case is like striking a deal; buying a mere bottle is just shopping – and middle-aged men hate shopping but love striking deals (leaving aside the question of whether they have actually struck one or not). Now it seems Majestic is booming, and unless the boom is solely due to the careful siting of branches near to power company millionaires' ghettos, then the corner has been turned for all of us.

Which countries does Majestic expect to provide the most exciting additions to its range over the next few years? 'California, Italy, France, Chile, South Africa, New Zealand and Spain,' Ms Wykes told me.

I can see why New Zealand is in there. Some of the best, and best-priced, sparkling wines in the world are coming out of New Zealand. And while Majestic has a couple, it doesn't have the one I regard as incomparable: Daniel Le Brun's.

Let me know when you're getting it in, will you, Tony? Put me down for a case. The way you price things in this area, I expect to pay around £130. Not bad for a dozen bottles of one of the loveliest bubblies on the planet.

Majestic Wine Warehouses
Odhams Trading Estate
St Albans Road
Watford
WD2 5RE

Tel 01923 816999
Fax 01923 819105

**SEE STOP PRESS SECTION AT END OF BOOK FOR
LAST-MINUTE ADDITIONS TO THIS RETAILER'S
RANGE.**

AUSTRALIAN WINE RED

Cape Mentelle Cabernet Merlot 1992   `14` `E`

Lush, controlled fruitiness with tannins smoothly operating in tandem.

Chateau Tahbilk Cabernet Sauvignon 1991   `14` `D`

Raw but brawny.

Chateau Tahbilk Shiraz 1991   `15` `D`

Spicy, plummy. Some good tannin.

Lindemans Bin 45 Cabernet Sauvignon 1992   `13.5` `C`

Good flavour and balance – good cheese wine.

Lindemans Pyrus, Coonawarra 1990   `16` `E`

Even at a tenner this wine's pedigree seems cheap. Deep rich fruit, brilliant soft tannins, restrained mint edge.

Penfolds Coonawarra Cabernet Sauvignon 1990   `17` `E`

Superb texture to this food ... I mean wine. It's as characterful, rich, smooth and deep as a sauce reduced by Nico Ladenis.

Penfolds Rawson's Retreat Bin 35 Shiraz/Cabernet 1992   `15` `D`

Ripe, soft fruit with some development ahead of it. Attractive berry flavours, well-structured and balanced. Very drinkable now but a 17/18-pointer in 3/4 years.

Preece Cabernet Sauvignon, Mitchelton 1992 `15` `D`

Lovely fruit, quite delicious and seductive. Complex, flavoursome, rich without being overripe.

Simon Hackett Cabernet Shiraz 1991 `13.5` `C`

Wyndham Estate Shiraz Bin 555 1993 `16.5` `D`

In spite of lacking an earthy dimension, this incredibly smooth and polished wine has such savouriness and depth it must rate highly at the price.

Yalumba Bush Vine Grenache 1993 `13` `D`

AUSTRALIAN WINE WHITE

Cape Mentelle Semillon/Sauvignon Blanc 1994 `17` `E`

Sublimely fruity and well-cut. Has an upper layer of creamy melon and a lower one of gooseberry. But this is not a stuff-yourself-full-of-calories slice of fruit cake; this is the product of a maitre patissier.

Chateau Tahbilk Marsanne 1992 `14` `C`

Sour/rich fruit of interest to grim-faced fish diners.

Lindemans Bin 65 Chardonnay 1994 `15` `C`

Lovely balance and structure. Vibrant, fruity, delicious.

Penfolds Bin 202 South Australian Riesling 1993 `14` `C`

Superb, rich aperitif. Delicious.

Penfolds Koonunga Hill Chardonnay 1992

Penfolds Rawson's Retreat Bin 21 Semillon/Chardonnay 1993

Fresh and lively yet a dollop of pineappley melon keeps intruding. Delicious refreshing wine.

Penfolds Semillon/Chardonnay 1993

Excellent recipe: fruit, acid, wood but will integrate and improve mightily over the next 1/2 years.

Penfolds South Australia Chardonnay 1993

Good wood and fruit integration leading to excellent food and wine integration.

Preece Chardonnay, Michelton 1993

Good but neither quirky nor as exciting as previous vintages.

Wyndhams Estate Bin 222 Chardonnay 1992

Has the depth and warmth plus the sheer fruity vitality to conquer even spaghetti a la vongole with a spicy tomato sauce.

CANADIAN WINE WHITE

Barrel Select Mission Hill Chardonnay 1993

CHILEAN WINE RED

Montenuevo Oak-Aged Cabernet Sauvignon 1992

Montes Alpha Cabernet Sauvignon 1990

Age for 5/6 years. Good tannins.

FRENCH WINE RED

Aloxe Corton Domaine Latour 1986

Good gamy aroma but thin fruit thereafter. Not worth the money.

Auxey Duresses Rouge, Faiveley 1992

**Beaume-de-Venise Cotes du Rhone
Villages 1990**

Delicious soft fruit with that dry, earthy touch of Beaumes.

**Bourgogne Passetoutgrains, Mongeard-
Mugneret 1993**

Mildly diverting but at a major incident price.

Bourgogne Pinot Noir, Faiveley 1992

**Cairanne J. Vidal-Fleury, Cotes du
Rhone 1985**

A wine for crusty old men in smoke-filled rooms. A lot of money for a late middle-aged dry stick like this. The earthiness has become all fruit with a dry edge. Handsome but what a price!

Chateau Beausejour, Fronsac 1992

Chateau Camplong, Corbieres 1993

Tannins here nicely evolving. Another year?

Chateau d'Aqueria, Lirac 1992 15 D

Very velvety but studded with sequins of tannin.

Chateau de Rully, Rully 1989 11 E

Some hints of character here.

Chateau Duplessis Hauchecorne, Moulis 1990 13.5 D

I'd cellar this wine for 4/5 more years and see how excitingly its tannins developed. It is drinkable now, especially with rare roast meat, but it is potentially more of a thriller.

Chateau Flaugergues, Coteaux du Languedoc 1993 16 D

Some chewy tannins here amongst the plum-edge blackcurrants and plum fruit give richness and depth to an essentially rustic style of wine. Great food wine.

Chateau Haut Bages Averous, Pauillac 1992 12 F

Chateau la Perriere Bordeaux 1993 14 C

Very soundly priced for such attractive claret styling. Begins soft, finishes savoury and tannic.

Chateau Meaume, Bordeaux Superieur 1990 13 C

Chateau Saint-James, Corbieres 1993 15 C

Refined earthiness.

Chateau Sainte Jeanne, Corbieres 1991 16 C

Brilliant wine. Rich and ready. Lovely tannic edge leading to dry blackcurranty fruit of some style. A very good price. Real quality here.

Chinon, Les Bardons 1992

Light, soft, raspberry/slate aroma and fruit – delicious! A beginner's Chinon (it's very easy-going on the palate) but very attractive. Fantastic bargain!

Chinon les Garous 1990, Couly-Dutheil

Black cherries, very dry and slate-like, yet soft and ripely finished. Lovely wine to drink cool with barbecued food. Indeed, I would consider the highest mark of a civilised host that he/she would serve this chilled with charcoal cooked lamb!

Coteaux de Tricastin, Domaine Vergobbi 1991

The new vintage is tasty (and at £3.99 still brilliantly priced) with a lingering, brambly, softly savoury flavour on the finish but it's lighter than the previous vintage. The gentle tannin and acid elements squabble a little and the completion of the wine is not flawless and as a result it is not so intensely arousing but . . . it's *still* a terrific red wine for the money.

Cotes du Rhone Villages, Vidal-Fleury 1990

Rich, soft – a great year.

Coudoulet de Beaucastel, Cotes du Rhone 1992

Domaine de Guingal Cahors 1990

Domaine des Schistes, Cotes du Roussillon Villages 1993

Some hints of richness here. Possibly needs more time in bottle to soften more. Open 2 hours before drinking.

Domaine Fouletiere 1991, Coteaux du Languedoc

Fortant de France Grenache, VdP d'Oc 1993
`15.5`

A wine to appal any tannin lover who prefers his fruit more mannered and stand-offish and demanding of bowing and scraping and ritual breathing before being prepared to reveal itself. This grenache is savoury cherry jam which bounces out of the bottle and slobbers over the tastebuds like a young pup – a glorious whore of a red wine.

Gigondas, Guigal 1990
`12.5` `F`

Great year but tannins still chewy here.

Les Jamelles Mourvedre, Vin de Pays d'Oc 1993
`13.5` `C`

I'd stick this in my coal hole and open it for Christmas around 1998 – it should be a 16-pointer by then.

Les Jamelles Syrah 1993, Vin de Pays d'Oc
`14` `C`

Ripe, soft, easy drinking.

Mas de la Garrigue, Cotes du Roussillon 1993
`13.5` `C`

This is tough and hearty and will suit appropriate food.

Mercurey Rouge Les Mauvarennes 1991, Faiveley
`12` `E`

Michel Lynch Bordeaux Rouge 1990
`13.5` `D`

Good solid claret with approachable, soft tannins and fruit.

Monastere de Trignan 1992, Coteaux du Languedoc
`14`

Chocolate edges here – good tannins – good developing fruit. Open 2 hours before serving with a casserole.

Oaky Claret `13` `C`

Regnie La Roche Thulon 1992, Louis Latour `13` `D`

Rully Rouge, Louis Pages 1991 `12` `C`

Saint-Julien 1993 `14.5` `E`
Real class, real flavour, real price. Has voluptuous fruit.

St Joseph 1990, Caves des Papes, Ogier `12` `D`

Vacqueyras Vidal-Fleury 1991 `12` `D`
Not as terrific as it has been. Still hints at savoury depth and real fruit but the emphatic style is missing.

VdP de l'Herault `13` `B`
Rough but very ready.

Vieux Chateau Valentin Premieres Cotes de Blaye 1990 `13.5` `D`
Some attractive savoury tannins – will age 2 years more and be better.

FRENCH WINE WHITE

Ardeche Chardonnay, Louis Latour 1993 `11` `C`

Baron de Hoen Tokay Pinot Gris Vendanges Tardives 1990, Beblenheim `12` `F`
Delicious, perhaps not as ready to drink as it will be in 7/8 years, and very expensive.

Bourgogne Chardonnay, 'Georges Faiveley' 1992

Bourgogne Chardonnay 'Paulee' 1992, I. Faiveley

Cante Cigale Rose de Saignee 1993, Vin de Pays de l'Herault

Light, fruity, fresh. Good fun with fish or without food.

Chablis Domaine Vocoret 1994

Just about acceptable – but what a price to pay for mere acceptability.

Chardonnay 1993, VdP d'Oc

Superb value for money: fruity, dry, subtle yet characterful. Good buttery side to it.

Chateau de Sours Rose 1993, Bordeaux

Chateau Haut Mazieres Blanc, Bordeaux 1992

Has an agreeable subdued richness of fruit which hints at real class.

Chateau La Fonrousse Monbazillac 1990 16.5 D

Beautiful bargain dessert wine with a burnt caramel and honey edge.

Chateau Meaume Bordeaux Rose 1994 13.5 C

A genuinely classy rose. I'm not overfond of the breed but this one at least pays its way fruitwise.

Chateaux Tanesse Blanc, Bordeaux 1993

Flavour here and a hint of class.

Chinon Rose 1992, Couly-Dutheil `14` `D`
Earthy, deliciously fruity and superbly ripe and zesty on the finish.

Cotes de Rhone Blanc, Domaine de la Meynarde 1994 `14.5` `C`
Softness, flavour. Great wine for trout and other freshwater fish.

Cotes de Rhone Blanc Vidal-Fleury 1994 `14` `D`
A touch pricey but has controlled earthy fruit and flavour, with some style. Good fish-stew bottle.

Delta Domaines Muscat 'Terres Fines', VdP de l'Herault 1994 `13.5` `C`
An excellent aperitif. Tickles the throat rather than tackling food.

Delta Domaines Picpoul 'Terres Fines' VdP de l'Herault 1994 `12` `C`

Domaine de Sours Bordeaux Blanc 1993 `14.5` `C`
Very classy fruit here: woody and expensive in feel.

Geminian Sauvignon VdP d'Oc 1993 `15` `B`
Good sauvignon expressiveness; restrained fruit with a melon edge. Crisp, well modulated acidity. A balanced, well-made, well-priced wine of some style.

Grand Ardeche Chardonnay, Louis Latour 1992 `13` `E`
Some woody richness of flavour here.

Lanine VdP des Cotes de Gascogne 1993 `14` `B`
An elegant, tightly fruity, unexotic Gascogne with wonderful clean, crisp fruit.

Le St Cricq Blanc de Blancs 1993

Bright, modern, very fresh with pear-drop undertones and appleskin overtones. Brilliant summer drinking.

Les Granges Touraine Chenin Blanc 1992

Les Jamelles Marsannes 1992, Vin de Pays d'Oc

Smells a little as if you should toss it in your eye rather than down the throat; reminds me of Optrex. The fruit is muted and rather nun-like in reserve.

Les Jamelles Viognier, VdP d'Oc 1993

Limoux, Toques et Clocher 1993

Macon Villages Les Chazelles 1993

Not bad, considering.

Mauzac Domaine Lamoure, VdP de l'Aude 1993

Moulin Touchais 1983

A deliciously different but expensive aperitif.

Muscat, VdP des Collines de la Noure 1993, Hugh Ryman

A vivid balancing act of ripe, sweet melon fruit and raunchy acidity. Terrific with hard fruit and hard cheese or blue cheese by itself.

Pinot Blanc 1993, Laugel

Powdery overtones on the melon/peach/apricot fruit. Finishes clean but slightly muted. Very good price. Excellent aperitif.

Pouilly Fume les Loges 1993, Guy Saget `12` `D`

Sancerre les Roches 1994, Vacheron `11` `E`

Comes on (smell) like a sancerre but not across (fruit).

**Sauvignon Blanc Comte d'Ormont 1993,
Guy Saget** `14` `B`

Tokay Pinot Gris 1992, Ribeauville `15` `D`

Superb. Streaks of apricot fruit, chewy yet not soft or flabby, mingle with the firm acids to make a superb aperitif.

Viognier Galet Vineyards, VdP d'Oc 1993 `13.5` `D`

The Spud-U-Like wine! The stones on the label ('galets') look unfortunately like potatoes. The wine offers more fruit, however.

GERMAN WINE   WHITE

**Cuvee Constantin Qualitatswein Trocken
1992** `12` `C`

**Grans Fassian Trittenheimer Altarcher
Riesling Kabinett 1992** `13.5` `D`

Put it down for 10 years for a 17-point wine to emerge, a golden butterfly from a tight chrysalis.

Grans Fassians Riesling 1993 `13` `D`

Needs 3/4 years more at least.

Jacob Zimmermann Auslese `15.5` `C`

Bargain. Complex fruit with a wonderful baked toffee fruit finish. Delightful for Chinese food – brilliant!

Jacob Zimmermann Kabinett 1993

Delicious aperitif for summer gardens / alfresco noshing.

Jacob Zimmermann Spatlese 1993

Great summer fun and for drinking with Chinese food – especially Peking duck with plum sauce.

Kirchheimer Schwarzerde Beerenauslese, Zimmermann-Graeff, Pfalz 1993 (half bottle)

Big-hearted sweetie which would be best left to develop over the next 10 years. Lay it down for the children's entrance to university?

Piesporter Goldtropfchen Riesling Auslese, Moselle 1990

Try it opening the Christmas presents as a wine for everyone. It has fruit, acid, balance, flavour, richness, subtlety and a mysterious lingering finish.

Trittenheimer Apotheke Riesling Auslese, Grans Fassians, Moselle 1989

Deep, flavourful, young yet middle-aged (will keep for 20 years or more). Great with grapes and cheese.

ITALIAN WINE RED

Barbera d'Asti Superiore, Bava 1990

Rich, very dry. It has the throaty wail of a low-registering violin. Excellent with food – real class. A lovely finish. Very good structure.

Bardolino Cavalchina 1994 `13` `C`
Dry cherries. Austere.

Capitel San Rocco Vino di Rispasso, Tedeschi 1990 `13.5` `D`

Castello di Nipozzano Riserva, Chianti Rufina Marchesi di Frescobaldi 1991 `14` `D`

Centine Rosso di Montalcino DOC, Banfi 1992 `15` `D`
Softness, richness, flavour (plums and dark cherries) and good fruit attack.

Col di Sasso, Vino da Tavola Banfi 1992 `10` `C`

Cortenova Merlot, Grave del Friuli Pasqua 1994 `13` `B`
Cheap but cheerful – cherry-ripe and bright.

Giordano Barbaresco 1986 `17` `C`
A lovely mature wine with restrained tannins, figgy fruit coated in plum and an earthy, subtly licorice finish. A superb wine for old codgers!

Montepulciano d'Abruzzo 1993, Barone Cornacchia `13.5` `C`
Humm. Great with pasta.

Recioto Della Valpolicella Halves 1988, Tedeschi (half bottle) `11` `D`
A sweet red wine which goes well with almond tart.

Salice Salentino Riserva, Taurino 1990 `14` `C`
Mature fruit with hints of earth.

Sangiovese di Romagna Riserva, San Crispino 1991

14.5 | D

Throaty yet seductive. Big sophisticated fruit with an earthy edge. A terrific food wine.

Santara Red 1993, Conca de Barbera, Hugh Ryman

14 | B

Good dry fruit, nicely shrouded in tannins yet soft and tongue-tickling. Very good value.

Taurino Notapanaro, Rosso del Salento 1986

16 | C

Rich, spicy, full of flavour and well-muscled fruit. Burnt edge to the finish which is quite delicious.

Valpolicella Classico, Tedescho 1991

12.5 | C

ITALIAN WINE   WHITE

Bardolino Chiaretto Cavalchina 1994

14.5 | C

A delicate dry rose with real flavour which never becomes cosmetic or too Barbie doll-flavoured.

Bianco di Custoza Cavalchina 1994

15 | C

Delicious example of custardy, nutty melon fruit never over-done.

La Prendina Bianco 1993

14.5 | D

Apples, currants and melons with a fruit finish which recalls no fruit on earth. Interesting wine for smoked fish (eel especially).

Pinot Nero Pavese 1993

11 | C

Vin Santo Brolio 1985, Ricasoli

An interesting example of a wine I usually detest. This has muted marmalade fruit and would be great with treacle tart or sticky toffee pudding.

MOROCCAN WINE — RED

Moroccan Red 15.5 B

Dry, earthy, plummy fruit – a touch of elegance amongst the dirt. Brilliant value!!

NEW ZEALAND WINE — RED

**Delegat's Proprietor's Reserve Cabernet
Sauvignon 1991** 14 E

NEW ZEALAND WINE — WHITE

**Coopers Creek Chardonnay, Gisborne
1994** 15 D

Delicious, restrained, classy. Never a dull note nor a harsh one.

**Coopers Creek Sauvignon 1993,
Marlborough** 14 D

Coopers Creek Sauvignon, Gisborne 1994 13.5 D

Not biting as decisively as it might at this price – but still a far from awkward wine.

Goldwater Chardonnay 1992, Marlborough `12` `E`

**Highfield Estate Sauvignon Blanc
Marlborough 1993** `14` `C`

Asparagus and spinach fruit of interest to anyone contemplating putting those two vegetables together in a salad.

Oyster Bay Chardonnay 1993, Marlborough `15` `E`

Balanced beauty. Tasteful fruit playing fast and loose with the acidity in fine style.

Oyster Bay Sauvignon 1993, Marlborough `14` `D`

SOUTH AFRICAN WINE   RED

Dieu Donne Cabernet Sauvignon 1993 `15` `D`

This has style and class and a nicely tannin-touched black cherry fruit. It will age well, very well, for 5/6 years.

SOUTH AFRICAN WINE   WHITE

Roodiberg Co-op Chardonnay 1992 `11` `C`

If honey went stale this is how it would taste.

SPANISH WINE   RED

**Alentejo Tinto Velho 1988,
J. M. da Fonseca** `13` `C`

Must be drunk with rich food.

Berberana Reserva Rioja 1988 `11` `D`

**Enate Tempranillo/Cabernet Sauvignon
Crianza 1992** `16` `D`

Has a rounded fruit edge which rolls off the palate like a replete
sultan (after an orgy) off his silken couch.

Gran Dolfos, Bodegas Farina 1989 `13.5` `C`

Has richness and flavour and some style. Best with forceful
cooking.

Rioja Vina Arisabel 1993 `13` `B`

Bit thin – but then so is the price.

Torres Coronas 1991 `14` `C`

Vina Real Gran Reserva Rioja 1982 `13` `F`

Delicious. Expensive.

SPANISH WINE   WHITE

Enate Chardonnay, Somontano 1993 `13.5` `E`

Some meaty fruit here.

**Monopole Barrel Fermented Rioja,
Cune 1992** `13` `D`

Delicious fish-stew wine.

Rioja Bianco Preferido, Berberana 1993 `10` `B`

Torres Sangredetoro 1991 `15.5` `C`

Licorice!? Very dry, starts well. Drink it in an hour – it fades.

Vinedos d'Avalos Rioja Crianzo Bianco 1987   `15` `C`

Wood aromas, somewhat rudely planed, but the fruit has vigour and attack and with creamy fish dishes or grilled chicken would be superb. Also good with barbecues.

USA WINE   RED

Atlas Peak Sangiovese, Napa Valley 1992   `11` `F`

Beringer Cabernet Sauvignon 1991   `16` `E`

Expensive but packed with personality and flavour.

Beringer Cabernet Sauvignon Private Reserve, Napa Valley 1989   `16` `G`

I hope this wine is in my Christmas stocking, but I wouldn't buy it for myself.

Beringer Howell Mountain Merlot, Napa Valley 1991   `14` `G`

Magnificently well-textured fruit, deep and dark. Very classy.

Beringer Zinfandel 1991   `13.5` `D`

Calera Pinot Noir, Central Coast 1991   `10` `F`

Coastal Ridge Cabernet Sauvignon 1992   `16` `D`

Beautifully dusky fruit, exotic, dry, full, spicy, complex and rich. Delicious.

Eagle Peak Merlot, Fetzer 1992   `14` `D`

Attractively well-developed fruit.

Ehlers Grove Cabernet Sauvignon 1992 `14` `C`

Good flavour – dryish but not without wit.

Ehlers Grove Pinot Noir 1993 `11` `C`

**Fetzer Valley Oaks Cabernet Sauvignon
1992** `14` `D`

Richness and depth.

Jade Mountain Syrah 1992 `10` `G`

Mondavi Reserve Napa Pinot Noir 1992 `10` `G`

**Ridge Santa Cruz Mountains Cabernet
Sauvignon 1992** `17` `G`

Yes, 17 even at this mountainous price, but the fruit is high-flying
too, with masses of flavour and depth, and great tannins.

USA WINE   WHITE

Andrew Quady Elysium Black Muscat 1993 `14` `D`

Cassis-like. Try it with blackcurrant fool.

Beringer Chardonnay, Napa Valley 1992 `13` `E`

Hints at class rather than exhibiting it full-bloodedly.

**Beringer Chardonnay Private Reserve,
Napa Valley 1993** `15` `G`

Delicious depth of flavour here: stylish, bold, posh.

Beringer Fume Blanc, Napa Valley 1993 `13` `D`

Curiously full-flavoured sauvignon. Suits rich fish dishes.

Calera Chardonnay, Central Coast 1993   14   F

A big wine with some finesse and elegance. Is this, though, worth £11? Nope. Is it fruity, woody, balanced, flavoursome and striking? Yep. Is it better than £20 white burgundies? It's different, that's for sure.

Coastal Ridge Chardonnay 1993   16   D

Oodles of buttery flavour with a hint of melon and orange peel. Delicious!

Electra Orange Muscat (4% alcohol) 1992   12   C

Drink it with ice cream.

Essensia Orange Muscat Halves, Andrew Quady 1993 (half bottle)   15   D

An unusually exquisite extraterrestrial monster which goes wonderfully with soft fruits.

Jekel Gravelstone Chardonnay 1992   12   E

Mondavi Reserve Chardonnay, Napa Valley 1992   14   G

Fancy fruit, fancy price.

FORTIFIED WINE

Delaforce 1975   16   G

Rolls smoothly around the palate. Lovely wine for cold winter evenings.

Los Arcos Dry Amontillado   17   E

Magnificent, oily, nutty, camomile-rich fruit. Drink very chilled with grilled prawns.

Lustau Old East India Sherry `15` `E`

Fruit cake-rich and delicious. Drink with a slice of Christmas cake.

Quarles Harris 1980 `13.5` `G`

Warres Warrior Vintage Character Port `16` `E`

Good value here: character, richness and depth for cheeses.

SPARKLING WINE/CHAMPAGNE

Ayala Champagne `10` `F`

Invariably delicious, this marque. Classic champagne.

Blanquette de Limoux, Cuvee Speciale 1988 `12` `E`

Bollinger Grande Annee 1988 `10` `H`

This is rich champagne, mature, compelling, complex; but at a price of such absurdity only nuts would buy it.

Chantelore Brut Blanc de Blancs (France) `14` `C`

Confectionery fruit fizz up front then pleasant fresh acid sidles in. An excellent summer garden aperitif – as long as you're not expecting a Bollinger clone.

Chantelore Rose (France) `14` `C`

Touch of ice-cream strawberry fruit in the middle. Good for gardens, hot days, and letting it all hang out.

Clover Hill 1991 (Tasmania) `11` `E`

De Telmont Grande Reserve Champagne   `14` `F`

Excellent. Good with smoked salmon.

Lancelot de Hoen Cremant d'Alsace   `14` `E`

Butter-biscuit fruit. Rather attractive in a raffish sort of way.

Nautilus Brut NV (New Zealand)   `17` `F`

This sleekly fruity, calm, well-balanced wine has considerable elegance and pulls off that remarkable trick which all outstanding bubblies do, of having a presence on the finish which is not mere carbonic gas and acidity but delicious soft fruit.

Oeil de Perdrix NV, Leonce d'Albe   `13.5` `F`

Sophisticated rose champagne for funerals and divorces.

Pongracz NV (South Africa)   `14` `E`

Austere and rather military in its briskness but a worthy Cape bubbly for all that.

Seppelt Chardonnay Blanc de Blanc Brut 1990 (Australia)   `13` `E`

Solid, dependable, gently citric bubbly.

Seppelt Great Western Brut   `14` `C`

Light and breezy.

Seppelt Great Western Rose   `15` `D`

Shadow Creek 1986 (USA)   `11` `E`

Taittinger NV   `11` `G`

Taltarni Brut Tache (Australia)   `14` `E`

A rose bubbly of restrained class.

ODDBINS

Oddbins is the wine retailer other wine retailers would be if they had the balls. And, it must be said, if they had behind them the benign and indulgent sponsorship of one of the world's largest booze companies. Oddbins is owned by the Seagram Corporation of America. This corporation has a charming, easily bored young man at its head, Edgar Bronfman, whom I met on several occasions a decade ago before he reached his present elevated position, and he, for me, represents the epitome of all that is so wonderfully wacky about the Seagram company and its myriad subsidiary interests. These interests now include expansion into the entertainment industry via Hollywood and thus it is entirely appropriate that a concern of such catholicity and wealth should be Oddbins' owners.

But not Oddbins' masters. Oddbins is surely its own master. Cynics would say this is only because everyone at corporate headquarters in the US has long given up trying to fathom the conspiratorial eccentricities of the British drinks market (Captain Morgan rum on Millwall's shirt fronts indeed!) and that, in any case, Oddbins is such a minor contributor to group profits, if at all, that its affairs probably don't even get reviewed at quarterly corporate board meetings. I daresay Edgar glimpses the newest Oddbins wine list, bold, bloody and bulging with the latest graphic incantations of cartoonist Ralph Steadman, says, 'Attaboys! Keep it up!' and immediately turns his attentions to the more soluble and exciting problem of whether Raquel Welch is the right actress to play Doc Holliday in a transsexual remake of *Gunfight at the OK Corrall.*

The secret of Oddbins is that it is the only wine retailer

who makes the customers feel more knowledgeable than it is itself. All great retail operations pull a similar psychological trick. M & S's clothes stores, for instance, have the brilliant knack of making customers feel that they *must* buy the stuff on the hangers before the store notices its mistake and puts the prices up. Oddbins, with its lagoons of marooned wines in boxes and tubs scattered all over the floorboards, its graffiti-dominated windows, its excruciatingly young assistants and their crumpled clothes bought at Oxfam and Save the Children shops, its sky-high shelves of wines inscribed with hilarious comments authored, it would seem, by the shop's own staff, all go to make the young to middle-aged man with a few bob to spend feel distinctly superior and relaxed. Spending money at Oddbins is a commercial exercise which makes you feel as virtuous as when you buy your copy of *The Big Issue*. (Don't tell Edgar this. He's quite likely to rattle his piggy bank and buy the magazine.) Surely, this well-heeled Young Turk of a customer tells himself, these delightful undergraduates don't *really* want the shop organised as higgledy-piggledy as all this, they simply don't know any better. No wonder the sort of bloke who drives a Porsche likes filling its boot with Oddbins wines (not difficult with such a car.)

What sort of wines? These were, not in any sales-volume order, the company's top-selling half dozen wines in spring this year:

1. Perrier Jouet NV champagne (£16.79).
2. Cuvee Napa Brut sparkling wine (£8.99).
3. Heidsieck Dry Monopole champagne (£12.49).
4. Lindemans Cawarra Colombard 1994 (£3.99).
5. Campo Viejo Rioja Reserva 1990 (£5.49).
6. Montana Sauvignon Blanc 1994 (£4.99).

Who said yuppy extravagance was dead? Three sparkling wines in a top-sellers list? It defies belief. Or maybe it's perfectly logical. Maybe it's Oddbins' just desserts for all the hard work it puts into promoting champagne. It's always pushing twelve bottles for the price of eleven deals and it has similar promotional offers on a regular basis. Champagne Charlie is alive and kicking at Oddbins and he is given plenty of good reasons to keep coming back. The average per bottle spend at Oddbins increased to £4.90 from £4.30 over the past year. The per bottle spend in the wine market as a whole went up during that period to £2.89 from £2.69.

Oddbins' strengths lie in the South of France, Burgundy, the US, Chile and Australia. 'We launched a large range of 1992 white burgundies, too,' PR manager and occasional fine wine buyer Katie MacAuley informed me. Also last year, it opened fifteen new shops and two more of the so-called Fine Wine shops, one in Edinburgh and the other in Glasgow. Whether Ms MacAuley's Gaelic origins had anything to do with the siting of these new ventures I cannot say but it is not without the bounds of possibility that it did. Oddbins is quite capable of flaunting the same quirky entrepreneurial streak that has always run, sparkling and rich, through the Seagram Corporation; a quality which means the risk-attendant personal hunch is to be preferred, now and then, over the highly researched and impregnably boring cert. This year, 1995, twelve new branches will be on line and two new Fine Wine Shops; Cambridge opens in April, Oxford in May – in time for the summer balls and punting parties. These latter will doubtless be able to float on the rivers of Perrier Jouet consumed.

That Oddbins has an emotional side was displayed when I spoke to the chain's Palate-in-Chief Steve Daniel, who told me how much he loved working for the company. 'Wine interests me not just as a wine buyer but as a wine enthusiast. That's why everyone works here, because we love the products. There's no thrill in our just stocking the same range as everybody else because there's not enough branches. We have 205 stores as opposed to 1,600 at Thresher. We've got to make it worthwhile for customers to seek us out.

'Any idiot can buy wines,' adds Steve. 'But at the end of the day you've got to sell them. We've got guys working for us out there who are interested and enthusiastic and knowledgeable. And over the thirty years that we've been around we've attracted the consumers who want our style of product. So we're in a great position. We've got the wines that with a bit of effort and hard work we can sell.'

Oddbins has, of course, its imitators. But no one can copy the ethos which makes the chain itself so genuinely different. The launch of the Greenalls Wine Cellar chain with a printed wine list which looked for all the world as if it was from Oddbins was, in Steve's view, pathetic.

'We just get so annoyed at things like that,' he muttered, visibly ruffled. 'Wouldn't it be nice if one of our competitors came up with something original for once? Why couldn't they just come up with a different concept? At least we'd respect them a little bit more. They all look at us and they all want our tiny 2 per cent of the market. Our style has evolved sort of organically over thirty years. These guys are just trying to replicate in six months something that took thirty years to do. They can't do it.'

Oddbins
31-32 Weir Road
Wimbledon
London
SW19 8UG

Tel 0181 944 4400
Fax 0181 944 4411

SEE STOP PRESS SECTION AT END OF BOOK FOR LAST-MINUTE ADDITIONS TO THIS RETAILER'S RANGE.

ARGENTINIAN WINE — RED

Trapiche Pinot Noir 1992 | 13 | C |

Delightful sweet fruit.

AUSTRALIAN WINE — RED

Angove's Nanya Estate Grenache/Pinot Noir 1992 | 8 | B |

This has to be the naffest Aussie red wine I have tasted for a some years. Sticking grenache with pinot noir is like asking Jayne Torvill to ice-dance with Paul Gascoigne.

Baileys 1920s Block Shiraz 1993 | 17 | E |

Like putting a cassis and chocolate cream fingered glove on your teeth. The rich tannins grip and don't let go.

Chateau Reynella Basket Press Shiraz 1992 | 16 | D |

Spicy, deep and so full of flavour you wonder for a moment — could grapes really be squeezed to yield fruit so rich?

Cockatoo Ridge Cabernet/Merlot 1993 | 14 | C |

Coldstream Hills Pinot Noir 1992 | 12 | E |

Ebenezer Barossa Valley Shiraz 1992 | 18 | E |

Utterly world-class fruit in romping form, subdued spice, soft tannins, great, great fruit.

Ebenezer Cabernet Sauvignon/Malbec/ Merlot/Cabernet Franc 1992

Jam and cream and strawberry-centred fruit. Dive in and enjoy yourself.

Geoff Merrill Mount Hurtle Grenache/ Shiraz 1992

Glenloth Cabernet/Shiraz/Cabernet Sauvignon

Good value here.

Hardys Chateau Reynella Shiraz, Stony Hill 1990

Gently tannic black cherry and plum fruit. Will improve for a few years yet but very good now!

Killawarra Cabernet Sauvignon/Shiraz 1992

Soft fruit you could pour over ice-cream. Good value.

Killawarra Shiraz/Cabernet 1992

Leasingham Cabernet/Malbec 1992

Ripe and full – complex, very highly flavoured. Delicious roast food wine.

Leasingham Shiraz, Clare Valley 1992 17 D

Brilliantly orchestrated fruit and tannins in rich voice together. Superb depth, complexity and flavour.

Leeuwin Estate Redgum Ridge Cabernet Sauvignon 1990

Delicious fruit, structure and style.

Lindemans Bin 45 Cabernet Sauvignon 1992   14 C

Attractive berry flavours and residual richness.

Lindemans Pyrus 1988   15 E

Lindemans St George Vineyard Cabernet Sauvignon 1989   16 E

McWilliams Mount Pleasant Cabernet Sauvignon 1992   15 C

McWilliams Mount Pleasant Cabernet/ Merlot 1993   13.5 C

Penfolds Bin 2 Shiraz/Mourvedre 1992   15 C

Plum and black cherries, muted spice. Delicious! Will develop and get even better.

Penfolds Bin 407 Cabernet Sauvignon 1990   16 E

Penfolds Coonawarra Cabernet Sauvignon 1990   17 E

The colour of crushed blackberries, subtle eucalyptus/leather aroma, sheer satiny acids and velvet-textured fruit touches – lovely tannicky finish.

Penfolds Old Vine Mourvedre/Grenache/ Shiraz, Barossa 1992   15 E

A flood of ripe fruit bolstered by friendly tannins which seem to me pretty as well developed as they could get for the best balance of flavours. In spite of what Penfolds say, drink this wine over the next year. The gloss of its fruit will fade if the tannins are allowed to tighten their grip over, say, 3/4 years.

AUSTRALIAN WINE

**Penfolds Rawson's Retreat Bin 35
Cabernet Sauvignon/Ruby Cabernet/Shiraz
1993**   `12` `C`

Soft and rather expressionless.

**Peter Lehmann Clancy's, Barossa
Valley 1992**   `15` `D`

Impressive smoothness and flavour.

Peter Lehmann Shiraz 1991   `16` `C`

Wonderful, rich, complex gravy.

Peter Lehmann Vine Vale Shiraz 1992   `15` `C`

Ripe and full of character. Abuzz with flavour.

Rothbury Estate Reserve Shiraz 1993   `14` `E`

Rich and jammy.

Rothbury Estate Shiraz 1993   `14.5` `D`

Soft, gripping fruit with a jammy centre.

**Saltram Mamre Brook Cabernet Sauvignon
1993**   `14` `D`

Saltram Shiraz 1993   `14` `C`

Wirra Wirra Grenache Shiraz 1994   `14` `E`

Lots of flavour, but restrained in temperament as though something holds it back (youth, most likely). The price will hold the thrifty wine-lover back, too.

Wirra Wirra R S W Shiraz 1993   `16` `E`

Rich and so fruity it weeps over the palate like a liquid blackberry bush.

Wirra Wirra The Angelus Cabernet Sauvignon 1993 | 14.5 | E |

Jammy and oddly cuddly. Not remotely standoffish.

Yalumba Menzies Coonawarra Cabernet Sauvignon 1991 | 16.5 | E |

Lovely class of fruit here, of such lingering, velvety smoothness you can't quite believe your palate's telling you the truth.

AUSTRALIAN WINE   WHITE

Aussie Rules Sauvignon/Semillon 1992 | 12 | D |

Bridgewater Mill Chardonnay 1992 | 12 | D |

Broke Estate Chardonnay 1993 | 12 | E |

Oily, delicious, woody, hints at bigness but, thankfully, doesn't deliver it.

Cockatoo Ridge Chardonnay 1994 | 13.5 | C |

Easy glug. Wish it was under £4, though.

Coldstream Hills Reserve Chardonnay 1992 | 13 | F |

Cullen Chardonnay 1992 | 14 | E |

Yes, it's delicious, elegant, sophisticated and I'm in love with the two women who make it. Okay?

Glenloth Dry White 1993 | 14 | B |

Lots of ripe fruit plus a touch of gooseberry and pineapple on the finish. Excellent value.

Glenloth Late Harvest Muscat 1993 | 14 | B |

Cheap thrills with hard fruit and cheese for company.

Heggies Vineyard Chardonnay, Eden Valley 1992 `13.5` `E`

Demure, classy, rather expensive.

Leasingham Clare Valley Semillon 1992 `13` `D`

Leeuwin Estate Chardonnay 1988 `12` `G`

Lenswood Chardonnay 1992 `10` `E`

Lindemans Cawarra Semillon/Chardonnay 1994 `14` `C`

Good with chicken casserole – has the weight of fruit to cope.

Lindemans Bin 65 Chardonnay 1993 `16` `C`

Lindemans Cawarra, Colombard Chardonnay 1993 `14` `C`

Mitchelton Goulburn Riesling `11` `C`

Mitchelton Reserve Chardonnay 1990 `16` `D`

Mount Hurtle Chardonnay 1992 `14` `C`

Oxford Landing Sauvignon Blanc 1993 `14` `C`

Penfolds Bin 202 South Australian Riesling 1993 `14` `C`

Superb, rich aperitif. Delicious.

Penfolds Koonunga Hill Chardonnay 1992 `14` `C`

Penfolds Rawson's Retreat Bin 21 Semillon Chardonnay 1994 `15` `C`

Great clash of soft mango/melony fruit and pineapple acidity. Slightly exotic, generous, bold, delicious.

Penfolds Semillon/Chardonnay 1993 `14` `C`
Excellent recipe: fruit, acid, wood but will integrate and improve mightily over the next 1/2 years.

Penfolds South Australia Chardonnay 1992 `16` `D`
Lovely polished, lush, woody fruit with touches of lemon, beautifully balanced. Elegant – a real alternative, at a far lower price, to fine burgundy.

Peter Lehmann Vine Vale Riesling 1994 `12` `C`

Rothbury Estate Barrel Fermented Hunter Valley Chardonnay 1994 `14.5` `D`
Bright, elegant. Hints at old-style white burgundy.

Rothbury Estate Reserve Chardonnay, Hunter Valley 1993 `14` `E`
Lots of flavour and taste; bruising depth.

Saltram Chardonnay 1993 `14` `C`
With a spicy fish gumbo this is your wine.

Saltram Mamre Brook Chardonnay 1993 `15` `D`
A completely precocious bastard! How can a wine so young be so cocksure? Lovely ripe fruit and undercutting lemony acids.

Saltram Riesling 1993 `12` `C`

Shaw & Smith Sauvignon Blanc 1994 `14` `E`
Herbaceous yet rich.

Valley Estates Rhine Riesling 1993 `13` `B`
Nice price for a nice mouthful of rich fruit polished up with some suggestion of freshness on the finish. Not a huge varietal success but a bargain aperitif.

Wirra Wirra Semillon Sauvignon Blanc 1994

Delicious wine for a mussel and potato stew. Rich-edged, finely balanced, echoes of sour melon – superb for food.

Wynns Riesling 1993

Yalumba Family Reserve Botrytis Semillon 1994 (half bottle)

Sweet but overpriced. Keep for 10 years to be an 18-point beauty.

BULGARIAN WINE RED

Stowells of Chelsea Cabernet Sauvignon (3 litre)

Dry, very good, rich, savoury-edged fruit – good with food.

CHILEAN WINE RED

Caliterra Cabernet Sauvignon 1991

Carmen Gold Reserve Barrel Select Cabernet Sauvignon 1993

This will be best kept for 2/3 years more. It has good tannins and excellent fruit now but will age beautifully.

Casablanca Miraflores Estate Cabernet Sauvignon 1990 13 C

Cono Sur Pinot Noir 1994 13.5 C

A very pleasing little drink. Beats tea any day.

Cono Sur Pinot Noir Reserve 1994   13.5 D
Expensive cherry fruit. Exceedingly drinkable but not sufficiently complex for the money to justify a higher rating.

Cono Sur Rauli Cabernet Sauvignon/Merlot   13 B

Cono Sur Reserve Cabernet Sauvignon 1992   12 D

Montes Alpha Cabernet Sauvignon 1990   13.5 E
Age for 5/6 years. Good tannins.

Nogales Cabernet Sauvignon 1993   14 C
Aromatic, soft, rich-edged. A most engaging wine.

Nogales Cabernet Sauvignon Gran Reserva 1990   16 C
Vivid fruit, good fruit and wood tannins well served by the acids. The result is an overall structure of impressive weight and class.

CHILEAN WINE   WHITE

Caliboro Blanco 1994   14 B
Good clean muscaty glug.

Caliterra Chardonnay 1992   14 C

Caliterra Sauvignon Blanc 1993   16 C

Carmen Chardonnay 1994   15 C
Squashed by a good butter mountain of fruit, the acid is not entirely flattened. Delicious.

Carmen Reserve Chardonnay 1994   15.5   C

Lovely melding of ripe fruit and complex acids. A balanced lingering wine of flavour and style.

Casablanca Chardonnay Lontue Valley 1993   13   C

Casablanca Santa Isabel Valley Sauvignon Blanc 1994   15   D

Expensive but extremely elegant and stylish. Better than any sancerre at the same price.

Casablanca Sauvignon Blanc Lontue Valley/Curico 1993   13   C

Casablanca Valley Chardonnay, Santa Isabel Estate 1993   15   D

Casablanca Valley Gewurztraminer 1993   12   D

Cono Sur Chardonnay 1994   14   C

Some attractive features here. Good grilled chicken wine.

Marques de Casa Concha y Toro Chardonnay 1994   16   D

Gorgeous, mouth-filling fruit with a creamy edge, a nutty undertone, great balance and purposeful style. Terrific stuff.

Santa Carolina Chardonnay, Los Toros Vineyard 1993   15   C

Santa Carolina Chardonnay Special Reserve, Santa Rosa Vineyard 1993   15.5   D

Santa Carolina Sauvignon Blanc, Lontue Valley 1993
`16` `C`

Brilliant construct: lemon, melon, peach, pineapple – all smoothed out and integrated. Classy bargain.

FRENCH WINE   RED

Carignanissime de Centeilles, Minervois 1992
`14` `C`

Chateau de Jau, Cotes de Roussillon Villages 1991
`14` `C`

Chateau Haut Bertinerie Blanc, 1er Cotes de Blaye 1992
`15` `D`

Fresh, light, very flouncey-skirted and fun.

Chateau Lilian Ladorys, St Estephe 1990
`15` `E`

Chateau Paul Blanc, Costieres de Nimes 1993
`15` `C`

A brilliant alternative to Cornas drinkers who find £10 rather too much.

Chateau Rollan de By, Medoc 1993
`13.5` `E`

A perfectly gentlemanly claret which is weighty now but its price, nigh on a tenner, represents very poor value. It will certainly age well for 7/8 years but, though good, its price is a real turn off.

Chateau Thieuley, Francis Courselle, Bordeaux 1992
`11` `E`

Chateau Villerambert Julien, Minervois Cuvee Trianon 1992
`13.5` `D`

Costieres de Nimes, Grand Plagnol 1992   `13` `C`

Some chewy, charcoal-edged fruit here. Good grilled sausage wine.

Cotes de Rhone Guigal 1990   `13` `C`

Crozes-Hermitage, Bernard Chave   `11` `D`

Crozes-Hermitage, Les Pierelle Belle 1992   `11` `D`

Crozes-Hermitages Clos des Grives 1992   `11` `E`

Cuvee de Grignon VdP de l'Aude 1994   `15` `B`

Simple rustic fruit, no razzamatazz? Yes, but consider the smoothness of this simple delivery – it's right on. A dry, plummy wine of distinction and unfussy class. A couple of years developing drinking in this '94 vintage.

Domaine de Lascaux, Coteaux de Languedoc 1993   `14` `C`

Brisk, savoury fruit.

Domaine de Lascaux, Les Nobles Pierres 1993   `14` `D`

Sunny and vibrant.

Domaine de Mas Carlot, Costieres de Nimes 1993   `17` `C`

Open a good couple of hours before drinking and get a massively soft, rich, aromatic, warm, friendly, beautifully integrated wine.

Domaine La Croix Belle, VdP de Cotes de Thongue 1994   `15` `C`

If you like your earth a bit fruity, and good and rich, this is your wine – beef casseroles too.

Domaine la Remejeanne, Cotes du Rhone les Arbousieres 1993 15 D

Real down-to-earth fruit here yet it's classy with it.

Domaine la Remejeanne, Cotes du Rhone Les Genevrieres 1993 15.5 D

Has an added oomph of licorice-edged fruit here. Lovely tannins.

Domaine Les Chenets Crozes-Hermitage 1992 14 E

Black-hearted fruit with smoked ham undertones.

Domaine Richaud Cairanne, Cotes du Rhone Cuvee l'Ebrescade 1993 13 E

Still evolving, slowly, in bottle.

Domaine Richaud Cariranne, Cotes du Rhone Villages 1993 13.5 D

Soft, approachable, with barely a hint of brusqueness.

Domaine Villerambert Minervois, Cuvee Opera 1992 13 C

Gevrey-Chambertin, Rossignol-Trapet 1991 12 E

Le Radical Cotes de Ventoux 12 B

Le Radical Grenache 1993 14 B

Very pleasant cherry fruit of a gently hairy mien.

Le Second de Reynon 1992 14 C

Mas Cal Demoura, Coteaux de Languedoc 1993 14 D

Rich, complex, warm tannins.

Merlot Galet 1994 `14` `C`

Soft with a typically merlot leathery edge with a subtle spiciness.
Good with grilled vegetables.

Meursault, Michelot-Buisson 1992 `13` `F`

Michel Lynch Bordeaux Rouge 1990 `13.5` `E`

Good solid claret with approachable, soft tannins and fruit.

Nuits St Georges, Clos de l'Arlot 1992 `10` `G`

Oddbins Red, VdP de Catalan 1994 `15` `B`

Lovely, ripe tannins, good rich fruit with soft, earthy touches.
Excellent all-round food wine.

St Joseph Vieilles Vignes, Cuilleron 1992 `12` `E`

Stowells of Chelsea Vin de Pays du Gard (3 litre) `14` `F`

Delightful smooth fruit with flavour and balance. A lovely touch
– a distant echo, really – of earth.

Syrah Galet Vineyards 1994 `14.5`

A handsome, rugged beast softened by rich tannins of some
gentility and a warm, savoury finish. A delicious soupy wine
for all sorts of lamb dishes.

FRENCH WINE   WHITE

Alsace Gewurztraminer, Schoffit 1992 `13` `E`

Alsace Pinot Blanc, Schoffit 1992 `12` `D`

Bourgogne Blanc Michelot 1992 `14` `E`

Bourgogne Hautes Cotes de Beaune, Jayer-Gilles 1991 `13` `F`

Chablis Premier Cru Montmains, Louis Michel `13` `F`

Chardonnay, Vin de Pays d'Oc, Andre Hardy 1994 `15.5` `C`

Lush creamy edge to fruit firmly held in place by nutty acidity. Brilliant for the money.

Condrieu Vieilles Vignes, Cuilleron 1992 `11` `G`

Croix Belle Rose, Cotes de Thongue 1994 `13.5` `C`

Character here, rare for a rose.

Domaine St Hilaire VdP d'Oc Chardonnay 1994 `16` `C`

Delicious woody overtone (though no wood is involved) to the rich fruit. Great balance and style. Impressive class for the money.

Gewurztraminer Cuvee Laurence Domaine Weinbach 1992 `18` `G`

Gewurztraminer, Hugel 1992 `15` `E`

Soft spicy nose, petal fruit and elegant weight.

James Herrick Chardonnay, VdP d'Oc 1994 `14` `C`

Better than previous vintages but not as remotely as impressive or weighty as the Andre Hardy d'Oc chardonnays.

La Revolution 1992 `12` `D`

121

Laperouse Blanc Val d'Orbieu & Penfolds, VdP d'Oc 1994

14 C

Rounded fruit flavours energetically supported by the elegance of the acids.

Le Second de Floridene Blanc 1992

16 D

Very classy wine: lush wood/fruit integration, calm acidity, overall purpose and style. Very attractive. Wonderful with seafood.

Macon Davaye, Domaine des Deux Roches 1993

14 D

Macon Davaye, Domaine des Deux Roches 1994

15 D

If you want a terrific white burgundy for the money, this is it. Has style, elegance, very attractive fruit and firm balance.

Menetou Salon Morogues, Pelle 1993

13.5 D

Menetou-Salon Cuvee Evelyn, Pelle 1994

13.5 D

Fruity and very attractive – overpriced.

Meursault Domaine Michelot 1993

12 G

Montagny Premier Cru, Domaine Maurice Bertrand 1993

12.5 E

Oddbins White, VdP des Cotes de Gascogne 1994

15 C

Delicate, fruity, not overly exotic or overripe, this is a lovely refreshing glug.

Pinot Blanc, Schoffit 1992

14 D

Pouilly-Fuisse Cuvee Vieilles Vignes 1992

13 F

Riesling, Hugel 1990 `13` `E`

Some petrolly undertones here.

**Riesling St Catherine, Domaine Weinbach
1993** `13.5` `G`

Riesling Tradition, Hugel 1990 `13.5` `F`

Citric petroleum and a good fruit finish.

**Saint-Aubin Les Charmois Premier
Cru 1993** `13` `F`

Delicious, but the price... the price stinks.

Saint-Veran Cuvee Prestige, Lasserat 1993 `13` `E`

**Saint-Veran Les Chailloux, Domaine des
Deux Roches 1994** `14.5` `E`

Another no-nonsense, excellent white burgundy at Oddbins.

**Saint-Verain, Domaine des Deux Roches
1992** `13` `E`

**Saint-Veran Vieilles Vignes, Domaine des
Deux Roches 1993** `15` `E`

**Sauvignon Blanc, Vin de Pays d'Oc
J. Lurton 1993** `14` `C`

**Stowells of Chelsea Vin de Pays du
Tarn (3 litre)** `12` `F`

Sound but dullish – not a lot of fruit.

Sylvaner Reserve Domaine Weinbach 1993 `14` `D`

Slick, rich-edged, lengthy, flavoursome. A great fish wine
(without the acidity this implies).

123

Terret Blanc, Vin de Pays d'Oc 1993 14 B

Modern pear-drop aromas and fruit, very perky and fresh too.

Touraine Sauvignon, Renaudie 1994 13 C

GERMAN WINE WHITE

Bacheracher Schloss Stahleck Riesling Kabinett, Toni Jost 1993 13 D

Lay down.

Burrweiler Altenforst Scheurebe Spatlese, Messmer, Pfalz 1994 12.5 E

Too young. Will improve in half a decade.

Burrweiler Schlossgarten Riesling Kabinett Halbtrocken, Messmer, Pfalz 1994 13 D

Will take at least 3 years to fully flower.

Durkheimer Fronhof Scheurebe Trockenbeerenauslese, Kurt Darting 1993 (half bottle) 16 E

Spiced apricots, grapefruit and a rich honey finish. Best kept for 10 years to become spectacular-er.

Durkheimer Hiochbenn Riesling Spatlese, Kurt Darting 1993 14 D

Honey-edged but try it with Thai food (meat dishes).

Durkheimer Spielberg Riesling Auslese, Kurt Darting 1993 14 D

Good with fresh fruit and cheese.

Haardter Burgergarten Riesling Kabinett, Muller-Catoir, Pfalz 1994

But 15 in 5/6 years? Maybe.

Haardter Herrenletten Grauburgunder Spatlese Trocken, Muller-Catoir 1993

Wonderful food wine – grilled chicken especially.

Haardter Herrenletten Riesling Spatlese Trocken, Muller-Catoir 1993

Haardter Herzog Riesling Spatlese Trocken Muller-Catoir, Rheinpfalz 1992

Haardter Mandelring Scheurebe Kabinett, Muller-Catoir 1993

A must for scheurebe fans.

Haardter Mandelring Scheurebe Spatlese, Muller-Catoir 1994 13 E

13 points now but 17/18 points in 4 years or so. Delicate as a snowdrop but with the force and assertiveness of a steel weapon. A beautiful wine with huge fruity charm. Firm acidity which will blossom later.

Hochheimer Reichestal Stahleck Riesling Kabinett 1993 14 E

Expensive – and rewarding to drink now as a black-mood-raiser but kept for 6/7 years it will be ambrosial.

Hochheimer Hofmeister Riesling, Franz Kunstler 1993

A delicious, fierce, lemon and mineral acid aperitif.

Muller-Thurgau, Messmer, Pfalz 1994

I'd leave it for a year or so and let it develop.

Mussbacher Eselshaut Rieslaner Spatlese, Muller-Catoir 1993

I'd drink it as an aperitif. But, as will all Muller-Catoir wines, it will improve for years and years.

Riesling Kabinett, Oberst Schultz-Werner 1993

Lay down for 5/6 years to get a 16-pointer.

Ungsteiner Honigsackel Riesling Auslese, Fuhrmann Eymael 1993

Delicious TV bottle.

Ungsteiner Honigsackel Riesling Spatlese, Fuhrmann Eymael 1993 15 E

A deliciously different aperitif. Thrilling.

Westhofener Aulerde Bacchus Kabinett, Wittmann, Rheinhessen 1994

ITALIAN WINE RED

Castel del Monte Rosso, Torrevento, Puglia 1993 15.5 C

Complex, characterful, lots of flavour. Dry, yes, but not dried out for the fruit is lengthy and rolls out along the tastebuds to an almost cassis-like finish.

Castelgiocondo Brunello di Montalcino 1988

Cent'are Rosso, Duca di Castelmonte, Sicily 1992
`15` `C`

Brighter, more perky, cheekier than most Sicilian reds, this wine has a lovely baked, black cherry finish.

Chianti Riserva Castello di Nipozanna, Frescobaldi 1990
`13.5` `D`

Raisiny-edged, figgy fruit.

Chianti Rufina, Castello di Nipozzana 1991
`13` `D`

Not as fierce or as brilliant as the previous 1990 vintage – which was great.

Primitivo del Salento 1993, Le Trulle
`13.5` `C`

Gamy, rich aromas and initial fruit attack and then nicely ripe cherries. Delicious.

Puglian Red, The Country Collection 1993
`14` `B`

Delicious, cherry-ripe value for money.

Riva Sangiovese di Romagna 1993
`15` `B`

Brisk cherry and plum fruit with a dry, lingering finish.

Riva Sangiovese di Romagna Superiore, San Crispino 1993
`14.5` `C`

Dry, warm, sunny, affectionate. Real flavour and heft, with a surprising lack of the usual earthiness. A smoothie with character.

Ronco delle Torre Cabernet Sauvignon 1990
`13` `D`

Tenuta di Pomino, Frescobaldi 1991
`13` `E`

Torre del Falco, Rosso della Murgia, Puglia 1994   14 C

Deep, dry, a real food wine with its tannic edge and depth of fruit. Marvellous with mushroom dishes.

Uva di Troia di Puglia, Cantele 1993   13 D

Of the quintet of Italian red wines I tasted at Oddbins on this occasion, this was the least successful – and the most pricey. For more money you get less character and tannin.

Valpolicella Il Garofano, Gaetana Carron, Cantine Ronco 1994   13 B

Slips down as effortlessly as a rat through a drain pipe.

ITALIAN WINE   WHITE

Albizzia Bianco di Toscana, Frescobaldi 1993   13.5 C

Pleasant, nut-edged crisp fruit.

Chardonnay del Salento, Kym Milne 1993   15 C

Pinot Grigio Bidoli Friuli 1994   13 C

Riva Albana di Romagna, Gaetana Carron 1993   15 C

Lovely nutty overtones to the rich-edged wine. Taken some months in bottle to reach this state of delicious drinkability.

Riva Trebbiano di Romagna 1994   14 B

Fresh, simple, nutty undertoned fruit.

Riva White 1993 `16` `B`

Such ripe fruit for the money! Fantastic ripe fruit! Fantastic! Ripe! Gorgeous! Unctuous!

Soave Il Garofano, Gaetana Carron Cantine Ronco 1994 `13` `B`

Terre Arnolfi Colli Amerini 1994 `12` `C`

Vermentino di Sardegna 1994 `12.5` `C`

MOLDOVAN WINE WHITE

Chardonnay Hincesti 1992 `11` `B`

NEW ZEALAND WINE WHITE

Montana Sauvignon Blanc 1993 `13` `C`

Stowells of Chelsea New Zealand Sauvignon Blanc (3 litre) `13.5` `G`

Keen, grassy aromas, good fruit, rather a quiet finish.

The Brothers Semillon/Sauvignon 1992 `14` `D`

SOUTH AFRICAN WINE RED

Beyerskloof Pinotage 1991 `14` `C`

Polished cherry fruit with a savoury edge.

Kanonkop Paul Sauer 1991 | 17 | F |
Big, serious, fruity, stylish, bold – world-class.

Stellenzicht Block Series Cabernet Sauvignon 1993 | 13 | C |

Stellenzicht Block Series Shiraz 1993 | 14.5 | C |
A 20-point wine by AD 2000 if we're lucky. But drinkable, by golly, today. It's smooth, rich and deeply flavoured (and anything can happen in the next four years).

SOUTH AFRICAN WINE   WHITE

Danie de Wet Chardonnay 1995 | 14 | C |
Delicate Danie belying his massive pit-prop of a frame to create a deft, subtle chardonnay of charm, reserve and stealthy mint.

De Wetshof Chardonnay d'Honneur | 15 | E |
Delicate, delicious, subtle and very soothing. Not a big, wildly expressive wine running riot with flavour, but uniquely and quietly impactful.

Eikendal Chardonnay 1994 | 15 | D |
Delicate, balletic, elegant – but with a delicious, haunting edge of big brassy richness.

Glen Carlou Reserve Chardonnay 1993 | 14 | E |
Highly priced but highly drinkable: classy, haughty, complex.

Swartland Reserve Chenin Blanc 1994 | 12.5 | C |

Swartland Reserve Sauvignon Blanc 1994 | 16.5 | C |
Lovely rich fruit with a winning dollop of herbaceous acidity lurking behind. Delicious, individual, special.

Van Loveren Blanc de Blancs 1994

Light, gentle aperitif style.

Van Loveren Colombard/Chardonnay 1994

A distant echo of spice in this gently fruity bottle – made for solo sipping or with poached fish. Oddbins blend.

Van Loveren Pinot Gris 1994

A truly wonderful rich edge to this wine's fruit. It lingers, too, and turns dry yet creamy and fruity with echoes of peach. This was blended to Oddbins' own specifications.

SPANISH WINE   RED

Agramont Cabernet/Tempranillo Crianza, Navarra 1991

Has a delicious crunchy edge to the rich, plum fruit.

Andelos, Navarra Tinto 1994

Simple, fruity, dry – good for pizza parties.

Campillo Rioja 1988

Garnacha 1993, Navarra

Superb fruit. Exceptionally rich and ripe without being over-blown.

Las Torres Merlot 1992

Palacio de la Vega Cabernet Sauvignon 1991, Navarra

Superbly bright, supporting tannins in dry, fruity wine of some class.

Palacio de la Vega Cabernet/Tempranillo Crianza 1992
`14.5` `C`

Fruit richly soldered to acids and tannins. And though brisk it slips down smoothly.

Palacio de la Vega Cabernet/Tempranillo, Navarra 1993
`16.5` `C`

Outstanding fruit for the money – lingering, flavourful, deep. Has plums, cherries and blackcurrants in soft, riotous array.

Palacio de la Vega Merlot 1992

Delicious fruit here which with the help of gentle coating by the tannins makes for a savoury wine of depth.

Palacio de la Vega Tinto 1993
`14` `C`

Ripe edge to blackcurranty fruit. Delicious.

Puelles Rioja 1993
`16` `C`

A lovely little wine. I say little because it is delicate rather than bruising and overwoody and this modesty is to be found in Jesus Puelles, its maker.

Rioja Cosme Tinto, Bodegas Palacio 1990

Solana Red 1993, Navarra
`16` `C`

Terra Seca Cabernet Sauvignon La Mancha 1994

Made by a jet-hopping Californian who seems to juggle with local character, tannin, acidity and luscious fruit and turn out a thoroughly tasty brew.

Torres Gran Coronas 1988
`15` `E`

Silken, soft, rich but very demure at the same time, this wine is a curiously un-Torres-like ensemble: it seems more like some

3rd growth Bordeaux from a once great chateau which has eccentrically produced a lovely wine.

Vega de Moriz 1993, Valdepenas `15` `B`

SPANISH WINE WHITE

Agramont Viura 1993, Navarra `14` `C`

Antea, Marques de Caceras 1992 `14` `C`
Classy richness with a curious creamy edge. Delicious with grilled chicken.

Jose Bezares, Rioja Blanco 1988 `14` `C`

Rioja Cosme Blanco, Bodegas Palacio 1993 `13` `C`
Echoes of wood and good fruit.

Santara Chardonnay 1994 `14` `C`
Varietal character edgily plump and ripe in the mouth, with a fresh finish.

Solana, Ribero 1994 `14` `C`
Very fresh and lemonic. A cool summer glug.

USA WINE RED

Fetzer Bontera Cabernet Sauvignon 1992 (Organic) `14` `E`
Simple, fruity, not fierce, balanced, subtle. A very savoury, delicious wine.

Fetzer Zinfandel 1993 `14.5` `D`

Big, bouncy, blissful – soft, sweet (in the most delightfully fruity way) yet dry to finish with controlled spiciness. Gently exotic and lithe, this is a delicious wine.

Franciscan Cabernet Sauvignon 1991 `13` `D`

Franciscan Oakville Estate Napa Valley Zinfandel 1993 `16.5` `E`

Dusty, rich, spicy, lots of dry brambly fruit and will improve for several years but great now with casseroles and roasts.

Franciscan Pinnacles Monterey Pinot Noir 1993 `13.5` `D`

Very pleasant, ripe, raspberry-tinged fruit which is amusing served chilled. Certainly a sparkier pinot than many red burgundies at the same money and more, but its fruit is pricey.

Havenscourt Barbera `12` `C`

Sweet cherry edge.

Havenscourt Cabernet Sauvignon `13.5` `C`

Havenscourt Gamay `11` `C`

Havenscourt Pinot Noir `12` `C`

Good gamy aroma.

Havenscourt Roti `14` `D`

A grenache, mourvedre and zinfandel blend. Soft and slightly spicy.

Havenscourt Sangiovese `14` `D`

Interesting alternative to chianti.

Havenscourt Syrah `14` `D`
Soft, plummy, very attractive rounded fruit.

Havenscourt Zinfandel `13` `C`
Sweet simple style of zin.

Lynmar Russian River Valley Pinot Noir 1992 `14` `F`
Out-smooths many a Volnay for the money – which is mountains, I know – but it is impressively textured.

Orion 1992 `13` `H`
100 per cent syrah and more crunchy, meaty and savoury than many a so-called great Rhone equivalent. I drank mine with a dish with a Madeira sauce. It was magnificent. But would I pay £24 for this bottle? Nope.

Pinot Meunier, Bonny Doon `11` `D`

Ravenswood Vintners' Blend Zinfandel 1993 `14` `E`
Flavour and soft depth – only a hint of the ferocity to be sometimes seen in zin.

Rex Hill Kings Ridge Pinot Noir 1993 `13` `D`

Sterling Vineyards Diamond Mountain Rand Cabernet Sauvignon 1991 `15` `E`
Brisk tannins here. Brilliant structure. Needs 3/4 years to become a really big wine of world class.

Sterling Vineyards St Dunstans Reserve 1991 `14` `D`
A stab at bordeaux. The grapes are cabernet sauvignon, merlot,

cabernet franc and petit verdot. Soft, easy-drinking plums are the result, with a touch of serious depth.

Sterling Winery Lake Pinot Noir 1993 | 12.5 | D

Interesting pinot noir – rather bright and rosy-cheeked but of some amusing immediacy and aromatic arousal. Finally it's an expensive toy – for pinot freaks only.

USA WINE   WHITE

Benziger Chardonnay 1991 | 15 | D

Loadsa fruit.

Beringer Fume Blanc, Napa Valley
1993 | 13.5 | D

Unusual grip to the fruit here.

Bloody Good White | 15 | D

Ca' del Solo Bloody Good White 1994 | 13 | D

Bouncy, fun, mightily overpriced.

Calera Chardonnay, California 1992 | 16 | F

Balanced and elegant, almost Chilean in feel, with a good, thumping, fruit finish.

Fetzer Bontera Chardonnay 1993 | 13.5 | E

A wine of subdued classiness, as fine Californian chardonnays go, but attractive and tasty.

Franciscan Chardonnay 1993 | 13 | D

Rather overwoody.

Franciscan Cuvee Sauvage Chardonnay 1992 `15` `E`

Immensely individual, with a raffish edge to the civilised cut of its fruit, but this is incongruity no more disconcerting than waist-length dread-locks on a media executive sharply suited in silk.

Kiona Late Harvest Gewurztraminer, Yukima Washington State 1993 `13.5` `D`

Kiona Late Harvest Muscat, Yukima Washington State 1993 `14.5` `D`

Would be scrumptious with soft goat's cheese and hard fruit.

Kiona Late Harvest Riesling 1993 `13.5` `D`

L'Ecole 41 Chardonnay 1992 `15` `E`

Upfront wood/fruit integration provides a powerful aroma but it needs more acidity to lengthen the weight of the finish. Aromatically, though, a triumph.

Landmark Overlook Chardonnay, Sonoma 1992 `14.5` `E`

Richer woodiness here for those who like this style. A touch brassy but not ugly.

Newton Chardonnay, Napa 1991 `13.5` `F`

Rich oils here but will they soothe the pocket as they soothe the tongue? At £12 I think they will ruffle it.

Rex Hill Kings Ridge Chardonnay, Oregon 1993 `15` `D`

Elegant woodiness and soft fruit, crisply undercut. Balanced, flavoursome, complex, stylish.

Ridge Santa Cruz Chardonnay 1990 | 13 | G

Rosato del Fiasco, Ca' del Solo, Bonny Doon Vineyard 1994 | 14 | D

In every sense, one of the most amusing, food-friendly roses on earth.

Sterling Chardonnay, Napa 1993 | 16 | D

A balanced, impressively refined wine with a gentle touch of wood, melon and good citric acidity. Not bold but very bonny.

Sundial Chardonnay 1993 | 13 | D

Big sunny fruit – expressive.

Wild Horse Chardonnay 1993 | 15 | E

Exceptional fruit for the serious white burgundy lover who prefers not to spend £25 on the French model.

SPARKLING WINE/CHAMPAGNE

Billecart-Salmon | 16 | G

Elegance, style, aplomb.

Bollinger Grande Annee 1988 | 10 | H

This is rich champagne, mature, compelling, complex; but at a price of such absurdity only nuts would buy it.

Bonnet Blanc de Blancs Champagne 1986 | 14.5 | G

Yeasty, yet this maturity has nicely lemonic undertones.

Cuvee Napa Rose | 14 | E

Great stuff.

Seaview Brut `15` `D`

Where available for under £5, one of the best sparklers on the market: stylish, refined, and quite delicious.

Seaview Pinot Noir/Chardonnay 1990 (Australian) `15` `E`

Segura Viudas `13` `D`

Seppelt Great Western Brut `14` `C`

Light and breezy.

Seppelt Great Western Rose `15` `D`

Seppelt Pinot Rose Cuvee Brut Sparkling (Australia) `15` `D`

Delicious. Real fruit here, justifying the colour.

Seppelt Premier Cuvee Brut `15` `D`

Lovely fizz, light and handsome.

Seppelt Salinger Sparkling Wine (Australia) `15` `F`

Seppelt Sparkling Shiraz 1990 `16` `E`

Fabulous roaring fruit.

SPAR

Spar possesses the most decisive name of any retailer in this book. It is short, monosyllabic, memorable and it rolls prettily off even the most untutored tongue. What does it mean? A spar, to a digger in the dirt, means a non-metallic mineral; to a sailor, a beam; to a pugilist, a scrap. However, the meaning given only in American dictionaries, my old *Websters Collegiate* in particular, is the most appropriate. Spar in that compendium is also 'A member of the Women's Reserve of the U.S. Coast Guard Reserve, known as SPARS, from the Coast Guard motto "Semper Paratus – Always Ready".'

Liz Aked, who runs Spar's wine buying department single-handed now that Philippa Carr has left to have a baby, may feel some kind of kinship here and, who knows, renewed warmth for her complex employer. She is, to be sure, *semper parata*. She needs to be. Spar is unlike any other retailer in this book, for it is not a chain of shops but a collection of franchises. And as such it cannot force its franchisees to buy from the central wine-buying set-up Ms Aked runs, it can only persuade them so to do by effectively supplying the wholesalers who in turn supply the various shops –1831 of which are licensed and run by independently minded men and women who are no doubt as wary of the notion of central control as any newly elected and touchy Eastern European republican president.

Nevertheless, Liz brims with confidence. What, I asked her, do you believe to be the special strengths of your wine range? 'It is,' she said, 'small but perfectly formed. It offers the best quality in its category.' A crisp response, but what does category mean? Category means 'the independent grocery sector'. (I hear you

141

stifling a yawn here but you ought to appreciate that there are people out there wearing Comme des Garcons suits and knitted silk ties who charge £5,000 a week to spout this kind of marketing speak, so hang about and we both might learn something.)

The organisation's top-selling wines are:

1. Liebfraumilch.
2. Lambrusco.
3. French Country Wine red.
4. French Country Wine white.
5. Claret.
6. Valencia white.
7. Bulgarian Country Wine red.

On the basis of this list we can only say for certain that Spar grocers are not bothered by wine snobs (who though a faster-dying breed than Scottish Conservative Party candidates are still to be encountered in hardy pockets up and down the country). Spar customers have straightforward tastes, for the most part, like low prices and, above all, enjoy drinking wine in moderation mostly with food. Many Spar shops stay open late (but then who doesn't nowadays?) and cater for the shopper who just wants to drop in for the odd bottle; many Spars enjoy seasonal upturns in trade, due to the proximity to the seaside or holiday area, which enable them to turn in a profit over the year even though business out of season may be thin. But it is, of course, this very unevenness of such shops' trade that deters competitors; the large supermarkets find the cramped conditions they would be forced to operate under uneconomic and the wine chains could not tolerate the seasonal fluctuations. This makes many a Spar an oasis in an otherwise barren retail landscape. And not only in rural, littoral and provincial areas. There is many a Spar to be found in corners of inner city areas, not far from the betting shop and the pub, and they prosper; they are mini-markets, the versatile corner shop. The only threat to them would come if Tesco decided to go mad with its Metro-Store shops and insinuate Mini-Metro-Stores into every available nook and cranny, and also if someone like Thresher (which seems prepared, at the pop of a cork, to launch yet another retail concept) decided to open seasonal or travelling branches. I daresay that if it were possible to acquire a liquor off-licence for a pantechnicon, then Thresher trucks would be as familiar a sight on certain roads as mobile libraries and fish vans.

The other aspect of the Spar shop's strength, which not even the implementation of the two outlandish ideas outlined above could mar, is the distinctly local nature of the shop's staff and, more often than not, its proprietor. A Spar shop may well sell local produce (sausages, butter, fish, meat), albeit on a small scale perhaps, which the giant superstore, ten miles away, cannot contemplate stocking.

However, nowhere in this scenario have I posited that it might be because of its range of wines that people patronise a Spar shop. No one, surely, visits a Spar grocery *because* of the wines? Curiously, however, if you put this question another way, and look at it from an angular perspective, you get an interesting answer. Does anyone visit a Sainsbury's solely for the wines? Or a Tesco or a Safeway? A few customers apart, we would surely agree that if these supermarkets were to become unlicensed then they would still stay in business as food stores – without doubt. We would all have to rely for the wines we drink on the high street chains or wine merchants. This is indeed what millions of customers of those supermarkets do already. But my belief is that a considerable proportion of Spar customers buy their wines at Spar and nowhere else. They certainly buy little from the high street chains and never from wine merchants and probably only occasionally from the supermarket if they've made the uncommon effort to shop there. For many people, the wine shop, however jazzy and seemingly informal its atmosphere, is still an intimidating arena to enter – as it is for many book buyers who prefer to purchase their reading matter from a W.H.Smith's rather than breach the more bookish interior of a Waterstones or a Dillons. The Spar customer is, then (if my thread is running logically true), likely to patronise the place because they can buy the wines they like at competitive prices and also do whatever convenience shopping they like. Or even, for that matter, do a weekly shop if there really is no superstore within reasonable reach or if they are not a car driver and the bus is too wearisome to use lugging two or three full carrier bags.

Little wonder that Spar needs a solid, well-chosen, competitive range of wines. And it is not restricted to the predictable bottles in the list above. As the list which follows demonstrates, there are many wines at Spar which even the most critical of palates would find difficult to fault (though it's my experience that too many people possessed of a critical palate use it to find faults exclusively rather than to discover delights generally). Liz Aked believes South Africa, Italy and Chile hold out great wines for the future which will fit in the Spar range (which means fitting the customers' pockets.). And she will, I am sure, continue the success of the group's initially cautious entry into the multi-purchase discount market. This encourages customers to buy, say, two wines for £5 or three wines for a tenner. Such promotional razzmatazz may be old hat for the big boys but this is innovation where Spar is concerned.

Spar Landmark
32-40 Headstone Drive
Harrow
Middlesex
HA3 5QT

Tel 0181 863 5511
Fax 0181 863 0603

AUSTRALIAN WINE RED

Hardys Bankside Shiraz 1992 `15` `D`

Tasty and richly centred. Very good fruit here with enough of a seriously dry edge to go with rich food.

Lindemans Bin 45 Cabernet Sauvignon 1991 `14` `C`

Soft, attractive, drinkable. Simple style, probably at its best with food rather than drunk alone. Try sausage and mash and onion gravy.

Lindemans Bin 45 Cabernet Sauvignon 1992 `14` `C`

Attractive berry flavours and residual richness.

Lindemans Cawarra Shiraz Cabernet 1994 `11` `D`

Lots of juice here but a lot of money for it. Curious lack of character and purpose.

Orlando R.F. Cabernet Sauvignon 1991 `16` `C`

Reaches an extreme of soft yet dry blackcurrant fruitiness with hints of spicy plum. A truly delicious wine.

AUSTRALIAN WINE WHITE

Lindemans Bin 65 Chardonnay 1993 `16` `C`

Deep bruised fruit – lovely and ripe – superb effect on the tongue.

Lindemans Cawarra, Colombard Chardonnay 1993   `14` `C`

Ripe fruit character with pineapple fruit-drop acidity. Delicious.

Orlando Carrington Rose   `13` `D`

BULGARIAN WINE   RED

Bulgarian Country Cabernet/Cinsault, Russe, Spar   `14` `B`

Dry, brisk, blackcurranty.

Bulgarian Merlot/Gamay, Russe 1993   `14.5` `B`

Spar's special blend and who would have thought merlot would settle happily down with gamay? Excellent value, this is brilliantly fruity, dry wine with great food versatility – good chilled. Better than most beaujolais.

Korten Cabernet Sauvignon 1991   `14` `B`

Ripeness and dryness, blackcurrant softness.

Spar Bulgarian Country Wine Cabernet/ Merlot   `10` `B`

BULGARIAN WINE   WHITE

Spar Bulgarian Slaviantzi, Country White, Muskat and Ugni Blanc   `13` `B`

A gentle aperitif.

FRENCH WINE

Baron Villeneuve de Cantemerle 1986   11 E

This has a lovely bouquet but the stalky fruit in the taste lets it down – especially at the money. However, can you wait 10 years? If you can, the wine will be terrific.

Cabernet Sauvignon VdP de l'Aude 1993, Spar   13 B

Good flavour here for food.

Chateau Bories-Azeau, Corbieres 1993   13 C

Chateau Clos de l'Eglise, Cotes de Castillon 1990   12.5 D

Coteaux du Languedoc (Spar)   14 B

Excellent value. Dry, fruity, balanced – only a bit more vivacity on the finish would top it off better.

Cotes de Catalanes, Spar   14 B

Nice touch of dry earth to the edge of the fruit. Rustic but great with bangers.

Domaine Montariol, Syrah VdP d'Oc   14 B

Soft berried fruit with a touch of fog balanced out by vigour and bite to the acidity. Most attractive.

Faugeres, Domaine de Moulin 1992   14 C

Rich, dry, earthy but never coarse. Good with food.

Hautes Terres, Coteaux de Tricastin 1994   12 C

Earthy.

Lussac St Emilion, Dulong 1992, Spar `13` `D`

Merlot Vin de Pays d'Oc, Spar `12.5` `B`

Oaked Merlot, VdP d'Oc Cuxac, Spar `11` `B`
Touch raw.

Spar Claret 1993 `12` `C`
Dry, very dry.

Spar Cotes du Rhone `10` `B`

Spar Fitou `13` `B`
Nothing wrong with this. Has a subtle, gamy, mushroomy undertone.

Spar Gamay, Vin de Pays du Jardin de la France `13` `B`

Spar VdP de la Cite de Carcassonne 1993 `13` `B`

FRENCH WINE WHITE

Chablis, Union des Viticulteurs de Chablis 1993 `11` `E`

Cotes de St Mont, Tuileries du Bosc 1992 `13` `C`
Fruit which doesn't turn crisp on the finish.

James Herrick Chardonnay VdP d'Oc 1994 `14` `C`
Pleasantly flavoured and comforting but somehow not as exciting as it pretends. Rates well, can't deny it that.

Muscat de St Jean de Minervois, Spar (half bottle) | 14 | B

Lovely pud wine or with blue cheese. Or as a stand-alone bottle for watching TV.

Oaked Chasan VdP d'Oc, Spar | 13 | C

Touch pricey.

Rose de Syrah, VdP d'Oc, Spar | 12 | B

Spar Chardonnay, VdP d'Oc | 15 | C

Delicious: clean, fresh, fruity (and a restrained nutty undertone). Terrific tipple by itself or with seafood.

Spar Muscadet | 10 | C

Spar Oaked Chardonnay, 1993 | 13.5 | C

Spar Rose d'Anjou | 11 | B

Spar VdP des Cotes Catalanes | 13 | B

Spar Viognier 1993 | 13.5 | D

An echo of peach. Dry, fresh, balanced.

Vin de Pays Du Gers | 12 | B

Vouvray Donatien Bahuaud 1993 | 13.5 | C

Restrained, honey fruit. A lovely aperitif.

GERMAN WINE   WHITE

Mainzer Domherr Spatlese, Muller | 13 | C

Not sweet enough for a pudding nor dry enough for a lot of food.

Niersteiner Spiegelberg Kabinett, Muller
1992
12.5 C

Pleasant aperitif in front of a roaring fire.

Piesporter Goldtropfchen Grans Fassien
1992
14 D

Brilliant balance of acidity, perkiness and fruit. Drinkable now with smoked fish or keep for 10 years or more.

Rosenlieb 5%, Spar
11 B

Sweet grapes, peachy, innocuous. Good for Gran.

Spar Hock
10 B

HUNGARIAN WINE   RED

Danube Hungarian Country Red, Spar
11 B

HUNGARIAN WINE   WHITE

Dunavar, Prestige Chardonnay 1993
14 C

Rich edge to the fruit. Brilliant with sauced fish dishes, crab, and chicken casseroles.

Spar Danube White
12 B

150

ITALIAN WINE RED

Montepulciano d'Abruzzo Tollo, Spar `12` `B`
Soft, jammy, great with pasta.

Pinot Negro Alto Adige, 1991 `11` `D`

Spar Merlot del Veneto `11` `B`
Ripe black cherry, rather stalky fruit.

Spar Valpolicella `12` `B`

ITALIAN WINE WHITE

Bianco di Custoza, Boscaini 1994 `13.5` `C`
Touch expensive, but clean and fruity.

Frascati Superiore 1994, Spar `11` `C`

**Frascati Superiore, Colli di Catone
1989** `10` `D`

Spar Soave `10` `B`

MORAVIAN WINE RED

Moravian Vineyards Czech Red, Spar `11` `B`

MORAVIAN WINE WHITE

Moravian Vineyards Czech White, Spar | 13 | B

40p more than it should be. But still balanced and clean fruitwise – only the price is skew-whiff.

PORTUGUESE WINE RED

Dona Elena Portuguese Red, Spar | 12 | B

Vinho do Monte Alentejo, 1991 | 14 | D

Expensive but greatly impressive. Has cherry/plum fruit which sweetly expresses itself on the finish and sustains the effect.

PORTUGUESE WINE WHITE

Dona Elena Portuguese White, Spar | 12 | B

Soft, fruity.

Duque de Viso Dao, Sogrape 1992 | 13 | C

Spar Alamo Vinho Verde | 12 | B

SOUTH AFRICAN WINE RED

Oak Village Vintage Reserve 1991 | 13 | C

Sable View Cabernet Sauvignon 1990

Curious but appealing clash of fruit styles in this wine.

Table Mountain Pinot Noir, Stellenbosch 1994, Spar

SOUTH AFRICAN WINE — WHITE

Sable View Chardonnay 1992

Lovely wine: full, ripe, mature yet fresh, youthful and lush. Lots of flavour, balance and true class.

SPANISH WINE — RED

Domino de Espinal, Yecla 1989

Brilliant value. Mature yet richly ripe fruit with undertones of vanilla, very soft yet dry. Terrific food wine.

Senorio de Nava, Ribero del Duero 1987

Leathery fruit, dry, yet soft and mature. Has berries, woodiness and a distinct herbiness. Great roast food and vegetable wine.

Spar Rioja

A revelation for those who think of this wine as oaky, vanilla-like, and heavy. This is a young specimen and totally unaffected in manner, nicely balanced and unhysterical. Good value.

Spar Valdepenas

Dry, dusty, spicy, good with casseroles.

Spar Valencia Red

One of the best-value reds in the land. An all-singing, all-dancing raspberry and blackcurrant double act. Marvellous simple stuff.

Vina Albali 1987

Rioja smell-alike but not taste-alike entirely. It is rich and dry, and typically vanilla-edged.

SPANISH WINE   WHITE

Valencia Dry White

Pleasant creamy fruit under the acidity. Good value.

Valencia Medium White

Valencia Sweet White

Grandma, over to you.

FORTIFIED WINE

Old Cellar LBV Port 1988, Spar

Brilliant rich, pruney wine. Great with Christmas cake or just as a heartening drink before . . . well, before anything really – even before getting married or shot (or both).

SPARKLING WINE/CHAMPAGNE

Asti Spumante `10` `D`

Marquis de Preval Champagne, NV `13` `F`

Not bad, not bad at all.

Moscato Fizz `10`

This shouldn't have a score in a wine guide because technically this wine, at 4% alcohol, is not wine. It is, in truth, partially fermented grape juice. I suppose the kids might like it, though, and old grans toothless from a lifetime of chewing sugar.

Orlando Carrington Brut (Australian) `15` `D`

Verve, style and value. Can't ask for more in a bottle of bubbly.

Seppelt Great Western Brut `14` `C`

Light and breezy.

THRESHER

One of the advantages of wine shops like Thresher was viciously demonstrated when a paragon of virtue who works for my ex-publisher, Faber & Faber, was mugged and found immediate human solace in a branch of the chain. The felon and his accomplice, lurking in a Ford Escort, found the victim no mere pushover for in spite of being cut and bruised she gave chase and noted the registration number of the getaway car. Apparently at least thirty good citizens piled into the Thresher shop to offer assistance and confirm the car's number but whether any wine was bought, opened and shared around is not recorded.

Thresher is an organisation quite likely, on the strength of the incident above, to launch a chain of shops expressly for the relief of distressed publishers. It already has a blooming family of subsidiaries which even a professional observer of the scene finds knotty to untangle: Wine Shops (846 branches), Drinks Stores (458 branches), Wine Rack (117 branches), Bottoms Up (72 branches), Food & Drink Stores (100 branches) and its latest enterprise called Home Run which flogs wine/pizzas/videos to would-be couch potatoes (a mere two branches as yet, one in Luton and the other, bizarrely, in Bournemouth).

The wines? Let me start in Bordeaux. Thresher has put together an interesting bunch of well-priced reds, only available to the store, by concentrating on minor spots like the Cotes de Bourg. This area, facing Margaux and the Haut-Medoc across the Gironde river, is fairly underdoggish but this is distinctly to the shrewd quaffer's advantage. Les Forges de Macay 1992 is a 14-pointer, and costs £5.49, and has an admirably tannic structure, implying staying power, but has more than you'd think of an immediately fruity finish. I also liked Chateau Sauvage 1990, a Premieres Cotes de Bordeaux, which has classic claret traits – from its violet scent and cigar-box hints to its stalky fruit which suggests that a decade of lush life lies ahead of it. This wine costs £6.49 and rates 15 points.

Other terrific red wines dot the shelves. Bulgarian Vintage Premiere Merlot 1993 belies its poncey moniker with handsomely textured fruit which is like a velvet jacket with patches of leather. It costs £2.99 and rates 15 points. The Valdemar Rioja is another soft, fruity touch, though less complex, and this costs £3.99 and rates 14. On the white side, newly arrived, there is Winelands Chenin Blanc 1995 which looks pedestrian to behold in bottle and in glass but turns out to be a classic solvent for those end-of-the-workday blues because the delicious melony fruit has more than a suspicion of crispness on the finish. The wine costs £3.49 and rates 14.5 points. The store also has a wonderful Moscatel de Valencia, at £3.39, which has a lovely waxy quality to its honey-drenched fruit making it perfect to accompany all manner of sweet festive fare. It rates 16.5 points.

The chain's top-sellers are:

1. Liebfraumilch.
2. Jacob's Creek Red.
3. Tollana Dry White.
4. Albor Rioja.
5. Lambrusco Bianco.
6. Tollana Red.

An equal spread, then – on the strength of the above – between men and women customers. This is a very healthy market base and it is not a balance all high street wine chains necessarily achieve so well. Thresher's range strengths – Eastern Europe, regional France, South Africa, Spain and Portugal, Australia and New Zealand as well as sparkling wine and champagne – give the group breadth as well as depth.

The chain believes that the most significant change in its business recently 'has been the successful initiative of matching wine with food'. But for me the more significant shift has been over a longer period of time and it involves, to quote the store's own, rather bland, words, the 'building on the awareness of the Thresher Wine Shop as the contemporary wine shop with a quality range through existing promotions and TV advertising'. Ten new branches were opened in Scotland and a marketing manager was hired from Jacobs – who make crackers. (Well, Thresher say they want to emphasise the matching of wine with food.) They also hired, to strengthen the wine-buying team, the energetic Lucy Warner from Victoria Wine.

No loss of dialogue with its suppliers, though. Last October, 'worried about the quality and direction that some of Miguel Torres' wines were taking', Thresher wine buyer Julian Twaites invited Senor Torres, wine-maker and driving force behind Spain's largest family-owned wine company, to a comparative wine tasting in London. Mr Twaites and Senor Torres got stuck into a range of wines from Australia, New Zealand, South Africa and, of course, Spain. The object was to demonstrate to one particular wine-maker – an adventurous, civilised, highly motivated and intelligent individual of considerable talent and versatility – that perhaps his wines weren't all that they could be and had been overtaken, in some instances, by new wines of which Senor Torres was unaware. Mr Twaites was 'alarmed that Miguel seemed to be taking his eye off the ball' (something Senor Torres would take deeply seriously since I can personally vouch for the fact that when playing tennis he never does) and as a result of the tasting, which revealed that Senor Torres had never heard about flying wine-makers and that the name Hugh Ryman was as foreign to him as a chip butty, certain Torres wines were shown to be not up to snuff. As a result, Gran Sangredetoro has already picked up pace and Gran Vina Sol, which Mr Twaites would like to see renamed Vina Sol Chardonnay is 'already . . . looking fatter'. Dialogue like this is a measure not only of how seriously a company like Torres takes Thresher as a buyer of its wines but how important the British wine market is as a whole. It also, of course, continues a historical process which has been going on for several centuries. The little group of islands known as Britain has had, since the demise of the ruling houses of ancient Rome and the disappearance of the monastic wine-making tradition, more influence over the taste of wine worldwide than any other single country. It is a trifle extravagant, perhaps, to compare Mr Twaites with Caligula and the Borgia popes, but in his wilder moments he might like to contemplate the similarities.

The Thresher organisation as a whole has a wild edge. It offers great breadth and this is increasing in spite of the marketing purist carping that this shape has been expensively purchased by the setting up of too many Thresher satellites. This is risky in a volatile market (and wine is subject to two volatile elements: changing drinkers' tastes and the new face each wine must put on every vintage, for better or worse, as a result of seasonal fluctuations). Unless each satellite is comfortably profitable in its own right or is tolerated as being less than this because its potential to become a long-term profit earner is great, then putting on the muscle of breadth risks losing the litheness of depth. It is certainly sound thinking to have one buying team service a number of differently styled branches, operating under various names, but the temptation is to diversify above the level which makes true commercial sense. Customers can get confused, let alone us poor wine writers.

Wine Rack and Bottoms Up are the two biggest subsidiaries. Let me look at them separately. Wine Rack's top six best-sellers are:

1. Domaine du Tariquet blanc.
2. Albor Rioja tinto.
3. Tollana Dry White.
4. Figaro rouge.
5. Jacob's Creek Red.
6. Macon Blanc Villages.

On the basis of these sound, very sound, wines I agree with Wine Rack when it says that its customers are 'predominantly the experienced sort from a managerial and professional background, aged between twenty-four and forty-five, and of both sexes'. The shop's range strengths are the same as Thresher's but one must add to this Alsace, Chablis, Rioja and the minor growths of Bordeaux. The most significant change in recent months in Wine Rack's business, so it tells me, is the growth in Alsace and New Zealand wines. This would enhance the store's case for the even male/female spread of its customer base, for the strong white wine profiles of both Alsace and New Zealand are spread equally between men and women who are experienced drinkers. Five new stores are planned for 1995 and each will, presumably, be true to the organisation's stated objective of developing Wine Rack 'as the classic wine shop, a true specialist in wine retailing which is at the same time not intimidating yet demonstrating care and enthusiasm for wine'. The word 'classic' worries me. I do not, in this context, know what it means. It summons up an image of old men in dark grey frock coats, dandruff dancing on their shoulders, muttering about rancid white burgundies. This cannot be what Wine Rack means for it is the complete antithesis of this in both style and temperament. Ah, words! All words are translations (as the saintly Johann Hamann said), and how true this is when it comes to wine writing.

Bottoms Up says it is 'the place to buy a case'. Does this make any sense? It offers, to be sure, something for the ear inasmuch as the felicity of the rhyme chimes agreeably (doubtless the most seductive factor in persuading those in power of its suitability as a slogan), but one must quibble at, or at least lay open to logical disputation, the raving dissonance between a shop selling wine by the case (or at least trying to flog its wine this way) and the name Bottoms Up. Surely, Money Down is a more pertinent title. Or how about Bottoms Up – Quids In? No doubt the chain's foreign suppliers, particularly the French and the Germans, have a quiet chuckle (inasmuch as either of these nationalities is given to quiet chuckling) when they literally translate the name – Bottoms Up – into their own languages. The wines in Bottoms Up best-sellers list, on the other hand, provide no laughs for either country:

1. Jacob's Creek Red.
2. Jacob's Creek White.
3. Tollana Dry White.
4. Domaine du Tariquet blanc.
5. Macon Blanc Villages.
6. Etchart Torrontes.

Well, the French might be able to afford a small smile (if the Aussie trio in front aren't too much for them to swallow), but who'd have thought they'd have an Argentinian hard on their heels (as they did when this list was compiled a few months back)? If these bottles follow the general sales pattern at Bottoms Up shops then it can be reckoned that probably over 50 per cent of the sales were in case lots. This increasing emphasis on sales by the case is, so Wine Rack tells me, 'the most significant change in our business in 1994'. The name is obviously no barrier, then.

Who is doing all this buying at Wine Rack? When I asked the store this they said 'predominantly big drinkers'. Make of this what you will. I take it to mean mainly men driving cars with large boots. Whoever they are, these 'big drinkers', they are certainly encouraging the chain to expand. Eight new branches opened last year with another ten in total planned for this year, 1995. The best sellers apart, where are they spending their money? On more expensive Australian bottles and wines from Spain, the cheaper regions of France, New Zealand, and they are cheerfully coughing up for champagne and sparkling wines.

Wine Rack will surely grow its sale-by-case market (watch out, Majestic), especially if it is as successful as it aims to be at the siting and effective launching of new stores.

They are also attempting to 'build the enthusiasm of branch

staff to nurture their customers'. This is essential in the case-sale market, for customers need tastings and genuinely informed and helpful staff if they are to become loyal customers of such a wine shop.

The future? This is interesting as far as new wines are concerned. Wine Rack thinks California will liven up, that Eastern Europe, Chile and South Africa will develop, that French regional wines will continue to grow in appeal and so will Australia, Portugal and Spain. However, it also believes, along with me, that New World rieslings will begin to make their mark and that 'new varietals and new varietal combinations' will become more of a vogue.

A vogue Thresher is threatening to kill altogether is the peculiarly British one of not complaining about what causes displeasure. This summer, the chain ran a TV commercial inviting customers to return any wine they didn't like. According to the press release sent to newspapers launching this initiative, 'Wine drinkers who find they don't like a bottle they've bought have . . . but two options – throw it down the drain or throw it in the cooking.' This, of course, is complete rubbish. You have the option, under The Return of Goods Act, to return the wine to the shop whence it came and have it replaced or to ask for your money refunded. Anyone who has ever gone back to a supermarket on this basis will know that the dosh is whipped out of the till instantly. Nevertheless, this is a 'novel idea', according to marketing director Mr Ralph Hayward – who adds further that Thresher 'are the first to come up with such a bold initiative'.

I have long urged readers to follow this course. Whether the wine is faulty, or corked, or simply not to your liking, the option to have it replaced with another bottle of the same wine, another bottle of comparable value, or to ask for your money back is no more than any customer should expect. I wish Thresher luck. But how will they deal with the individual who says that the Dom Perignon 1985 he paid £60 for didn't go with the fish fingers it was purchased to partner? Such a customer may well insist on his moolah being returned rather than be Dommed again.

Interesting times ahead for Thresher's sales assistants.

Thresher, Wine Rack, Bottoms Up
Sefton House
42 Church Road
Welwyn Garden City
Herts
AL8 6PJ

Tel 01707 328244
Fax 01707 371398

SEE STOP PRESS SECTION AT END OF BOOK FOR LAST-MINUTE ADDITIONS TO THIS RETAILER'S RANGE.

ARGENTINIAN WINE WHITE

Etchart Cafayate Chardonnay 1993 `13.5` `C`
Tasty.

AUSTRALIAN WINE RED

Chapel Hill Shiraz 1992 `14` `E`
Smooth and flowing, beautifully executed, rich, finely textured.
You wallow in it.

Penfolds Bin 2 Shiraz/Mourvedre 1993 `15.5` `C`
Integrated, soft, very brisk and bright yet with a firm finish.
Good food Aussie.

Penfolds Bin 35 Shiraz Cabernet 1992 `15` `C`

Penfolds Bin 407 Cabernet Sauvignon 1990 `16` `E`

**Penfolds Coonawarra Cabernet Sauvignon
1990** `17` `E`

Penfolds Kalimna Shiraz Bin 28 1992 `15` `D`
Superb style, flavour, weight, balance of elements (fruit, acid,
tannins), the whole of which makes for perfect casserole
compatibility.

**Penfolds Old Vine Mourvedre/Grenache/
Shiraz, Barossa 1992** `15` `E`
A flood of ripe fruit bolstered by friendly tannins which seem to
me as pretty well developed as they could get for the best balance

of flavours. In spite of what Penfolds say, drink this wine over the next year. The gloss of its fruit will fade if the tannins are allowed to tighten their grip over, say, 3/4 years.

Petalluma Coonawarra 1992

Expensive dollop of minted blackcurrant. Too expensive? Not quite. Its class keeps its rating respectable.

Red Cliffs Coonawarra Cabernet Sauvignon 1992

Subdued mint on the velvet blackcurrant fruit. Impressive, good value, lots of flavour.

Red Cliffs Coonawarra Cabernet Sauvignon 1991

Riddoch Coonawarra Cabernet Shiraz 1990

Riddoch Coonawarra Shiraz 1992

Yes, there's flavour but yes, there's a price tag. I'm nit-picking? Maybe, but when this soft-hearted beauty meets food I fear for its sanity.

Rosemount Cabernet Sauvignon 1993

Calm and impressive but almost *too* neatly turned out – it's like an answer to an exam question.

Rosemount Estate Merlot 1993

Soft, savoury, quick – then comes back at your throat with a light grasp of tannin. Too soft for hard grub? Yes.

Samuels Bay Grenache, Barossa 1994

Brilliant rich fruit of real staying power. Superb mouth-filling richness, softness, textural ripeness and intense style. Lovely grub.

Samuels Bay Malbec, Padthaway 1994   13   D

Rich, aromatic, pricey – and falls apart at the end.

St Hallett Shiraz, Barossa 1992   14   E

Soft-hearted as a new father. Stop blubbing, you wimp!

Stowells of Chelsea Shiraz Cabernet (3 litre)   14   G

Rich fruit with earthy undertones. Has a long, meaty finish with a firm, purposeful balance of fruit and acid.

Tollana Black Lace Shiraz 1992   14   C

Breezy cherry finish to some depth of fruit.

Tollana Cabernet Sauvignon 1992   15   C

Lovely bright, almost zippy finish to some herby, soft fruit of weight and distinction. Delicious.

Tollana Cabernet/Shiraz 1992   13   C

Tollana Red   14   C

Better than before, this non-vintage wine. Not as jammy and light as it was, it's now even got a touch of the soil.

AUSTRALIAN WINE   WHITE

Bridgewater Mill Riesling 1993   14   C

Attractive but a curious expression of the grape.

Brown Brothers Orange Muscat & Flora 1994 (half bottle)   13.5   C

For pudding freaks.

Chapel Hill Riesling 1993

Jacob's Creek Chardonnay 1994

Lots of the usual rich fruity attack underpinned by a delicious freshness. Good, balanced, good with food.

Jacob's Creek Dry White Semillon Chardonnay 1994

Getting feebler, this blend. Still tasty, but at well over four quid this is not great value.

Katnook Estate Coonawarra Chardonnay 1992

A cool, classy wine but overpriced somewhat.

Katnook Estate Coonawarra Sauvignon Blanc 1993

A cat got in amongst the fruit too – and peed a little.

Lindemans Bin 65 Chardonnay 1993

Deep bruised fruit – lovely and ripe – superb effect on the tongue.

Lindemans Padthaway Chardonnay 1992

Moyston Semillon Chardonnay 1994

Vim and verve.

Oxford Landing Sauvignon Blanc 1993 14 C

Impressive: good fruit, acid, style and great with fish (like grilled sole).

Penfolds Bin 202 South Australian Riesling 1993 14 C

Superb, rich aperitif. Delicious.

Penfolds Bin 21 Semillon/Chardonnay 1993 15 C

Penfolds Koonunga Hill Chardonnay 1994 14 C

Solid batter – off the back foot at this price but it's still in the crease.

Penfolds Rawson's Retreat Bin 21 Semillon Chardonnay 1994 15 C

Great clash of soft mango/melony fruit and pineapple acidity. Slightly exotic, generous, bold, delicious.

Penfolds Semillon/Chardonnay 1993 14 C

Excellent recipe: fruit, acid, wood but will integrate and improve mightily over the next 1/2 years.

Penfolds South Australia Chardonnay 1992 16 D

Lovely polished, lush, woody fruit with touches of lemon, beautifully balanced. Elegant – a real alternative, at a far lower price, to fine burgundy.

Riddoch Chardonnay 1991 15 D

Riddoch Coonawarra Sauvignon Blanc 1994 15 D

A curious, rich, flavoured style of sauvignon. A superb wine for rich fish dishes and fish soups.

Riddoch Riesling 1993 13 C

Samuels Bay Colombard, Barossa Valley 1994 13 D

Floppy-eared and playful but an expensive bunny.

Samuels Bay (unoaked) Riesling 1993 13 E

St Hallett Chardonnay, Barossa 1993　`14` `E`

Expensive, but explicit: fruit-packed, dry, purposeful.

St Hallett Poachers Blend 1993　`15` `C`

Feast your larynx here – throat-clenching flavour. Great with lobster, scallops, squid.

Stowells of Chelsea Semillon Chardonnay (3 litre)　`14` `G`

Presence and lift, style and purpose – this fruit knows where it's going. Good with food and mood.

Tollana Chardonnay 1994　`14` `C`

Delicious, ripe, almost baked fruit.

Tollana Colombard Chardonnay 1993　`14` `C`

Assertive fruit, nicely acidically balanced.

Tollana Coonawarra Riesling 1993　`13` `C`

Tollana Dry White 1994　`14` `C`

Fresh and fruity. A much better blend than previous vintages – more of a sparkle to its eye.

Tollana McLaren Vale Oak Aged Chardonnay 1993　`15` `C`

Lots of rich swirling fruit. Stylish, full, great with roast chicken.

Tollana Medium Dry White 1993　`13` `B`

More interesting fruit than the dry version.

Tollana Semillon/Chardonnay 1993　`12` `C`

Tyrrells 'Old Winery' Chardy 1993　`13` `D`

Lemony but not quite a lemon.

Wynns Coonawarra Riesling 1993
Ripe, balanced wine to enjoy by itself.

AUSTRIAN WINE WHITE

Lenz Moser Gruner Veltliner 1994
Good fruit – good price.

BULGARIAN WINE RED

**Bulgarian Russe Cabernet Sauvignon/
Cinsault**
Lovely dry-edged but intensely fruity wine which has serious
glugging candidature as well as stretching the broad hand of
friendship to food.

**Bulgarian Vintage Premier Merlot, Iambol
Region 1994**
Dry, gently leathery. Tasty.

Cabernet Sauvignon, Pulden 1989

**Iambol Vintage Premiere Cabernet
Sauvignon 1994**
Rugged edge to soft fruit. Good solid fruity wine.

**Stowells of Chelsea Cabernet Sauvignon
(3 litre)**
Dry, very good, rich, savoury-edged fruit – good with food.

Vintage Premier Cabernet Sauvignon 1993

Vintage Premier Merlot 1993

Bargain fruit. Some serious dry touches to a lovely, rounded depth of flavour. Excellent with cheeses.

BULGARIAN WINE WHITE

Khan Krum Chardonnay 1990 `12` `C`

Slaviantzi Country Wine `9` `B`
Try it behind your ears.

Yantra Valley Bulgarian Dry 1994 `12.5` `B`

Yantra Valley Bulgarian Riesling 1994 `12` `B`

CHILEAN WINE RED

Caliterra Reserva Cabernet Sauvignon 1992

Red, smooth, deliciously soft berried fruit with an engaging rich meaty edge. This edge is subtle but persistent. An elegant wine which makes every concession to be liked. Available in Wine Rack and Bottoms Up stores.

Chilean Cabernet Sauvignon
Biscuity, chewy fruit.

Las Colinas Merlot/Cabernet Sauvignon 1993

Solid yet free of any hardness, smooth and fruity. Basic but very drinkable – especially with simple meat dishes.

Las Colinas NV

Delightful little wine with perky fruit, good balance and effective tannic styling. Excellent with food (roasts, etc).

Santa Carolina Malbec 1993

Touch haughty for no apparent reason.

Santa Carolina Pinot Noir Reserve 1994

Not bad, but too light and unconvincing on the finish (in spite of a middle whack of real gamy fruit).

Santa Carolina Special Reserve Cabernet Sauvignon 1990

Bright and blooming with fruit.

Valdivieso Merlot, Lontue Region 1993

Gripping, rich, assertive, well-plotted from start to finish. A good thriller.

CHILEAN WINE · WHITE

Errazuriz Sauvignon Blanc 1994

Has cool class by virtue of its hint of richness to the bright fruit. Classic sauv blanc? Maybe not. But delicious with food.

Las Colinas Chilean White 1993

Brilliant price for a superbly well-constructed mouthful of fruit – richly edged and full without being blowsy.

Las Colinas Riesling 1994

Rich edge to the fruit makes it a good fish-stew wine.

Las Colinas Sauvignon/Semillon 1994

Superb double act of grape varieties singing softly and deliciously together. Great summer drinking with fruit, acid and overall pleasing zippiness.

Santa Carolina Chenin Blanc 1994

Out-Loires the Loire here, for the money. Richness, depth, good with chicken dishes.

Santa Carolina Gran Reserva Chardonnay 1993

Rich, slightly exotic, complex, serious, fun, compelling. Pricey but worth it.

Santa Carolina Special Reserve Sauvignon Blanc 1993

Great stuff. Exceptional.

Villa Montes Chardonnay, Cuvee Ryman-Montes Curico 1994

Elegant fruit here.

Villa Montes Sauvignon Blanc, Cuvee Ryman-Montes Curico 1994

Marzipan fruit.

Villard Sauvignon Blanc, Aconcagua 1994

Richness, flavour and style.

ENGLISH WINE   WHITE

Heritage Fume 1992   16   D

A strikingly clean and elegant English wine of considerable class.

It sits, deliciously, between the sancerre of old and New Zealand sauvignons blancs of the 1990s. Available at Thresher Group stores only.

Mersea 1992 `14` `D`

Well-structured from start to finish, with nice Ortega (grape variety) richness showing through on the fruit. Available at Bottoms Up stores.

Moorlynch Estate Selection 1992 `11` `D`

Grapefruit on the nose leads to some soft fruit on the middle palate. But what fruit this wine has, has a bland quality. Available at Bottoms Up stores.

Northbrook Springs Medium Dry 1992 `12` `D`

Expensive for the sweet fruit on offer. Available at Bottoms Up stores.

Pilton Manor Dry Reserve 1991 `12` `D`

A bit muddy on the front and a bit short on the finish. Rather expensive for the fruit on offer. Available at Bottoms Up stores.

Sharpham Barrel Fermented Dry 1993 `13` `E`

Very attractive grapefruit and ginger fruit, and well-structured, but over-priced for the quality of fruit on offer. Available at Bottoms Up stores.

Sharpham Estate Selection 1992 `12` `D`

Gingery nose and fruit which has some richness. Available at Bottoms Up stores.

Valley Vineyards Fume 1992 `16` `E`

Beautiful, elegant, stylish and clean with lovely fruit and a good structure. Will age well too. Available at Bottoms Up stores.

Valley Vineyards Hinton Grove 1992   `14` `D`

Attractive 'off-dry' wine with pleasantly rounded, soft fruit. Available at Bottoms Up stores.

Valley Vineyards Regatta 1992   `13` `D`

This wine has a minerally character, some weight of fruit and a balanced structure. In short, it is well made – very clean. Available at Bottoms Up stores.

Wickham Fume 1992   `15` `D`

Lovely style of fruit, clean, fresh and gently nutty. This wine's available at the House of Commons bar and I hope MPs choke on it considering the unfair duty levels English wine-makers are forced to swallow. Also available at Bottoms Up stores.

Wickham Vintage Selection Dry 1993   `13` `D`

A delicate, attractive nose leads to ripe fruit and some weight on the finish. Good structure. Available at Bottoms Up stores.

FRENCH WINE   RED

Alicante, VdP de l'Aude 1994   `15` `D`

Deep and brown-soup fruity. Real flavour here of some dimension.

Berloup St Chinian 1991   `11` `C`

Chateau Bonnet, Reserve Andre Lurton 1990   `15` `D`

Excellent value with its dry yet soft style.

Chateau Bouscasse, Madiran 1991   `15` `D`

Interesting wine. It will certainly age for the next 3/4 years, broaden in flavour and deepen in appeal. It has active tannins, rich, charcoal fruit with good berry concentration, a distinct leathery overtone and a strong, lingering finish with resolute tannins not easily giving up. My sort of wine, the price is excepted. It is £1.50 more than it deserves to be. That said, if cellared properly it could be very good indeed and a reputation-enhancing bottle for the uncelebrated tannet grape which predominantly makes up the blend.

Chateau Brulesecaille, Cotes de Bourg 1991
 16.5 D

Burnt quail and excellent with it. Real depth here, even 2 hours before drinking. Leathery, mouthfilling, great tannins, great fruit, great dryness and flavour.

Chateau Coucheroy, Pessac Leognan 1990
 16 D

Chateau d'Arsuc, Haut-Medoc 1990
 15 E

Chateau de Francs, Cote de Francs 1989
 15 E

Chateau de la Liquiere, Clos de l'Olivette Faugeres 1993
 16.5 D

Such fabulous dusty fruit it brings tears to the eyes, not just joy to the palate. Great dry food wine. Decant 5 hours beforehand and then just jump in with all senses alert and primed. Not at Thresher Wine Shops.

Chateau de la Riviere, Fronsac 1992
 14 C

Classic Fronsac tannin with a beefy broth of fruit.

Chateau de Lastours, Corbieres 1989
 13.5 D

Not so upfront as the '91, nor so compelling. Bottoms Up only.

Chateau de Lastours, Corbieres 1991 `15.5` `D`

Superb dry fruit with flavour, depth, aroma and lingering possessiveness of the back teeth. Wine Rack only.

Chateau de Laurens Faugeres 1993 `15.5` `C`

Dry but not dry-stickish. Fruity but never sweet. Handsome but not foppish. A lovely soft wine of real class.

Chateau de Violet, Minervois 1992 `13` `D`

Soft, ripe plums.

Chateau Grand Prebois Cotes du Rhone AC 1992 `13` `D`

Chateau Guibon, Bordeaux AC 1992 `14` `C`

Chateau Les Ollieux Romanis, Corbieres 1990 `12` `C`

Chateau Macay, Cotes de Bourg 1992 `13` `D`

Chateau Mercier, Cotes de Bourg 1993 `13` `D`

Dry, well-flavoured. Very good with roasts.

Chateau Ramage La Batisse, Haut Medoc 1989 `15` `E`

Chateau Sauvage, Premieres Cotes de Bordeaux 1990 `15` `D`

Chateau St Auriol, Corbieres 1992 `14` `D`

Soft, deep, velvety, balanced and classy.

Chateau St Esteve Cotes du Rhone 1991 `13` `C`

Chateau Suau, Premieres Cotes de Bordeaux 1991 `11` `D`

Chorey Les Beaunes, Tollot Boeuf 1992 `11` `F`

Very pleasant – till you have to put your hand in your pocket.

Claret `12` `C`

Claret Bordeaux Superior 1991 `12` `C`

Corbieres l'Estagnon 1991 `12` `B`

**Cotes de Nuits Villages, Domaine d'Arlot
Clos du Chapeau 1991** `12` `F`

Some hints at striving to make a burgundy here. But what a price!

Cotes de Ventoux 'La Mission' 1994 `13.5` `B`

Tasty, simple, proper.

Cotes du Rhone J. P. Bartier 1992 `11` `C`

Cuvee Pierre Sicard, Minervois 1991 `12` `C`

Domaine de la Rectorie, Banyuls 1993 `14` `D`

A red pud wine? Yes. And no. Try it with fruit and cheese.

**Domaine de Peyre Rose Coteaux du
Languedoc, Cuvee Syrah Leone** `11` `E`

A £3.29 wine at best. Has some dark, attractive fruit but little spunk.

**Domaine de Rivoyre Cabernet Sauvignon
1993** `14` `C`

Light yet chewy with excellent varietal character which is never tart or crude green-peppery.

Domaine du Grand Bosc, Fitou 1991 `11` `C`

Domaine Font de Michelle Chateauneuf-du-Pape 1992 `14` `F`

An expensive bottle but a decently fruity one with a complex finish.

Domaine Gauby Cotes du Roussillon 1991 `14` `D`

Country fruit with avenues of aristocratic tannin and acidity. Delicious. Wine Rack only.

Domaine Ste Eulalie, Minervois 1992 `11` `C`

Fitou, Mme Claude Parmentier `10` `C`

Fleurie, Cellier de Samsons 1992 `10` `D`

L'Estagnon Rouge `13` `B`

Le Cordon Lot 37 1993 `14` `C`

Les Aubuis, Caves Rabelais Chinon 1993 `11` `C`

Les Forges de Macay, Cotes de Bourg 1992 `14` `D`

Has a good fruity finish to the dry, tannic structure.

Les Oliviers Chateauneuf-du-Pape 1993 `12.5` `E`

Macon, Regional Classics 1994 `12` `C`

Some reasonable fruit.

Macon Rouge, Jean-Paul Bartier 1993 `10` `C`

Macon-Bray Domaine de la Combe 1991 `10` `D`

Mas Faussie, Peyriac 1994 `14` `C`

Classy yet with an earthy edge of character. Delicious with roast, herby lamb. Wine Rack only.

Mature Claret

Merlot Galet 1994

Very soft but never gooey. Delicious fruit.

Morgon Duboeuf, Jean Descombes 1994

Morgon is one of the few Beaujolais crus to have real meat and savour to its fruit. This is no exception.

Rasteau, La Ramillade 1991

Delicious and impressively classy rusticity, but hopelessly overpriced by at least £2. Even so it's worth 14 points because it's better than some Chateauneufs.

Sablet, La Ramillade 1991

Sauvigny les Beaune 1990

Sirius Red

Some weight of fruit but rather disappointing structure. Some aroma, too, but ill-defined. A formula wine made to a recipe, like tinned food.

St Amour, Domaine de la Pirolette Georges Duboeuf 1992

Stowells of Chelsea Vin de Pays du Gard (3 litre)

Delightful smooth fruit with flavour and balance. A lovely touch – a distant echo, really – of earth.

Val du Torgan

Bright with a rustic edge.

Vin de Pays des Coteaux de Peyriac 1993

Hammy, dry, plummy, light, cheap. It is rated as a light

wine and deserves its rating, but it is not heavy with fruit or complex.

FRENCH WINE   WHITE

Alsace Tradition Turckheim 1992   12 C

Blanc de Blancs Medium Dry   11 B

Blanc de Blancs Dry   13.5 B
A zippy wine of deep appeal to those prising apart fresh shellfish.

Bordeaux Blanc 1993   11 B

Bordeaux Sauvignon 1993   13 C
Some attractive fruit here.

Chablis Premier Cru Beauroy 1992   13 E

Chateau Bonnet Entre Deux Mers 1993   12 C

Chateau Bonnet Entre Deux Mers Oak Aged 1992   11 E

Chateau Bonnet Rose Bordeaux Clairet 1993   12.5 C

Chateau Climens 1991 (half bottle)   12 F
Better value than a £3 bottle of Moscatel de Valencia? Nope. A treat strictly for aficionados.

Chateau de Coucheroy 1992   14 D
Like it, don't love it (not at six quid) but I do like it.

Chateau de la Jaubertie Sauvignon 1993 `14` `C`
A highly drinkable rose.

Chateau de Rouergue 1992 `11` `C`

Chateau la Lezardiere Entre Deux Mers 1993 `13` `C`

Chateau Pascaud Villefranche, Sauternes 1992 `11` `G`

Chateau Rouergue Entre Deux Mers 1993 `12.5` `C`

Chateau Villotte Bordeaux 1993 `12` `C`

Domaine de Tariquet, VdP des Cotes de Gascogne 1994 `14.5` `C`
Real fruit and zippy style here. Flavoursome enough to go with food – fresh enough to be a good glass by itself.

Laperouse Blanc Val d'Orbieu & Penfolds, VdP d'Oc 1994 `14` `C`
Rounded fruit flavours energetically supported by the elegance of the acids.

Le Cordon 1993 `13` `C`

Macon Villages, Regional Classics 1993 `12` `C`
Regional yes. Classic no.

Mas Faussie VdP des Cotes de Peyriac 1994 `13` `D`
Serious mask of fruit worn here – with little relieving acidity. Suit Brookside fans.

Mouton Cadet 1992 `10` `D`
Barely recommendable. And what a cheek at the price.

Muscadet 1993 `10` `C`

Muscadet Chateau de la Cornilliere 1993 `13` `C`
Some fine fruit on display here.

Petit Chablis Chateau de Maligny 1991 `12` `E`

Petit Chablis Goulley 1993 `12` `D`
Drinkable but pricey.

Picpoul de Pinet 1994 `12.5` `C`
A real tasty country bumpkin – but not a tasty country
bumpkin price.

Pinot Blanc d'Alsace, Turckheim 1993 `14` `C`
Soft apricot touches to the fruit. Delightful drinking.

Pouilly Fuisse 1993 `11` `D`

Premieres Cotes de Bordeaux AC `12` `C`
Pud wine.

Premieres Cotes de Bordeaux Sichel `12` `C`
Pudding wine but better with blue cheese.

**Riesling Trimbach 1989, Cuvee Frederic
Emile** `12` `G`

Rivesaltes Vieille Reserve 1980 `12` `D`
Raisiny and sweet.

**Sauvignon Touraine La Chapelle de
Cray 1993** `15` `C`
A class act. A bit restrained on the fruit for those used to New
Zealand but this example is in good voice nevertheless. Has a

crispness of attack which is deeply delicious – and good news for shellfish marriage brokers.

Soleil d'Or Chardonnay VdP d'Oc 1994   13.5   C
Real flavour here.

Stowells of Chelsea Vin de Pays du Tarn (3 litre)   12   F
Sound but dullish – not a lot of fruit.

Turckheim Gewurztraminer 1993   13   D
Very tasty.

Turckheim Tokay Pinot Gris 1993   12.5   D

VdP du Gers, Au Loubet 1993   13   B
Bargain – simple, cheap glugging.

Vendange Blanc VdP Catalan 1993   13   C

White Burgundy 1993   10   C

Zind Humbrecht Tokay Pinot Gris Vieilles Vignes 1991   15   G

GERMAN WINE   WHITE

Bereich Bernkastel G. Prinz 1992   11   B

Bereich Nierstein, Regional Classics 1993   12.5   B

Deinhard Vintage 1993   13   B
Oh! If only it had more of the vibrant acidity it needs to make it really exciting!! But future vintages may redress this.

Dr Loosen Riesling 1992   15   D

Keep for 3/4 years but if you must drink it now, chill it and serve with smoked salmon.

Dr Loosen Riesling Kabinett 1992   16   D

Real sherbet lime undercutting the fruit. Superb aperitif and wonderful with smoked fish.

Hock, Regional Classics   13   B

So much better priced than many a Liebfraumilch and more appealing.

Kirchheimer Schwarzerdener Kerner Spatlese 1992   13.5   C

Aperitif – a really interesting one.

Liebfraumilch, Regional Classics 1993   13   B

Not as sweet as some.

Liebfraumilch Rheingau Langenbach 1993   14   B

An excellent step-up to real Liebfraumilch for the young wine drinker moving on from sweet wines. This has real character.

Niersteiner Gutes Domtal 1994   12   C

Niersteiner Spiegelberg Silvaner 1994   13   C

Chilled with pea soup? Eccentric pairing but then so is life and wine writing.

Piesporter Michelsberg, Regional Classics 1994   12   C

Good, simple, summer evening aperitif.

Stowells of Chelsea Liebfraumilch (3 litre)   12   F

As reasonable a proposition as you get with this beast.

Wormser Liebfrauenmorgen Kabinett 1994 `13.5` `C`

Delicious aperitif – or try it with smoked salmon.

HUNGARIAN WINE   RED

Butlers Blend Red `10` `B`

Soft, soggy, simple.

Villany Hills Cabernet Sauvignon 1992 `15` `B`

Villany Hills Merlot 1992 `12` `B`

HUNGARIAN WINE   WHITE

Butlers Blend White `13` `B`

Delicious, rich-edged aperitif and soup and salad wine. Curious
sticky-toffee edge to the fruit but it finishes admirably cleanly.
Also good with fish and chips and squid dishes.

**Cool Ridge Barrel Fermented Chardonnay
1994** `14` `C`

Rich and ready for all sorts of flavourful food – smoked fish and
fish cakes, shrimp risotto, asparagus, mussels, even lamb chops.
A versatile friend to food, this wine.

Disznoko Tokaji Furmint 1993 `12` `C`

**Domaine Boyar Tasgovischte Chardonnay
1994** `14` `B`

As fresh, bright and breezy as the label. Thoroughly modern
slurping.

Gyongyos Chardonnay 1994 `12` `B`

Not as lively as previous vintages.

Hungarian Muscat 1991 `13` `B`

A delicious, light aperitif. Has musky, spicy, dry-elderberry overtones.

Muscat 1993 `14` `B`

Dry, very appealing spicy melon fruit. A good aperitif.

Pinot Blanc 1992 `12` `B`

Sauvignon Blanc Gyongyos Estate 1994 `12` `B`

Going over the £2.99 barrier has not meant an increase in quality. Good, but not as exciting as previous vintages.

ITALIAN WINE RED

Alasia Dolcetto d'Asti 1994 `13` `C`

Barco Reale 1993 `13` `D`

Chianti Rufina Selvapiana 1990 `15` `D`

Chianti Rufina Grati 1991 `13` `C`

Merlot, Friuli-Grave 1993 `12` `B`

Light, with some fruit.

Parrina Rosso 1991 `12` `C`

Tastes like a light chianti. Basic, sound and a touch expensive.

Primitivo del Salento 1993, Le Trulle `13.5` `C`

Gamy, rich aromas and initial fruit attack and then nicely ripe cherries. Delicious.

**Recioto della Valpolicella, Amarone
Classico 1988** `10` `E`

Rosso Piceno, Umani Ronchi 1992 `12` `C`

Salice Salentino Riserva, Taurino 1990 `15.5` `C`

Mature fruit with hints of earth. Smashing.

ITALIAN WINE WHITE

Alasia Cortese del Piemonte 1994 `13` `C`

Alasia Muscate Sec 1994 `11` `C`

Bottoms Up stores.

Bianco di Custoza 1992 `14` `C`

Delicious zip here.

Castello di Neive Arneis 1993 `13` `D`

Elegant lemony fruit.

Frascati Superiore Satinata Catone 1994 `11` `C`

Orvieto Classico Antinori Abbocatto 1994 `12` `D`

Sweet to finish – soft, good for soft-gummed nonagenarians.

Orvieto Classico Campagnole 1994 `13` `C`

Balanced, fruity – touch pricey.

Selva d'Oro VdT di Toscana 1993 `11` `C`

Soave, Regional Classics 1993 `12` `C`

Has flavour.

Vernaccia di San Gimignano Riserva 1992 `12` `D`

Vernaccia di San Gimignano 1993 `13.5` `D`

Nutty and fresh, citric echo on the finish. Costs, but it is a fine
partner for spaghetti alla vongole.

MOLDOVAN WINE   RED

Rochu de Hincesti 1992 `14` `B`

Cheering, burnt cherry/plum fruit. Pleasantly dry.

MOLDOVAN WINE   WHITE

**Hugh Ryman Chardonnay/Sauvignon
Blanc, Hincesti Region 1993** `13` `B`

Rkatsiteli `14` `B`

Lemon zesty wine of great charm.

NEW ZEALAND WINE   RED

Awatea Cabernet/Merlot 1992 `11` `F`

Very drinkable but almost unthinkable at nigh on £13.

Delegat's Cabernet/Merlot 1994 `13.5` `D`

Bright jammy finish to easy-drinking fruit which has a serious tang – but only a tang, not more.

Palliser Estate Pinot Noir 1993 `10` `F`

Mildly diverting – for a second or two. (But for an eleven-quid wine you want major diversionary fruit which lingers.)

NEW ZEALAND WINE WHITE

Cooks Bay Chardonnay 1992 `15` `D`

Cooks Gisborne Sauvignon Blanc 1992 `13` `D`

Hunters Chardonnay 1991 `14` `E`

Yes, it's tasty, but a tenner's worth of fruit? No way, Jose.

Hunters Sauvignon Blanc 1993 `15` `E`

Balanced, sane, very pure and clean. Preaches fruit without screaming it.

Jackson Estate Sauvignon Blanc 1993, Marlborough `16` `E`

Not huge grassiness here, just gentle soothing fruit and balanced stylishness. One of the most elegantly purposeful of sauvignons blancs around. Will repay cellaring for 2/3 years. Very fine.

Kapua Springs Dry White, Gisborne 1993 `13` `C`

Kapua Springs Medium Dry White, Gisborne 1993 `11` `C`

Montana Chardonnay, Marlborough 1994 `12` `C`

Montana Sauvignon Blanc 1993

Pleasant working herbaceous acidity. Marvellous with shellfish.

Palliser Estate Chardonnay 1993

Drinkable but the price tag is a millstone.

Stoneleigh Riesling, Marlborough 1993

Elegant, deliciously vegetal/fruit bouquet. Ripe sour melon fruit with a crisp-ish finish. Good fish wine. Good clean fun – a touch respectable but it will suit vicars.

Stoneleigh Sauvignon Blanc 1993

Stowells of Chelsea New Zealand
Sauvignon Blanc (3 litre)

Keen, grassy aromas, good fruit, rather a quiet finish.

Timara Medium Dry White 1993

A soft and gentle introduction to New Zealand.

Villa Maria 'Lightly Oaked' Chardonnay
1994

Decent rather than dazzling. Thresher, Wine Rack and Bottoms Up.

Villa Maria Private Bin Riesling 1993

Delicious riesling which totally converts German riesling haters to the NZ style. This is rich, dry, lingering, not tart or a prick tease. This is good fruity wine. Great with mackerel.

Villa Maria Riesling 1993

Excellent aperitif.

Villa Maria Sauvignon Blanc 1993

They always get enough lift from the fruit here to balance out the grassy acids. Superb.

Wairau River Chardonnay 1993 `10` `E`
Far too pricey.

Wairau River Sauvignon Blanc 1993 `14` `E`
Delicious; expensive.

PORTUGUESE WINE RED

Alandra, Hordade do Esporao `15` `B`
Floral notes to a dry wine which is robustly capable (although
it is not a hugely rich wine) of tackling spicy food.

Bairrada Reserva Dau Ferraz 1989 `13` `B`

Bright Bros Douro 1992 `14.5` `C`
Bright by name, bright by nature. But tannins intrude, brisk
and food friendly, and the fruit is beautifully developed.

Cabernet Sauvignon Esporao 1993 `13.5` `C`
Touch pricey for the level of hail-fellow well-met fruit (casual
but delicious).

Dao Dau Ferraz Reserva 1989 `14` `B`

Dom Ferraz Reserva, Barraida 1989 `13` `B`

Dom Ferraz Reserva, Dao 1989 `14` `B`

Esporao Reserva 1990 `15` `D`
Oh, what a silly label for such a delightful bottle of fruit.
Criminal!

J.P. Tinto

Light but quite delicious and fruity without a trace of tannic harshness, oxidation or sourness. Has a plum quality to it. A true quaffing masterpiece.

Joao Pato Tinto 1991

Real duck soup: dry, rich, gripping, savoury, deep. Growls with fruit.

Monte Velho 1993

Friendly, delightfully friendly. But a loose embrace, rather than a firm handshake.

Quinta de Lamelas Douro 1993

A distant tang of chocolate, plus some grip from the dry fruit.

Ramada

Cherries and raspberries dryly expressed. Soft creamy touch to this fruit. Delightful quaffing wine.

Ramada Vinhode Mesa

PORTUGUESE WINE WHITE

Albis 1992

J.P. Branco

Delicious cheapness – not of fruit, but of your pennies.

Monte Velho Regenguas 1993

Delicious with fried fish, spicy and bold – like the wine, fine to finish but bold to begin.

SLOVAKIAN WINE · RED

St Laurent, Slovakian `12` `B`

SLOVAKIAN WINE · WHITE

Gruner Veltliner `11` `B`

SOUTH AFRICAN WINE · RED

Boschendal Le Pavillon `13.5` `C`

Very light but there is dark at the end of the tunnel if you keep the wine a year or so.

Paarl Heights Red, Boland Wynkelder 1994 `15` `B`

Soft, spicy, ripe-edged fruit of considerable charm and vibrancy for the money.

Stellenryck Cabernet Sauvignon 1989 `11` `E`

Intense blackcurrant aroma and flavour, somewhat soft and affectionate and arguably *too* friendly for the money – especially as the fruit is drying out and losing elasticity. The tannins are disintegrating and give the wine, without food, the bitterness of wood. It is a drinkable wine, and not unpleasant, but £9 for fruit this ragged and infirm is asking too much.

Stowells of Chelsea Pinotage (3 litre) `13.5` `F`

Soft, not as vivacious – nor with as big a finish -- as some, but attractive and well-balanced.

Thelema Cabernet Sauvignon/Merlot 1993　14　E

Classy, soft, bordeaux (mature)-style wine with a warmth and richness of true depth and style. Bottoms Up only.

Winelands Cinsault/ Tinta Barocca　14　C

Unusual marriage but delicious. Very smooth and rolling. Aromatic, pungent, purposeful.

SOUTH AFRICAN WINE　WHITE

KWV Chenin Blanc 1993　13　C

Some attractive rich fruit here.

KWV Sauvignon Blanc 1995　13.5　C

Thresher, Wine Rack and Bottoms Up.

Lesca Chardonnay, Danie de Wet 1994　16.5　E

A delicious, warm, charming, subtle, forgiving, purposeful, elegant wine of some class – just like the woman it was named after. Only at Wine Rack.

Paarl Heights Colombard, Paarl 1994　13.5　B

So close to scoring more points.

Stellenbosch Dry White 1994　14　B

If only the label of this wine looked less like a Kaffe Fassett knitting pattern and more like the nicely fruity, warm and attractive young thing in the bottle.

Stellenvale Chardonnay 1993　12.5　C

Woody but not totally wise. The finish lets it down.

Stowells of Chelsea Chenin Blanc (3 litre)   `14` `F`

Comes out bright and clean – here is fruit and zip and real style.

Swartland Reserve Sauvignon Blanc/
Chardonnay 1994   `13.5` `C`

Not a marriage of grape varieties which normally conveys an advantage to either but in this wine there is significant balance and attractive fruit.

Winelands Chenin Blanc 1995   `14` `B`

Bright and breezy, delicious with its typically South African, pear-drop edged tropical fruit and great freshness. Aromatic, fruity, good value. Dull words for a far from dull wine.

Winelands Medium Dry White 1994   `10` `B`

A barely exciting tipple.

SPANISH WINE   RED

Agramont Tempranillo/Cabernet, Navarra
1990   `14.5` `C`

Dry, tannic development finishing off lovely, fruity intro and a rich middle passage.

Albor Campo Viejo 1992   `14` `C`

Albor Rioja 1994   `15` `C`

Delicious, vanilla-tinged plum fruit. Joyous style.

Baron de Lay Rioja Reserva 1987   `15` `D`

Berberana Tempranillo, Rioja 1991 `15` `C`

In the demure new style but still with delicious wood/vanilla echoes.

Campo Viejo Reserva Rioja 1988 `15` `C`

Chivite Reserve, Navarra 1989 `14` `C`

Finishes on the up, this wine – leaves you feeling cheerful. Mature yet never overripe or jammy.

Conde de Valdemar Rioja 1991 `15` `D`

Apple peel and blackcurrant with a touch of raspberry. Not a heavy one but it has presence and style in the throat.

Conde de Valdemar Rioja Crianza 1989 `16` `C`

Conde de Valdemar Rioja Crianza 1991 `14` `C`

Ripe, figgy, chocolatey.

Copa Real `15.5` `B`

Superb value: lots of generous fruit which never yields either to the tannins or the acidity – so it's serious company for intellectuals discussing rugby football as well as food.

Copa Real Plata `16` `B`

Sixty penn'orth more than its partner but a good deal more than 60p's worth more fruit. More developed tannins here, with a gripping finish.

Domino de Espinal Yecla 1990 `13` `B`

Mature yet still flexing its muscles.

Don Darias `14` `B`

You know how sometimes you meet an upfront fruity person whose ribald sense of humour almost makes you blush but you can't help yourself falling completely under his or her spell? So it is with this wine.

Don Domingo `14` `B`

Monte Ory Tempranillo/Cabernet Sauvignon, Navarra 1993 `14` `C`
Solid and fruity with a dry undertone.

Santara 1993 `14` `B`
Seriously good, right-on fruit. Dry, full, rich yet very quaffable. A great pasta wine.

Senorio de Sarria, Cabernet Sauvignon Navarra 1987 `14` `D`
Expensive but full of fruit.

Torres Gran Sangredetoro Reserva 1989 `14` `D`
Flavour, well-matured and nicely the right side of ripeness. It's dry and food-friendly, too, with good balance.

Torres Sangredetoro 1991 `13` `C`
Tasty but not compelling. Too many reasons to drink elsewhere at £4+ to rate this wine higher.

Valdemar Tinto, Rioja 1993 `14` `C`
Soft.

Valdemar Tinto, Rioja 1994 `14.5` `C`
Excellent: smooth, dry, polished, rounded yet characterful.

Valencia Red `14` `B`
Simple, soft, fruity, with enough dry finish to invite a second glass.

Vega Camelia, Rioja 1992   15   B

Vina Albali Reserva, Valdepenas 1987   15   C
Creamy, touch of vanilla. Delicious.

SPANISH WINE   WHITE

Casal da Barca Ribeiro 1992   13   B
Delicious fish wine.

Colegiata Blanco Do Toro 1993   11   C
Expensive for the plainness of style. Must be £2.99 to be realistic.
A plain wine of little exciting fruit. It is one of those wines which
taste sublime on holiday but lose their sexiness on their way to
the airport.

Copa Real   13   B
Zip and fruit. Good value.

Moscatel de Valencia   16.5   B
Wonderful waxy quality to the honey-rich fruit. Drenches the
tastebuds in flavour.

Senorio de Elda Moscatel Alicante 1993   13   C
Amusing aperitif, well chilled. Honey edge to the finish.

Torres Gran Vina Sol, Chardonnay 1992   14   D
Well-constructed, naturally fruity and has a classy feel.

Torres Vina Esmeralda 1993   12   D
Go for the '94 vintage of this wine in preference to the '93.

Torres Vina Sol 1993   13.5   C

Valdemar Rioja 1993

USA WINE RED

Arciero Zinfandel

Soft, quiet – very unadventurous. The fruit is squashed flat. A total beginner's zin.

Duxoup Dry Creek Valley Syrah 1993 `13` `F`

Silly pretensions here which almost but not quite mar an impactfully jammy wine with a soft, sweet fruit finish with well-held tannins.

Duxoup Pinot Noir 1992 `11` `F`

A lot to pay to swallow a pun on a Marx Bros movie.

Firestone Merlot 1992 `13.5` `E`

Impressive and evolving, thanks to its tannins, all the while. Don't like the price. Bottoms Up only.

Kings Canyon Unoaked Cabernet Sauvignon 1994 `14.5` `C`

A solid opening of aroma and brambly fruit, coming up behind which are depth and flavour enough to take a rich casserole or a plate of cheeses.

Morgan Pinot Noir 1992 `13` `F`

Yes, it's pinot and it has a handsome, dusky, truffley side. Bottoms Up only.

Newtonian Cabernet 1991 `15.5` `E`

Delightfully classy style of fruit with flavour and depth, balance and cool, very cool, hauteur. Coonawarra meets Barolo.

Voss Zinfandel, Alexander Valley 1992

A tenner's worth of zin: tannic (yet running with flavour, fruit and softness), balanced, finishing dry and finely wrought overall.

Widmer California

Buzzes with rubbery, cherry fruit; stands a better chance against beefy, spicy grub than those Aussies.

USA WINE WHITE

Kah-Nock-Tie Sauvignon Blanc 1992

Delicious, pricey but delicious.

Kings Canyon Chardonnay 1994

Lots of fruit, dry, controlled, meaty-edged. Good grilled chicken wine.

Kings Canyon Sauvignon Blanc 1994

Lots of modern, exotic fruit character laid on thick. But not so thick the acidity can't bite. This is a cool dude's wine if I ever tasted one.

Kings Canyon White Zinfandel 1994

Might be fine extremely chilled on a hot summer's day.

Matanzas Creek Winery Sonoma Valley Chardonnay 1993

Silly price for an unspectacular wine which will, it is true, age and improve for 5/7 years.

Newtonian Chardonnay 1992   13 E

Not as overwhelmingly great as I thought it would be, with the burgeoning reputation of this vineyard. The style is quiet (so quiet it is certainly a chardonnay for those drinkers who say they dislike New World oaked chardonnays) and whisperingly impressive. But without food it lacks the complexity or weight to combat the price.

Prosperity White, Santa Ynez Valley 1994   16 C

Wonderful ripe blend of grapes. Has rich texture to the wine mingling modern zip with heavy old-fashioned jammy fruit. Curiously delicious. Great with Thai food – mussels with lemon grass especially!

FORTIFIED WINE

Cavendish Late Bottled Vintage, Vin de Liqueur 1963   14 D

Intensely sweet, great with Christmas cake.

Cavendish Port LBV 1963   15 D

A hugely caramel and sticky toffee wine which with Christmas pud aflame might prove rather fine.

Charter LBV Port 1987   13 E

Skeffington 1977 Vintage Port   13 G

SPARKLING WINE/CHAMPAGNE

Asti, Regional Classics (Italy)   12 C

Bollinger Grande Annee 1988 `10` `H`

This is rich champagne, mature, compelling, complex; but at a price of such absurdity only nuts would buy it.

Castellblanch Extra Brut (Spain) `13` `D`

Chassenay NV Champagne `13` `F`

Croser Brut 1992 `15` `F`

Nutty, slightly toasty edge. Delicious. Sophisticated.

Hamm Reserve Premier Cru Champagne `13` `G`

Hamm Reserve Premier Cru Champagne Brut `13` `G`

Only at Bottoms Up.

Jean de Praisac NV Champagne `12` `F`

Le Mesnil Blanc de Blancs, Champagne `14` `G`

Mature, stylish champagne.

Montoy Champagne Brut `13.5` `F`

Moscato Sweet Spumante, Regional Classics (Italy) `12.5` `C`

For the sweet-toothed. And very well priced.

Seaview Pinot Noir/Chardonnay 1991 (Australian) `16` `E`

Rounded yet fresh and refined – classy, cool, excellent ripe edge to the fruit plus brilliant acids.

Seppelt Blanc de Blancs Brut 1990 (Australia) `13` `E`

Solid, dependable, gently citric bubbly.

Seppelt Great Western Brut　　14　C

Light and breezy.

Seppelt Great Western Rose　　15　D

Tremendous rose for the money – elegant, rich-edged cherry
fruit, good acid balance.

Seppelt Salinger Brut 1990 (Australia)　　13　E

Has a subtle saline quality – almost like a sparkling fino. Good
with smoked salmon.

Seppelts Salinger Sparkling Wine
(Australia)　　15　F

UNWINS

I cannot quite fathom this retailer out. It is not for want of trying. I often hang around outside the odd branch disguised as a local in an attempt to get a picture of the typical customer, but I am rarely successful – certainly I don't come away with a clear image in my mind of the sort of thirsty soul who patronises these 305 establishments. When once, unshaven, I donned old jeans, sneakers and an oily sweater in order to pass unremarked amongst its customers as I sussed out one branch I found it was strictly patronised by pin-striped nobs off the 5.45 from Waterloo and I stood out like a bloody mary at a temperance convocation. I left before the manager, a kindly but suspicious soul, could ask me to do so or, worse, make secret signals to the local constabulary and have me thrown out. It would, of course, only have made matters worse if I had protested I was a *Guardian* journalist seeking the truth.

Unwins has 29 branches in London, 5 in Middlesex, 10 in Bedfordshire, 8 in Berkshire, 17 in Buckinghamshire (8 in Milton Keynes alone), 8 in Cambridgeshire, 22 in Essex, 17 in Hampshire, 24 in Hertfordshire, 46 in Kent, 2 in Leicestershire, 7 in Norfolk, 2 in Northamptonshire, 12 in Oxfordshire, 31 in Surrey, 2 in Wiltshire and 50 in Sussex (including, perhaps not surprisingly, 10 in boozy Brighton).

Its top half-dozen best sellers are:

1. La Mancha Red.
2. La Mancha White.
3. Liebfraumilch.
4. Frascati Superiore.

5. Chardonnay White Burgundy.
6. Stockman's Bridge White.

I must say that I doubt very much if the chaps I saw in the branch I visited bought any of these wines. They were strictly a claret and port crowd and, to be sure, Unwins believes the strength of its range lies in these wines as well as in champagne, southern France and, to some extent, Australia. Nothing revolutionary about any of these areas; indeed, there is a tendency on Unwins' part to play safe both in the wines chosen and the way they are presented. But things are changing. The shops may not be such heady places to buy wine as, say, Wine Rack or Oddbins, but things are looking up with odd splashes of colour supplied by more adventurous bottles (see below). And the wine list, which was once suspected, in spite of it being in colour, of having been designed by someone still trapped in the days of black and white television, is a breezier document all round. The new summer list was neatly laid out, still a bit prim typographically, but it was interspersed with readable articles on wine producers – including the unforgettable Mau family of Gironde-sur-Dropt. I once enjoyed a spectacular dinner with several generations of the family, and half-way through the meal the oldest member showed us the highly aromatic fruits of his recent gallstone operation. The old bordeaux we were drinking at the time went rather well with them and, for a moment, the farmyard chicken, the sweetbreads and the wild mushrooms the size of satellite TV dishes we were eating, were overpowered.

The new Unwins will not create so dramatic an impact.

On the expansion front, seven more branches were added to the figure above. Three of these were so-called Wine & Food stores which are 'proving an increasingly important part of our estate' in the words of the company. Two new wine buyers were hired, there was 'an increasing search for undiscovered wines and exciting one-off parcels ' and 'more dynamic merchandising techniques were introduced'.

The chain also made an effort to reduce its profit margin on some wines in a bid to compete with the big boys. La Mancha at £1.99 being a case in point.

Bill Rolfe, one of Unwins' wine buyers and marketing manager, also told me that the company 'now has the ability to organise The Wine & Spirit Education Trust diploma courses on our own premises, with the backing of the Trust, which enables us to put many more employees through the course'.

He was also reassuring about new ways forward. 'We have established a new idea called "Undiscovered Wines". This is a promotional idea which is the result of our endeavour to find new, little-known wines from various parts of the world and bring them to our customers at attractive prices. This also encompasses the purchase of one-off parcels of wine.' The first of these bottles I tasted earlier this year was a red wine from Faugeres (in the Midi). Domaine Coudougno 1992 it was called (and there may still be the odd bottle around on an Unwins shelf somewhere). It was refined yet earthy, blackcurranty with soft tannins, and it left an impression of muscled litheness. An impression, I must add, which disappears a couple of hours after opening, so it was not a heavy breather requiring decantation; it was a wine to be opened and knocked back with the usual gritty substances. It rated 15.5 points and cost £3.99. This sort of wine certainly makes life more fun for the customers; they have reason to keep coming back to the shop if it has regular new, cheap, extremely drinkable wines from obscure areas. Where will many of these new wines comes from?

South Africa, southern France, South America and Italy, it seems. Certainly these are the countries Mr Rolfe expects to provide the most exciting additions to Unwins' range over the next few years. It must be said that, at present, his wine range from these regions is extremely predictable and safe – Canepa from Chile, several KWV wines from South Africa, and Cahors, Fitou, Minervois and Cotes du Roussillon as far as southern France is concerned.

But it's those customers I keep coming back to. Who are they? What do they like about Unwins?

The answer, having thought about it a while, is to be found totally in my experience with the besuited commuters. They like their Unwins because it's safe, doesn't thrust dangerously weird bottles at you, many of the names of the wines on the shelf are known and, most importantly, the shop is on the way home. Bringing home the bottle is as heartfelt a modern ritual as bringing home the bacon was to an earlier generation. Unwins branches are well sited to meet these ritualists' needs.

Unwins Wine Group Limited
Birchwood House
Victoria Road
Dartford
Kent
DA1 5AJ

Tel 01322 272711
Fax 01322 294469

SEE STOP PRESS SECTION AT END OF BOOK FOR LAST-MINUTE ADDITIONS TO THIS RETAILER'S RANGE.

AUSTRALIAN WINE RED

Lindemans Bin 45 Cabernet Sauvignon 1992 `14` `C`

Attractive berry flavours and residual richness.

Lindemans Pyrus, Coonawarra 1990 `16` `E`

Even at a tenner this wine's pedigree seems cheap. Deep rich fruit, brilliant soft tannins, restrained mint edge.

Penfolds Bin 35 Shiraz Cabernet 1992 `15` `C`

Penfolds Rawson's Retreat Bin 35 Cabernet Sauvignon/Ruby Cabernet/Shiraz 1993 `12` `C`

Soft and rather expressionless.

Penfolds Stockman's Bridge `12` `C`

Simple fruit – a touch expensive.

Wakefield Cabernet Sauvignon 1990 `15.5` `D`

Big friend of a wine. Rich, velvety, stylish – a deeply flavoured glug. Great with roasts and grills.

AUSTRALIAN WINE WHITE

Lindemans Bin 65 Chardonnay 1994 `15` `C`

Good as ever it was. Oily, ripe, balanced, very fruity. Lovely with grilled chicken.

Penfolds Bin 21 Semillon/Chardonnay 1993

Fresh and lively yet a dollop of pineappley melon keeps intruding. Delicious refreshing wine.

Penfolds Koonunga Hill Chardonnay 1992

Penfolds Koonunga Hill Chardonnay 1994

Solid batter – off the back foot at this price but it's still in the crease.

Penfolds Semillon/Chardonnay 1993

Excellent recipe: fruit, acid, wood but will integrate and improve mightily over the next 1/2 years.

Penfolds Stockman's Bridge

Stowells of Chelsea Semillon Chardonnay (3 litre)

Presence and lift, style and purpose – this fruit knows where it's going. Good with food and mood.

Wakefield White Clare Crouchen/ Chardonnay 1991

Lychees and pears – very dry. Classy feel to it.

AUSTRIAN WINE RED

Winzerhaus Blauer Zweigelt 1993

A superb wine, chilled, for rich fish dishes, chicken and oriental duck. A light, fruity, supple wine – much more attractive than the beaujolais it could easily replace.

AUSTRIAN WINE   WHITE

Eiswein Neusidlersee Burgenland 1992   `14` `E`

A great wine in 2015. But why wait? It's gorgeous now with strawberries and cream.

Gruner Veltliner Weinviertel Region Estate Bottled, 1993   `14` `C`

As delicious as ever.

BULGARIAN WINE   RED

Merlot Reserve Stambolovo Region 1988   `13` `C`

CANADIAN WINE   RED

Calona Vineyards Rougeon, British Columbia 19488   `8` `D`

Unspeakably dull and poorly made – and far from cheap.

CANADIAN WINE   WHITE

Calona Pinot Blanc, British Columbia   `11` `D`

Not bad for £3.29 – but at £5.99 it's nuts (without being nutty).

CHILEAN WINE RED

**Canepa Cabernet Sauvignon Maipo
Valley 1993**   `13` `C`

CHILEAN WINE WHITE

**Canepa Sauvignon Blanc Sagrada
Familia 1993**   `14` `C`

A very well turned out sauvignon with enough fruit to please the palate and sufficient commanding acidity to tickle the tastebuds.

ENGLISH WINE WHITE

Denbies Chardonnay 1992   `13` `C`

Better than muscadet any day.

FRENCH WINE RED

Beaujolais Villages E. Loron 1993   `10` `C`

**Bourgogne Passetoutgrain Vieilles Caves
de Bourgogne 1992**   `10` `C`

Bourgueil Les Barroirs, Couly-Dutheil 1993   `14` `D`

Delicious. Try it chilled with salmon (grilled).

Buzet 'Renaissance', Les Vignerons Buzet 1993 `12` `C`

Cabrieres Rouge, Coteaux du Languedoc 1993 `13.5` `C`

Cahors, Les Cotes d'Olt 1990 `14` `C`
Drunk with food, this dry wine ignites.

Chateau de Crouseilles, Madiran 1989 `13.5` `E`
Big, juicy food wine.

Chateau du Bois Bousquet, Mauregard 1993 `14.5` `C`
Lovely effect of velvety tannins. Classy.

Chateau Ducla Bordeaux 1991 `12` `D`
Touch bony for my taste.

Chateau Mingot Cotes de Castillon 1992 `13.5` `C`
Good sound fruit.

Chinon Les Gravieres, Couly-Dutheil 1993 `13.5` `D`
Strawberryish and dry.

Corbieres, Coteaux du Languedoc 1993 `14` `C`
No casserole would be ashamed to be seen with this dry, fruity, rustic-edged wine. It doesn't bite but it does purr – a little.

Cotes de Gascogne `12` `B`

Cotes du Frontonnais, Michel de l'Enclos 1992 `12.5` `C`

Cotes du Roussillon 1993 `13` `C`

Domaine Coudougno Faugeres 1992 | 15.5 | C

Excellent! Refined earthy blackcurrant, soft tannins, muscle yet litheness. Tends to get flabby and lose its concentration if not drunk in 2 hours.

Domaine de l'Estagnol Minervois | 12 | B

Domaine des Caunettes Hautes Cabardes 1992 | 12 | C

Domaine St Denis Cabernet Sauvignon, VdP d'Oc | 13 | C

Lots of attractive fruit here.

Fitou 1991 | 13 | C

Very attractive fruit here.

Fitou Chateau de Segure 1991 | 14.5 | D

Interesting tannins here, a touch austere for the tender-palated. Lay it down for 2 years at least. Or drink it with rare beef.

Macon Superieur E Loron 1994 | 10 | C

Pinot Noir Cuvee a l'Ancienne 1989 | 10 | D

Sauvignon Bordeaux 1994 | 10 | C

St Joseph Louis Mousset 1991 | 13.5 | E

Impossible to dislike this hearty, sweet-finishing wine. Expensive.

Vieux Chateau Negrit, Montagne St Emilion 1992 | 13.5 | D

FRENCH WINE WHITE

Blanc de Blancs Yvon Mau | 12 | B

Sound rather than exciting.

**Buzet 'Renaissance', Les Vignerons de
Buzet 1993** | 13.5 | C

Solid performer with chicken dishes.

Chablis, Domaine de Corbeton 1992 | 10 | E

Chardonnay A. Bichot 1993 | 13 | D

Some signs of life here.

Chateau Ducla Entre Deux Mers 1993 | 12.5 | D

**Cotes de Gascogne Domaine Lasserre du
Haut 1992** | 12 | C

**Domaine Colin Rosier Chardonnay, Vin de
Pays d'Oc** | 10 | C

**Domaine de Saumelongue VdP de l'Herault
Sauvignon Blanc 1994** | 14.5 | C

Dry, nutty, clean. Delicious.

Mauregard Tour le Pin 1993 | 13 | C

Good and clean. Great with sole.

**Muscadet de Sevre et Maine Sur Lie
Domaine de Plessis, J. P. Petard 1994** | 10 | D

Pinot Blanc Woelfelin 1993 | 12 | C

Clean and distantly lemony.

Sancerre Les Roches Vacheron 1993 `11` `E`

Not bad. But a tenner's worth of fruit? No way.

Sauvignon Blanc Bordeaux 1993 `12` `C`

GERMAN WINE WHITE

Hock `12` `A`

Good value. And so much more acidically intriguing than many Liebfraumilchs.

Mainzer Domherr Kabinett Mont Royal Barois 1994 `12` `C`

Sweet aperitif.

HUNGARIAN WINE WHITE

Gyongyos Estate Chardonnay 1993 `12` `B`

Losing freshness.

Gyongyos Estate Sauvignon Blanc 1993 `14` `B`

Some attractive herbaceous fruit nicely undercut by the acidity. More characterisic of the grape than the '92.

ITALIAN WINE RED

Barbera del Piemonte, Giordano 1993 `12` `C`

Sweet and jammy.

Barbera del Piemonte Giordano 1992 `13` `C`

Breganze Bartolomeo 1993 `13` `C`
Brilliant with pasta.

Merlot del Veneto 1992 `12` `B`

Montepulciano d'Abruzzo Miglianico 1993 `15` `C`
Lovely soft fruit at heart, cherries and plums, but there's a brisk
dry edge giving it true complexity and depth. Bargain.

ITALIAN WINE WHITE

Frascati Superiore, Tullio San Marco 1994 `11` `C`

Orvieto Classico San Marco 1994 `12` `C`

Pinot Grigio del Veneto Cesari 1994 `11` `C`

Tocai Via Nova, 1993 `12` `C`

**Verdicchio dei Castelli di Jesi Classico
1993** `11` `C`

PORTUGUESE WINE RED

Alta Mesa Estremadura 1994 `14` `B`
Simple, soft, ripe, very fruity, delicious chilled and poured over
parched tongues.

Beira Mar Sarrafeira 1980 `15` `D`

Borba 1994 `14` `C`

Delicious plummy fruit. Dry yet mellow.

Borba VQPRD 1992 `14` `B`

Dao Reserva, Dom Ferraz Caves Primavera 1990 `13.5` `C`

Dry. Good with casseroled meats.

Dom Ferraz Reserva, Barraida 1989 `13` `B`

Garrafeira Reserva Particular, A. Bernadino 1984 `12` `D`

Old but still youthful and far from past it.

Pedras do Monte, Terras do Sado 1994 `15.5` `C`

Light but very effectively fruited and well shaped. Plum and cherry flavours – good lightly chilled.

Quinta do Manjapao, Torres Vedras 1992 `12.5` `C`

Sweet finishing.

Quinta do Vale da Raposa, Douro 1994 `13` `D`

Terras de Xisto Alentejo 1993 `14.5` `C`

Beauty. Great fruit and structure.

PORTUGUESE WINE WHITE

Ramada Estremadura 1994 `14` `B`

Lively, fruity, balanced, clean. Terrific for moules marinieres.

Vinho Verde 'Octave' Borges `10` `C`

SOUTH AFRICAN WINE RED

**Cape Cellars Cabernet Sauvignon, Breede
River Valley 1992** `13` `B`

SOUTH AFRICAN WINE WHITE

**Cape Cellars Chardonnay, Coastal
Region 1992** `12` `B`

KWV Sauvignon Blanc 1995 `13.5` `C`

Pearl Springs Chenin Blanc 1994 `10` `B`

Pearl Springs Sauvignon Blanc 1994 `12` `B`

**Stowells of Chelsea South African
Sauvignon Blanc (3 litre)** `13` `F`

Quiet but sound. Not a lot of zip but subdued soundness.

SPANISH WINE RED

Don Fabian Tempranillo Navarra 1994 `14.5` `C`

Bustling, no-nonsense fruit, brambly and dry with a brisk and
softly finishing tannic dusting. Has style, character and is a great
casserole partner.

Encanto Red Wine `14.5` `A`

Utterly simple, fruity and with some lingering dryness. Good for

parties, pizzas and pastas. And for those watching the pennies.
A really good deal for the dosh.

Faustino Rivero Ulecia Rioja 1992   14   C
Coconut fruit to eat with Thai chicken dishes.

La Mancha   14.5   A
Cheap, fruity, balanced. Bargain.

Raimat Abadia, Costers del Segre 1994   16   C
Real class for under a fiver. Rich, creamy, handsomely wooded
fruit of depth, flavour and great food friendliness. Gripping
finish, too.

Raimat Tempranillo, Costers del Segre 1991   14.5   D
A decent tempranillo of dryness and good savoury fruit. Has
smoothness and gentle richness.

Stowells of Chelsea Tempranillo La Mancha (3 litre)   15   F
A bright, cherry/plum dry wine of really good fruit, balance and
a really attractive finish.

Torres Coronas 1991   14   C

SPANISH WINE   WHITE

Castillo Fuentemayor Oak Aged Rioja 1990   12.5   D
Drink it with prawn curry.

Dona Isabella Viura Navarra 1994   12.5   C

El Coto Rioja 1992   13 C
Curiously fresh rioja, good with shellfish.

Encanto White Wine   13 A
Fresh, fun, fruity. Excellent party plonk.

La Mancha   10 A
This wine is simply not performing as well, fruit-wise, as last year and this is reflected in the rating – despite being Unwins' second most popular wine.

Raimat Chardonnay, Costers del Segre 1994   13 D
Mite too expensive for the style which is fruity and full of flavour but not complex.

USA WINE   RED

Blossom Hill California   12.5 C
Sweet and almost flowery.

Columbia Crest Merlot, Columbia Valley Washington State 1990   14 E
Very pleasing complex fruit: polished, soft and subtly rich.

USA WINE   WHITE

Blossom Hill, California   12 C

Sutter Home Chardonnay 1994   12.5 C

SPARKLING WINE/CHAMPAGNE

Bollinger Grande Annee 1988 `10` `H`

This is rich champagne, mature, compelling, complex; but at a price of such absurdity only nuts would buy it.

Chardonnay Blanc de Blancs 'Le Baron' `13.5` `D`

Gently peachy fruit. Splendid aperitif.

Clairette de Die Methode Dioise Ancestrale, Georges Aubert `13` `D`

Good and peachy for sweet-toothed tipplers.

Duchatel Brut `10` `F`

Touch raw for me.

'Mayerling' Cremant d'Alsace `14` `E`

Like a fine quality cava. Excellent value.

Seaview Pinot Noir/Chardonnay 1990 (Australian) `15` `E`

Mature, fruity, classy. Great value.

VICTORIA WINE

The recipient of a letter from The Victoria Wine Company, founded five years before Dickens gave up the ghost in 1870, is offered food for thought over and above whatever tidbits its actual contents might provide. The design of the letterheading itself provides a feast of speculation. The philatelic impression of the head of the youthful Queen Vic (who was, in fact, forty-six in 1865) which adorns this letter paper – her regal Grecian profile staring wanly out from a royal red background – drives the ponderer to chew mightily. And what he chews on is this: what manner of business lies behind so fustily composed a representation? There is surely only one conclusion. This is a business living in the past – a past when royalty stood for something; stood indeed for the majesty of a whole era. This business – head office in Dukes Court no less – simply cannot forget when it was founded.

But, I hear you say (or is it a pshaw!), this may be the impression given by a mere letterhead – not to mention the carrier bags, wine lists and shop fascias which have been spotted carrying the royal profile – but when you visit a Victoria Wine branch or one of the new Victoria Wine Cellars establishments (that damned word cellars again! When will these retailers twig that cellars is a dead word?) you can hardly say this is a company which lives in the past. Look at all those . . . whoa. Hold on here. You said a mere letterhead. Before we go on to discuss the Victoria Wine company, let me tell you that there is no such thing as a mere letterhead. A letterheading is a window into the deepest soul of a company – or an individual for that matter. Hours, days, maybe even weeks, are spent over the design of the imagery and typefaces at the top and the bottom of such sheets of paper. Thus a letterheading is no small matter to be passed over as if it were an incidental blot in a copybook. Victoria Wine is telling us through its letterhead that this is how it really feels about itself and, equally crucially, this is how it wants the outside world to feel about it.

Victoria Wine (owned by the large Allied Domecq group) is a monument to the past; but such constructions where modern retailing is concerned should be strictly for private viewing only – never for constant public display. The company may be unable to forget that it was formed on the crest of the wine wave which so stirred British wine-drinking habits as a result of William Gladstone's dramatic reduction of the duty on French wines in 1860, but for today's drinker of a wonderfully fruity £3 new world red this history is gloriously irrelevant. The phrase 'monumentally boring' was coined expressly to cover situations like this. Which is why many retailers avoid it. Budgens, the southern supermarket chain, was formed in 1872 (thirty-seven years before Sainsbury's kicked off). Yet neither one of these old codgers offers us this reminiscence on its letterhead. Victoria Wine is actually telling us via its letterhead, and through its very name, that nothing has really changed. And nothing, in many respects, seems to have done. The earliest Victoria Wine letterhead I have seen is on an 1896 wine list (Kangaroo Port from the colonies a snip at 23 bob the dozen!) and the same Queen is still there – a woman angelically trapped in time.

And so we come to the crux of the problem. Is Victoria Wine similarly trapped? Or can it become, in spite of its regal aegis, the most glittering, most exciting chain in the high street? The chain whose competitiveness the supermarkets will fear most?

It cannot, in my view, achieve these things unless it divorces its royal mistress. In order to release all the creative energies confined within the myriad corridors of its head office and lying in confinement at all its 1500-odd branches, Albert's widow must be elbowed.

Off with her head! And the sooner the better. The wound

will quickly heal. The patient will swiftly recover. The weight that has been lifted will take years off the company.

So simple an execution. So simple a stroke. John Arlott, in his foreword to a book devoted to the history of Victoria Wine (*Wine for Sale* by Asa Briggs, Batsford 1985), wrote that 'The triumph of Victoria Wine has always been to tread an immaculate middle path. They have ensured that the ordinary man has neither been overawed by their shops, nor ashamed to be seen going into them.' In ten short years, however, that middle path has, thanks to supermarket wine, narrowed horribly and become uncomfortably overcrowded.

Not that the company hasn't tried to tread new paths. It became the first wine chain to open a branch in Calais (Tesco and Sainsbury's also have wine shops in the vicinity) and the shop concentrates on New World wines not given much, or in some cases any, distribution in France. Also, there are now forty Victoria Wine Cellars shops (with the aim of reaching 150 within the next three years) and they compete directly with modern whizzkids like Oddbins, Wine Rack, and Greenalls' me-too bid for modernity – the newly launched and tiny Wine Cellar chain. No middle path here. This is, or it certainly pretends to be, the fast track. But what of the 822 Victoria Wine Shops, the 504 Victoria Wine drinks stores and the 179 Haddows (a Scottish flowering)? Some great wines; some very pleasant people behind the counter (who are given tremendous support to learn as much as they can about wine through officially sponsored courses supported by audio tapes and teaching packs); but that old royal relic is still there, looking askance. When I asked PR manager Nicola Harvey to spell out what was planned for the future of these various enterprises she replied in detail. 'A considerable investment programme is planned,' she told me, 'to refit the shops over the next few years with priority to convert the ex-Augustus Barnett premises into the correct refit style, expand the number of Victoria Wine shops and develop a new refit style for our wine-led off-licences. These shops will have an increased wine range and more wine-orientated promotions. Staff training and customer services will be increasingly emphasised.'

It is no surprise that with so many off-licence style outlets (also selling beers, soft drinks, crisps and confectionery), Liebfraumilch is the company's number one best-selling wine. The next five, however, number amongst them less predictable bottles and this suggests a very wide spread of customers from the easy drinker to the more complex food and wine matcher looking for a bargain. These five wines, subject to the usual seasonal shifts, are:

2. Casa Barco Spanish red.
3. Soave.
4. Hock.
5. Beaubourg Vin de Pays rouge.
6. Bulgarian Cabernet Sauvignon.

Other wines, as with all the retailers' top-sellers lists in this book, come and go out of the top category, and in Victoria Wine's case four other major sellers are Sansovino Lambrusco, Valpolicella, Brokenback Ridge Australian Red and the Castillo de Liria medium dry white. Only one French wine in its top ten? That's an interesting statistic. My bet, also, is that Victoria Wine will become, at some point in the not too distant future, the first British retailer to list a South African white amongst its top sellers. A wine like Landema Falls Colombard-Chardonnay at £2.99 is the perfect candidate to hit this top spot. It has lush fruit with a crisp undertone and the soft melon fruit is not overdone. It is a very attractive 15.5 point bargain which appeals to both sides of the house; conservatives will like its breezy fruit which suits a sipping situation and socialists can employ it as a party wine for riotous gluggers. Overall, Victoria Wine offers a decent range from South Africa, is well represented in Australia and Chile and is making an impressive effort with red bordeaux.

Interesting wines from New Zealand come and go also. Cooks

Riesling/Chenin 1993 from New Zealand was on special offer during April for £3.19. This represented an odd bundle of fruit, the nature of which taxed me greatly before I felt comfortable about its rating (13 points). Was it dry? Was it off-dry? Was it fruity or was it merely posing? There seemed an awkward side to the wine which needed food to smooth out and in the end I decided that with a *spaghetti alla vongole* it would be utterly delicious and thoroughly prove its value. Easier to rate (at 16.5 points) was Corbans Private Bin Merlot 1992. This was a sinfully imbibable New Zealander and one to drool over, but somewhat more difficult to buy even when it went on sale; only fifty cases of the wine were shipped to the UK and although Victoria Wine had every one I suspect there were wine nuts out there trying to snap up every bottle from the few branches which stocked it. This wine was like quicksand in a blackcurrant patch. It dragged the tastebuds down and drowned them in fruit. This fruit had a seductive edge, soft and gently leathery, and its lusciousness was evident the moment the cork was drawn; the perfume was like cassis; the final texture warm velvet. It did not last long on shelf. It did not stay long in bottle. It did not possess the tannin or acid to give it cellaring potential, so it needed to be stowed intestinally – within an hour or so of being opened and preferably with loving companions to share it with. It cost, alas, £7.99 but then it is somewhat of a limited edition. No doubt Victoria Wine will ship future vintages of this wine and though these may not come up to the '92's lusciousness, they should certainly be worth looking out for. It is a measure of the confidence of the chain's wine buyers that they can do good business with small, one-off parcels of wine like this.

These buyers, who, at time of writing, are Geraldine Jago, Joanne Convert, Rosemary Neal and Thomas Woolrych, backed by Hugh Suter as wine development manager, not only have skill and experience (many retailers can boast wine buyers with both) but, equally importantly in the highly competitive environment in which they operate, are given the scope to develop their own ideas. Following her own nose is a professional wine buyer's first instinct, however much she may have to fulfil the mundane needs imposed by filling the gaps in a wine range with Liebfraumilch as its number one best-selling wine. Big Frank's Red & White from southern France and Ed's Red from Tarragona are proofs that this freedom is resulting in some forcefully innovative, appealingly fruity and well-priced wines.

Behind that staidly coiffured Queen could there be an iconoclast with a shaven head gently stirring?

The Victoria Wine Company
Dukes Court
Duke Street
Woking
Surrey GU21 5XL

Tel 01483 715066
Fax 01483 755234

SEE STOP PRESS SECTION AT END OF BOOK FOR LAST-MINUTE ADDITIONS TO THIS RETAILER'S RANGE.

AUSTRALIAN WINE

Barramundi Shiraz/Merlot [14] [C]

Vibrant, spicy, fun.

Basedow Cabernet Sauvignon 1992 [17] [D]

Creamy digestive-biscuit middle to this impressive wine which is aromatic fore and ripely sweet aft. Superb. Available from Victoria Wine Cellars and Wine Shops.

Basedow Shiraz 1992 [14.5] [D]

Lots of flavour, a distant, spicy echo, and a rich finish.

Basedow Shiraz 1993 [16] [D]

Blackberry, raspberry, dry, plummy – it's got the lot, with a shroud of rich figs. Available from Victoria Wine Cellars and Wine Shops.

Brokenback Ridge Shiraz/Cabernet [13.5] [B]

Ripeness of flavour pleases (cherry/plum).

Brown Brothers Shiraz/Cabernet 1983 [10] [E]

Good price for such a mature, teeth-grippingly (yet soft) tannic performance. Floods of flavour and style. Available from Victoria Wine Cellars and Wine Shops.

Brown Brothers Tarrango 1993 [15] [C]

Vivid, striking, softly smoky and rubbery and so gluggable it's sinful.

Deakin Estate Cabernet Sauvignon 1994 [12.5] [C]

Hardys Bankside Shiraz 1992 `15` `D`

Tasty and richly centred. Very good fruit here with enough of a seriously dry edge to go with rich food.

Hardys Cabernet/Shiraz Stamp Series 1992 `14` `B`

Some steamed fruit and soft spice – good big pasta party wine.

Hardys Nottage Hill Cabernet Sauvignon/ Shiraz 1993 `16` `C`

Controlled soft spice laid on smooth blackcurrant fruit. Delicious, firm, well-styled.

Katnook Cabernet Sauvignon 1990 `14` `E`

Expressive but expensive. Available from Victoria Wine Cellars and Wine Shops.

Katnook Merlot 1990 `15` `E`

Ripely integrated fruit character which is softly tannic and flavourful. Available from Victoria Wine Cellars and Wine Shops.

Leasingham Classic Cabernet Sauvignon, Clare 1992 `15.5` `E`

A tenner's worth of fruit! (Plus weight, tannins, a perfect structure, finish and lingering memorability.)

Montana Cabernet Sauvignon 1992 `14` `C`

Must be drunk with beef stew or ham dishes.

Nottage Hill Cabernet Sauvignon 1992 `15.5` `C`

Still sporting a day-old growth of beard to the smooth fruit (courtesy of the tannins). Lovely performer – one of the best made cabernets sauvignons around for the money.

Orlando RF Cabernet Sauvignon 1991 `16` `C`

Aromatic, rich, balanced, classy, dry (good tannins) and

altogether sweetly turned out. Scores extra point here because it's under a fiver.

Penfolds Bin 2 Shiraz/Mourvedre 1992

Plum and black cherries, muted spice. Delicious! Will develop and get even better.

Penfolds Bin 35 Shiraz Cabernet 1992

Ripe, soft fruit with some development ahead of it. Attractive berry flavours, well structured and balanced. Very drinkable now but a 17/18-pointer in 3/4 years.

Penfolds Coonawarra Cabernet Sauvignon 1990

The colour of crushed blackberries, subtle eucalyptus/leather aroma, sheer satiny acids and velvet-textured fruit touches – lovely tannicky finish.

Penfolds Kalimna Shiraz Bin 28 1992

To be poured into jugs at sausage-and-garlic-and-olive-mashed-potato parties and the cataractic torrent of this brambly, velvet fruit left to get on with it.

Penfolds Koonunga Hill Shiraz Cabernet 1992

Shouldn't be over a fiver.

Penfolds Old Vine Mouvedre/Grenache/ Shiraz, Barossa 1992

A flood of ripe fruit bolstered by friendly tannins which seem to me as pretty well developed as they could get for the best balance of flavours. In spite of what Penfolds say, drink this wine over the next year. The gloss of its fruit will fade if the tannins are allowed to tighten their grip over, say, 3/4 years.

Riddoch Shiraz 1992

Soft, spicy fruit, initially dry then turning soft, this is a handsome specimen.

Ryecroft Peppertree Shiraz/Cabernet 1991

Lovely plummy finish, soft and rich, to a dry, forcefully flavoured wine which stays the right side of ripeness.

Stowells of Chelsea Shiraz Cabernet (3 litre)

Rich fruit with earthy undertones. Has a long, meaty finish with a firm, purposeful balance of fruit and acid.

Woodford Hill Cabernet Sauvignon/Shiraz 1992

Good and fruity with some well-intentioned fruit.

Wynns Coonawarra Estate Michael Shiraz 1991

Horrendous price for a delicious wine of substance and real minty Coonawarra typicity.

AUSTRALIAN WINE WHITE

Barramundi Semillon/Chardonnay

Rich, fruit-salad nose. Lots of pineapple acidity and great, swinging melon/mango fruit. Smashing wine to let the heart soar.

Basedow Chardonnay 1993

Big, grassy, rich – like a Texas oil millionaire. Available in Victoria Wine Cellars and Wine Shops.

Basedow Semillon 1993 `15` `D`

Woody, wavy, rich. Probably magnificent with lemon chicken. Available in Victoria Wine Cellars and Wine Shops.

Colonnade Chardonnay 1993 `14` `D`

Available in Victoria Wine Cellars and Wine Shops.

Deakin Estate Chardonnay 1994 `13.5` `C`

Good fruit and oak. Chardonnay oaked-style for beginners.

Deakin Estate Colombard/Chardonnay 1994 `14` `C`

Has both sides of the grape: delicious pointed acidity, warm soft fruit. Great with fish dishes.

Deakin Estate Sauvignon Blanc 1994 `14` `C`

Soft edge but a crisp middle. Distinctive, and tasty with mussels.

Green Point Chardonnay 1993 `14` `E`

Pricey, but good fruit. Available at Victoria Wine Cellars and Wine Shops.

Hardys Moondah Brook Verdelho 1993 `14` `D`

Highly attractive aperitif. Rates 16 with a fish salad with bitter leaves and a lemony dressing.

Hardys Nottage Hill Chardonnay 1994 `17` `C`

Best vintage yet. Lovely textured, oily fruit, never overdone or blowsy and a buttery, melony finish of surefooted delivery. Terrific value for such classy drinking.

Hardys Rose 1995 `12` `B`

Hardys Stamp Series Grenache Shiraz Rose | 13.5 | C

Upfront pong of artificial soft fruit but the finish is dry and flavourful.

Jacobs Creek Semillon/Chardonnay 1993 | 13 | C

Jacobs Creek Chardonnay 1993 | 14 | C

Jacobs Creek Dry Riesling 1994 | 12 | C

Katnook Botrytised Chardonnay 1992 (half bottle) | 13 | D

Rich and very honeyed but not complex enough yet, maybe in 10 years? Available from Victoria Wine Cellars and Wine Shops.

Lindemans Padthaway Chardonnay 1992 | 15 | E

Rich, oily, big – like a Texan wildcatter on a Saturday night. Great with grilled chicken, this wine.

Moondah Brook Chenin Blanc 1993 | 14.5 | D

Lovely, dry, waxy, honeyed edge to fruit – typically chenin blanc. But – and it's a bonny but – the fruit is warm and sunny, not dry and flat.

Ninth Island Chardonnay 1994 (Tasmania) | 14 | E

Very limited availability, this wine – a pity, for although it's pricey it's tasty, individual, and firmly structured.

Nottage Hill Chardonnay 1993 | 15 | C

Penfolds Barrel-Fermented Semillon 1994 | 14 | D

Nice wood touches on the fruit – not solid and oaken but soft and balsa. Will develop in bottle well for a couple of years.

Penfolds Bin 21 Semillon/Chardonnay 1993
`15` C

Fresh and lively yet a dollop of pineappley melon keeps intruding. Delicious refreshing wine.

Penfolds Koonunga Hill Chardonnay 1994
`14` C

Engagingly rich and oily textured, sunny and powerful.

Rowan Chardonnay, Victoria 1992
`14` D

Some sweet fruit on the finish. Good wood integration and style to the overall structure.

Stowells of Chelsea Semillon Chardonnay (3 litre)
`14` G

Presence and lift, style and purpose – this fruit knows where it's going. Good with food and mood.

Wolf Blass Semillon/Chardonnay 1993
`14` C

Flavour, freshness and style.

Wolf Blass South Australia Riesling 1993
`13.5` C

BULGARIAN WINE RED

Bear Ridge Gamza
`12` B

Bulgarian Country Wine, Merlot/Pinot Noir Sliven
`16` B

Only the Bulgars would stick two such unlikely grapes together and produce a serious wine. This is a really fruity yet dry miracle for the money.

Debut Cabernet Sauvignon 1993 `13` `B`

Very sound.

**Russe Cabernet Sauvignon Reserve
1989** `17` `C`

Superb value for money. Minty attack on the nose, rich damson
and blackcurrant on the tongue, and a dry, lingering finish in
the throat. Utterly delicious.

**Stowells of Chelsea Cabernet Sauvignon
(3 litre)** `14` `F`

Dry, very good, rich, savoury-edged fruit – good with food.

BULGARIAN WINE   WHITE

Bear Ridge Bulgarian Dry White 1993 `13` `B`

Bear Ridge Chardonnay `13` `B`

Pleasant, inoffensive, fruity.

Rousse, Muskat and Ugni Blanc `13.5` `B`

Very pleasant aperitif.

CHILEAN WINE   RED

Caliterra Cabernet Sauvignon 1991 `16` `C`

Dry, lovely dry blackcurrant fruit. Very classically moulded
and finished.

Canepa Zinfandel 'Winemaker's Selection' 1994 `16` `C`

Firm, rich cherry/plum centre, controlled spice, soft, concentrate. Only at Victoria Wine Cellars and Wine Shops.

Concha y Toro Casillero del Diablo Cabernet Sauvignon 1992 `15` `C`

Vivid yet subtle. Gluggable yet thought-provoking. Rich yet refined. Delicious paradox.

Concha y Toro Marques de Casa Concha Cabernet Sauvignon 1991 `16` `D`

There is a beaut of a finish to this impressively fruity wine which gives it true style and class.

Cono Sur Pinot Noir Reserve 1993 `14` `D`

Very attractive chilled with a spaghetti and bacon and raw mushroom salad. Limited stocks.

Cousino Macul Antiguas Reservas Cabernet Sauvignon 1990 `16` `D`

This is sheer class in a glass for half what stuffy frogs charge for the same grape in the same splendid fruit.

La Fortuna Malbec 1994 `14` `C`

Curls your toes with its richness. Pity it's not a quid cheaper.

CHILEAN WINE WHITE

Caliterra Sauvignon Blanc 1994 `13` `C`

Losing the brilliance of its finish now it's ageing.

Canepa Oak Aged Semillon 1994 | 14.5 | C

Solid, with fleeting hints of excitement. Well-balanced, though, and classy. Selected stores.

Casablanca Sauvignon Blanc 1994 | 14 | C

Depth of fruit, breadth of acidity, weight of flavour – well in tune with itself, this wine. Limited stocks.

Concha y Toro Casillero del Diablo Sauvignon Blanc 1994 | 15 | C

Lovely rich rolling fruit of assertiveness and style. Dee-dee-delicious.

Concha y Toro Marques de Casa Concha Chardonnay 1994 | 16 | D

This is how properly to barrel ferment to achieve loving integration of wood and fruit! Great class and sophistication at a snip of a price.

Errazuriz Sauvignon Blanc 1994 | 14.5 | C

Has cool class by virtue of its hint of richness to the bright fruit. Classic sauv blanc? Maybe not. But delicious with food.

Santa Monica Chilean Riesling 1994 | 14 | C

Alsace meets New Zealand but comes from Chile. Available at Victoria Wine Cellars and Wine Shops.

Villa Montes Sauvignon Blanc, Curico 1994 | 13 | C

ENGLISH WINE   WHITE

Penn Vineyard Dry White, English Table 1993 | 15 | D

Balanced, even-tempered fruit with a definite firm edge and firm style. Well-made and highly drinkable. Available at Victoria Wine Cellars.

FRENCH WINE   RED

Abbaye St Hilaire, Coteaux Varois 1993   `13` `B`

Lighter than previous vintages. Selected stores.

**Alsace Pinot Noir Cuvee Medaillon d'Or
Pfaffenheim 1992**   `14` `D`

Rich gamy fruit with raspberry undertones. Delicious chilled. Available from Victoria Wine Cellars.

**Beaujolais, Philippe de Courcelettes
1994**   `11` `C`

Beaujolais Villages, Jouvet 1994   `11.5` `C`

Big Frank's Red   `15` `D`

**Cabernet Sauvignon VdP d'Oc, Val
d'Orbieu 1994**   `13` `B`

Sweet edge to the fruit.

Calvet Reserve, Bordeaux 1993   `11` `D`

Chais Cuxac Merlot, VdP d'Oc 1993   `13.5` `C`

Soft, jammy. Wine Cellars only.

**Charles de France, Pinot Noir, Boisset
1993**   `11` `D`

Selected stores.

Chateau Carignan, Bordeaux 1990

Stunningly ready fruit. Totally integrated fruit and tannin. Drink now for instant happiness.

Chateau Carignan Premieres Cotes de Bordeaux 1992

Touch too much money for the simplicity of the fruit. Might repay laying down for a couple of years though. Selected stores.

Chateau Chante Alouette, Premieres Cotes de Blaye 1990

Delicious soft, integrated fruit with a serious depth of flavour and style. Great stuff! Can bat against the Aussies!

Chateau d'Arcins, Haut Medoc 1992

Chateau de Capitoul, La Clape, Coteaux de Languedoc 1993

Juicy yet dry. Selected stores.

Chateau de Chantemerle, Bordeaux 1993

Good, dry, fumacious edge to the fruit.

Chateau de la Jaubertie, Bergerac 1991

Victoria Wine Shops only.

Chateau La Diffre, Seguret, Cotes du Rhone Villages 1994

Brambly, flavour-packed, dry, gently earthy – outstanding vintage of this wine.

Chateau la Jalgue, Bordeaux 1994 13 C

Tasty and dry. Roast beef wine.

Chateau Laclaviere, Cotes de Francs 1990 `13.5` `D`
Pity it's so pricey, for it is very personable.

Chateau Le Leret, Cahors 1992 `13` `C`
A most easy-going Cahors. Not a challenge to any set of tastebuds. Selected stores.

Chateau Maragou, Cotes de Francs 1993 `13.5` `C`

Chateau Mauleon, Cotes de Roussillon Villages 1993 `15.5` `C`
Rich, dry deep, savoury. Great casserole companion.

Chateau Michelet, Bordeaux 1994 `13.5` `C`
Good, chewy fruit here. Great with roast meat or vegetables.

Chateau Mirefleurs, Bordeaux Superieur 1992 `12` `C`
Soft and cuddly – most uncoy for a '92 Bordeaux.

Chateau Peyros, Madiran 1989 `14.5` `D`
Loaded with soft, delicious fruit which surprises with a whack in the throat as it goes down dry and leathery. Victoria Wine Cellars only.

Chateau Teyssier, St Emilion 1990 `13.5` `E`
Rich and fruity. Overpriced.

Chateau Vaudieu, Chateauneuf-du-Pape 1992 `13` `E`
Lovely drinkable fruit but twice the price it should be. The Diffre (qv) is much better value.

Claret, Victoria Wine `13.5` `C`
Light but authentic. Also available in 1.5 litre sizes at Victoria Wine Cellars and Wine Shops.

Cornas, Allemand 1991

Big thumping hairy-chested brute with soft berries, brambly and rich, mingling with chocolate and figs. Only the price is cause for regret. Available from Victoria Wine Cellars.

Costieres de Nimes 1994

Brambly, dry fruit with some depth to it.

Cote Rotie Guigal 1990

Super ripe fruit. Lush and lovely. Only at Victoria Wine Cellars.

Cotes de Brouilly, Philippe de Courcelettes 1993

Available from Victoria Wine Cellars and Wine Shops.

Domaine Cazal Minervois 1993

Wine Cellars only.

Domaine de Larrivet, Graves 1992

Domaine de Rivoyre Cabernet Sauvignon, Vin de Pays d'Oc H. Ryman 1992

Ripe and bright.

Domaine de Saint Laurent Vin de Pays des Coteaux du Libron 1993

By the time this book comes out, the 1994 vintage will probably be on the shelves, but this wasn't available for tasting before going to press.

Domaine de St Hilaire Cabernet Sauvignon, VdP d'Oc 1992

Deeply dry and meaty blackcurrant fruit – rustically edged but royally intentioned.

Domaine de Tauch Corbieres 1993

Soft, gluggable, yet with just enough depth to match the flavours of food. Selected stores.

Domaine Sallele Syrah 1993

Good rounded fruit.

Domaine Serres-Mazard Corbieres 1992

Most unusual medical pong. Fruit's okay. Victoria Wine Cellars only.

Faugeres Gilbert Alquier 1993

High-priced but highly fruity, dry, rich, deep and individual. Wine Cellars only.

Fitou Mme C. Parmentier

Fleurie, Georges Duboeuf 1994

French Full Red Vin de Pays de l'Herault

Delicious. Excellent value. Simple but effective. Also available in 1.5 litres.

Galet Vineyards Oak Aged Merlot, VdP d'Oc 1994

Hammy edge to the rich fruit gives the wine flavour, style and great casserole compatibility. Selected stores.

Gigondas Les Perdrix 1994

Lovely – with 2 years or so development in bottle. Selected stores.

Hautes Cotes de Beaune, Dennis Carre 1992

Available from Victoria Wine Cellars.

Hautes Cotes de Nuits, Oak-Aged, Les Caves des Hautes Cotes 1992 `14` `D`

Interesting wine. Not classic pinot noir but an impressive red for all that. Available from Victoria Wine Cellars and Wine Shops.

Hermitage Guigal 1990 `12` `G`

Only at Victoria Wine Cellars.

La Cuvee Mythique VdP d'Oc 1993 `14` `D`

Classy, very classy. Victoria Wine Cellars only.

Meffre Cuvee Syranne, Cotes du Rhone 1993 `14` `C`

Has backbone and bite. The spine is the fruit, the teeth the tannin. Attractive bottle. Only at Victoria Wine Cellars and Wine Shops.

Merlot Fortant de France, VdP d'Oc 1993 `13` `C`

Michel Lynch Bordeaux Rouge 1990 `13.5` `E`

Good solid claret with approachable, soft tannins and fruit.

Minervois Caves des Hautes Coteaux `13` `B`

Morgon, Les Vignerons du Prieure 1993 `11` `D`

Available from Victoria Wine Cellars and Wine Shops.

Oak Aged Claret, Philippe de Noange `13` `C`

Pommard Jouvet 1990 `10` `F`

Dull. Pricey. At selected Victoria Wine Shops only.

Riverbed Vineyards, VdP d'Oc Meffre 1994 `12` `B`

St Joseph Medaille d'Argent 1990 $\boxed{15}$ $\boxed{E}$

A rich, hammy wine with lovely husky-edged fruit. Pricey but plush and plump. Only at Victoria Wine Cellars and Wine Shops.

Stowells of Chelsea Vin de Pays du
Gard (3 litre) $\boxed{14}$ $\boxed{F}$

Delightful smooth fruit with flavour and balance. A lovely touch – a distant echo, really – of earth.

Syrah Galet Vineyards 1994 $\boxed{14.5}$ $\boxed{C}$

A handsome, rugged beast softened by rich tannins of some gentility and a warm, savoury finish. A delicious soupy wine for all sorts of lamb dishes.

FRENCH WINE WHITE

Alsace Pinot Blanc Pfaffenheim 1993 $\boxed{13}$ $\boxed{C}$

Faint echoes of lush apricot fruit. But I'd like more acidity at this price. Available at Victoria Wine Cellars and Wine Shops.

Baron Philippe Sauternes 1991 (half bottle) $\boxed{11}$ $\boxed{D}$

Selected stores.

Bordeaux Blanc 1994 $\boxed{13}$ $\boxed{B}$

Good sound stuff at a good sound price. Neighbourhood Drinks Stores and Haddows only.

Bourgogne Chardonnay, Boisset Charles
de France, Boisset 1993 $\boxed{10}$ $\boxed{D}$

Chablis AC La Chablisienne 1993 $\boxed{12}$ $\boxed{E}$

Gets another point at M&S where it's a quid less.

FRENCH WINE

Chablis Premier Cru, Les Vaudevey, Bacheroy-Josselin 1993 `10` `F`

Chardonnay Fortant de France 1994 `14` `C`

Tasty depth of fruit and good flavour. Selected stores.

Chardonnay Galet Vineyards 1994 `14` `C`

Ignore the overcooked spuds on the label – drink this rich-edged wine with chicken casserole or risotto. A tasty wine here.

Chateau de la Jaubertie Sauvignon 1993 `14` `C`

A highly drinkable rose.

Chateau de la Louviere, Graves 1993 `13` `E`

Chateau de Vaudieu Blanc, Chateauneuf-du-Pape 1993 `14` `E`

Delicious touch of soft earthiness to the vigorous fruit, which is impressive without being overstated.

Chateau Haut Bonfils Oaked Sauvignon 1994 `13.5` `C`

Nice touch of sympathetic wood.

Chateau Haut Bonfils Sauvignon Blanc 1993 `11` `C`

Chateau La Diffre, Seguret, Cotes du Rhone Villages 1993 `12` `C`

Chateau la Tuque, Bordeaux 1994 `13.5` `C`

Chateau St Gallier, Graves 1994 `14` `D`

Quietly classy. Victoria Wine Cellars only.

Chateau Terres Douces Cuvee Prestige 1994
`15.5` `C`

Brilliant ripe fruit well hemmed in by the acidity – this makes for an impressively balanced bottle.

Cinquante Chardonnay/Sauvignon VdP d'Oc 1993 (50cl)
`13` `B`

Amusing, mildly, and a good size.

Domaine de Biau, VdP des Cotes de Gascogne H. Ryman 1994
`13.5` `C`

Fails by a squeak to make 14 – although it will improve in bottle over the Christmas period and be in finer fettle. Selected stores.

Domaine de la Croix Bergerac, H. Ryman 1994
`13.5` `C`

Some touches of elegance here, though the final flourish is taut.

Domaine de la Tuilerie Chardonnay VdP d'Oc 1992
`14` `C`

Domaine de la Tuilerie VdP d'Oc 1994
`15` `C`

Lovely rich fruit with a clean finish, Has an engaging serious/funny side – like Clive James.

Domaine de Rivoyre Chardonnay, VdP d'Oc 1993
`16` `C`

Full ripeness of melons in the mouth. Quite superb and polished with tongue-tingling acidity. Stylish, explicit, fine.

Domaine l'Argentier Terret, VdP Cotes de Thau 1993
`14` `B`

By the time this book comes out, the 1994 vintage will probably be on the shelves, but this wasn't available for tasting before going to press.

Domaine Pre Baron, Sauvignon de Touraine 1994 `13` `C`

Selected stores.

Domaine Souchais Muscadet Sur Lie 1994 `12` `C`

Selected stores.

Big Frank's White VdP d'Oc 1994 `15.5` `C`

A nice blend of freshness and fruit: citric edged ripe melon and banana with a pineapple finish. Delicious swigging for a hot summer's day (or night).

Galet Vineyards Chardonnay, VdP d'Oc 1994 `14` `C`

Solid. Punches its weight – at the price.

Galet Vineyards Grenache Blanc, VdP d'Oc 1994 `13.5` `C`

Gewurztraminer, Cave Vinicole de Turckheim 1992 `13` `C`

Lay down for 3 years. Rich but not balanced yet.

Grenache Blanc Galet Vineyards 1994 `14.5` `C`

Odd, but oddly delicious. It has a creamy, pineapple-edged fruitiness which rolls around the palate like a pear-drop.

James Herrick Chardonnay, VdP d'Oc 1994 `14` `C`

A fiver on the price tag but not quite a fiver in the bottle.

La Serre Chardonnay VdP d'Oc 1994 `14.5` `C`

Good class of chardonnay here.

La Serre Sauvignon VdP d'Oc 1994   `14` `C`

Fancy – another estimable sauvignon blanc from the south of nowhere. A crisp, flavourful wine of restrained class.

Laperouse Blanc Val d'Orbieu & Penfolds, VdP d'Oc 1994   `14` `C`

Rounded fruit flavours energetically supported by the elegance of the acids.

Macon Vinzelles Les Cailloux Blancs 1994   `12` `D`

Selected stores.

Marsanne VdP d'Oc 1994   `14` `C`

Marsanne is a grape. This example does not reveal all the variety's charms but it does give a good account of itself and would be superb with chicken dishes. Well-priced. Victoria Wine Cellars only.

Montagny Premier Cru, Oak Aged Buxy 1992   `12` `D`

Selected stores.

Muscat Cuvee Tradition, Turckheim 1993   `11` `C`

Available at Victoria Wine Cellars and Wine Shops.

Muscat de Beaumes de Venise, Cuvee Antoine 1992   `15` `E`

An exceptional dessert/blue cheese wine. Waxy and honeyed, it has a gorgeous, uplifting richness which will age brilliantly well beyond AD 2000. Selected stores.

Muscat de Rivesaltes Mimosas, Dessert Wine (half bottle)   `10` `B`

This wine, usually an outstanding honey monster, is, in this example, curiously waxy and almost soapy in feel.

Riesling Grand Cru Shoenenbourg, Turckheim 1990 `13` `E`

Delicious mineral undertones flirt with the fruit – but it's the price which brings a blush to the drinker's cheeks. It needs at least 5 years more ageing to sprout fully into life. Victoria Wine Cellars only.

Rolle, VdP d'Oc 1994 `13` `C`

Attractive.

Sancerre Cuvee de Chene de Saint Louis 1994 `11` `D`

Overpriced – vastly.

Sauvignon de Bordeaux 1994 `13.5` `B`

Lively acid, good fruit, effective styles. Excellent price to go with shellfish.

Stowells of Chelsea Vin de Pays du Tarn (3 litre) `12` `F`

Sound but dullish – not a lot of fruit.

Sur Lie, Vin de Pays d'Oc, Mme C. Parmentier 1993 `10` `C`

By the time this book comes out, the 1994 vintage will probably be on the shelves, but this wasn't available for tasting before going to press.

Syrah Rose Fortant de France 1993 `13` `C`

Vendange Tardive Gewurztraminer, Cuvee Ste Catherine Pfaffenheim 1990 (half bottle) `10` `F`

Waxy, floral, gently honeyed. Bad value for good fruit. Available at Victoria Wine Cellars and Wine Shops.

Vin de Pays de l'Herault French Dry White `13` `B`

There's a touch of sweet and sour fruit on the rather loose edge. Good value but somewhat limp in the final analysis, though fish and chips will work well with it.

Vin de Pays de l'Herault Medium Dry `13` `B`

GERMAN WINE WHITE

Forster Jesuitengarten Riesling Spatlese 1988 `10` `E`

Uninteresting, why bother?

Kabinett, Bornheimer Adelberg 1992 `10` `B`

Niederhauser Hermanshohle Riesling Spatlese, Nahe 1988 `15.5` `E`

Complex, vibrant wine with lots of soft, orchidaceous fruit, nuts and richly textured acidity. Wonderful wine to treat the long-distance lawn mower or lorry driver with after a hard drive.

Serriger Heiligenborn Riesling Spatlese 1983 `15` `D`

Superb petrol and honey fruit. Wonderful with shrimps and garlic.

Serriger Herrenberg Riesling Spatlese, Bert Simon 1985 `10` `D`

Dull, usual thing.

Spatlese, Bornheimer Adelberg 1990 `13` `B`

Not a bad aperitif.

**Trittenheimer Apotheke Riesling Auslese,
Friedr. Wilhelm Gymnasium 1988**   14   E

Lovely aroma of muted lemon sherbet – rich fruit with the
petally echo. A wine for cheese and a bunch of grapes.

HUNGARIAN WINE   RED

Cabernet Sauvignon Szekszard   14   B

Soft and flavoursome.

Country Red Villany 1993   13   B

Attractive, bustling fruit.

Merlot, Danubiana Bonyhad 1993   13.5   B

Soft, very pleasant. Hints of savouriness about the fruit.
Selected stores.

**Villany Cabernet Sauvignon, Szekszard
1993**   15.5   B

This wine has no right to be as brisk, as tasty, as correct and as
serious as this for the money.

HUNGARIAN WINE   WHITE

Chapel Hill Irsai Oliver 1993   15   B

Excellent with scallops (cooked anywhich but with cheese).

Chapel Hill Irsay Oliver   11   B

Chapel Hill Rheinriesling 1994 `12.5` `B`

Chapel Hill Sauvignon Blanc 1994 `13` `B`

Taut – good with shellfish.

Chardonnay Balaton 1993 `11` `B`

By the time this book comes out, the 1994 vintage will probably be on the shelves, but this wasn't available for tasting before going to press.

Country White Magyar Vineyards `11` `B`

Gyongyos Sauvignon Blanc H. Ryman `13` `B`

Real gooseberry character.

Oak Forest Hungarian Chardonnay 1994 `14.5` `B`

Excellent rich-edged fruit with true chardonnay depth and flavour. Selected stores.

ITALIAN WINE   RED

Aglianico del Vulture, Riserva, Pipoli 1986 `14` `D`

Perfect cheese wine with its ripe maturity and well-finished fruit/acid balance.

Barbera d'Asti Ceppi Storici 1991 `13.5` `C`

Rich but not overdeep or over-ripe. Good with light meat dishes. Touch pricey for the style.

Bardolino Pasqua 1994 `14` `B`

Delicious, simple, cherry-fruited drinking – chilled with pasta.

Barolo 1991 `13` `E`

In the lighter style (in all but price). Selected stores.

Cabernet Riserva Alto Adige, Baron Felix Longo 1991 `12.5` `C`

Interesting, authentically individual, but recognisable cabernet wine. Needs food, but better, it needs to get to at least AD 2000 to really let rip. One for the millennium, this wine. Selected stores.

Ceppi Storici Oak Aged Barbera 1991 `13` `C`

Overpriced but decidedly attractive – especially with tarragon chicken. Selected stores.

Chianti Colli Senesi, Castello di Montano 1993 `13.5` `C`

Excellent dry fruit. Selected stores.

Chianti Piccini 1993 `12` `C`

Light, with a background of dry plumminess.

Chianti Rufina Riserva, Fattoria di Galiga 1990 `13.5` `C`

By the time this book appears, the 1991 vintage may be on the shelves – not yet tasted as at 27 June 1995.

Colle del Talo, Vino da Tavola, Castello Vicchiomaggio 1990 `14` `D`

Prunes and violets, rich, dark, satisfying, classy, well-balanced.

Cortenova Merlot 1993 `13` `B`

Some attractive fruit with faint savoury echoes.

Fattoriadi Galiga Chianti Riserva 1990 `16.5` `C`

A staggeringly approachable Rufina chianti: polished, fruity, soft, yet serious. Quite delightful. Gorgeous dry/sweet fruit with a licorice edge. Victoria Wine Cellars only.

Lambrusco Grasparossa di Castelvero   13   B

Yes, Lambrusco! It finishes yet (and bubbly) but the fruit is soft
and yielding. Works well with cold meat starters.

Merlot/Sangiovese, Casal del Giglio 1993   16   B

Black cherries, plums and blackberries with a shroud of rich
tannin. Austere but very impressive. Interesting and very successful marriage of French and Italian grapes: dry, firmly fruity,
balanced, very effectively built from first to last. Available from
Victoria Wine Cellars and Wine Shops.

Monferrato Rosso   15.5   B

A lovely warm wine of great charm and flavour for the money.
Great wine for maudlin Italian dishes.

Montepulciano di Abruzzo 1993   13.5   C

Comes so close to notching up 14 I feel guilty. Selected stores.

Parducci Petite Syrah 1993   14   D

Big, gravy-like bouquet, dry-edged soft.

Primitivo del Salento, Le Trulle 1993   13.5   C

Gamy, rich aromas and initial fruit attack and then nicely ripe
cherries. Delicious.

Rosso del Veneto 1993   12.5   B

Soft and sweet for pastas.

Sangiovese di Toscana, Cecchi 1993   14.5   C

Lovely ripe yet earthily edged wine of some class. Delicious with
cheese dishes.

Sqinzano, Mottura   13   B

Pleasing fruity lift to the fruit on the finish.

Valpolicella Classico Zonin 'Il Maso', 1993   `12` `C`

Valpolicella Pasqua 1993   `12` `B`

Vermiglio di Ripanera, Vino da Tavola   `14` `C`

Delicious. Soft plummy fruit of vivid freshness.

Vigneti di Marano, Amarone della
Valpolicella, Boscaini 1990   `14` `E`

Acquired taste, but worth acquiring: almondy, cherryish, dry
yet very soft with a hint of raisin. Available from Victoria
Wine Cellars.

ITALIAN WINE WHITE

Asti Mondoro

20 points (for grans), 10 points (for the rest of humanity).
Definitely a must for Christmas for ladies over 95 years of age.
Great packaging. Great sweet fruit.

Bianco di Custoza 1993

Lemony, light.

Bianco di Verona, Fabiano 1993   `13` `B`

Lightly scented, medium dry. Good for Lieb lovers trying to
break out. Selected stores.

Chardonnay del Salento, Vigneto di
Caramia 1993   `14` `D`

Expensive, but the fruit is rich, the structure sound, the effect
satisfying. Available in Victoria Wine Cellars only.

Chardonnay del Piemonte Castelvero 1992

By the time this book comes out, the 1993 vintage will probably be on the shelves, but this wasn't available for tasting before going to press.

Chardonnay del Salento, 'Le Trulle' 1993 `13.5` `C`

This vintage is not as highly rated as once it was, because the fruit is beginning to crumble – it's getting too old.

Dry Muscate di Puglia 'Le Trulle' 1993 `13` `B`

Delicious little aperitif.

Frascati Superiore Pallavicini 1994 `13.5` `C`

Soft and supple with a sweet edge. Touch pricey for the style. Selected stores.

Gambellara Classico Zonin 1993 `13` `C`

Some flavour. Suits rich fish dishes. Victoria Wine Cellars only.

Lugana, Pasqua 1993 `13` `C`

Elegant lemony wine.

Monferrato Bianco `13.5` `B`

Oh! How pleasant and agreeable this simple wine is! I sigh for a rough edge, so anodyne is it.

Puglian Rose 'Le Trulle' 1993 `12` `B`

Puglian White Country Collection 1993 `15` `B`

A rich ripe melon edge to crisp finishing fruit.

Soave Classico Superiore, Anselmi 1993 `13` `D`

This is a delicious and gracefully forward soave but such is the pricey pretension of its two labels that you wonder if the fortune this added to the price couldn't have been better used reducing it. Available in Victoria Wine Cellars only.

Soave, Pasqua `13` `B`

Not bad, not great, but not bad for dear old soave which in this example at least is neither dear nor old.

Verdicchio Classico Villa Pigna 1993 `12` `C`

Available in Victoria Wine Cellars and Wine Shops.

Villa Fontana, Fontana Candida 1993 `13` `C`

MEXICAN WINE — RED

L. A. Cetto Petite Syrah 1993 `15` `C`

Delicious individuality. A sunshine wine with oodles of fruit and uncommon smoothness and satiny texture. Great depth of flavour. Victoria Wine Cellars only.

MOLDOVAN WINE — WHITE

Hincesti Moldovan Chardonnay, Hugh Ryman 1993 `12` `B`

Getting a touch creaky in the joints.

Kirkwood Chardonnay, Ryman 1994 `14` `B`

Curiously delicious, dry, vegetal edge. Good fruit, good price. Selected stores.

MORAVIAN WINE — RED

Moravia Hills Dry Red `13` `B`

MORAVIAN WINE · WHITE

Moravia Hills Dry White `12` `B`

MOROCCAN WINE · RED

Domaine Cicogne Moroccan Red `14.5` `B`
Rich, oxidised edge to the attractive fruit gives it a raisiny quality. Great with roast and grilled foods. Only at Victoria Wine Cellars and Wine Shops.

NEW ZEALAND WINE · RED

Church Road Cabernet Sauvignon, Montana 1992 `14` `E`
Ripe, stylish, balanced – pricey. Only at Victoria Wine Cellars.

Corbans Merlot 1992 `15` `E`
Curious clotted cream and raspberry meringue fruit. Rather delicious. Available from Victoria Wine Cellars and Wine Shops.

Stoneleigh Cabernet Sauvignon 1992 `12` `E`
Sadly, hugely overpriced. Yet it is excruciatingly soft and drinkable.

Vidal Hawkes Bay Cabernet/Merlot 1992 `13` `E`
This has sweetly impressive fruit but a sourly unimpressive price tag. Available from Victoria Wine Cellars and Wine Shops.

NEW ZEALAND WINE WHITE

Church Road Chardonnay, Hawkes Bay 1993   16   E

Elegant, classy fruit with highly effective wood integration. Striking balance of components (fruit/wood/acid) and a delicious wine results. Available at Victoria Wine Cellars and Wine Shops.

Cooks Riesling/Chenin Blanc, Gisborne 1993   13   B

Nautilus Chardonnay 1993   12   E

Very limited availability, and it flatters to deceive. Great aroma, disappointing finish.

Nobilo Sauvignon Blanc 1993   14   D

Delicious ripe (lychee and pear) touch to the typical herbaceous fruit.

Shingle Peak Chardonnay 1994   13   D

The fruit is a mite hidden by the acidity but the pendulum will decidedly swing the other way if this promising specimen is cellared for 1/2/3 years.

Shingle Peak Riesling 1993   15.5   D

Clean fresh aroma and taste, with a hint of tangy excitement. Excellent crisp fruit on the tongue, young gooseberries with a touch of minerality. Delicious, classy.

Shingle Peak Sauvignon 1994   14.5   D

Clean, gooseberry fruit, fresh as a dew-drenched daisy escaped the lawnmower. Crisp, mineral, almost slaty undertones. Bit quiet on the finish. Impressive up front but a bit expensive.

Stoneleigh Sauvignon Blanc 1993　13　D
Very grassy, very clean, very fresh. Good with oysters.

Timara Medium Dry White 1993　13　C
A soft and gentle introduction to New Zealand.

Vidal Hawkes Bay Sauvignon Blanc 1993　10　D
Slightly honeyed undertones on the grassiness we have come to expect of New Zealand sauvignon blancs. Distinguished feel to the wines. Delicious with grilled fish. Available at Victoria Wine Cellars and Wine Shops.

Villa Maria Chardonnay Private Bin 1993　15　D
Rich fruit with a sour edge which is highly attractive paired with rich fish stews. Available at Victoria Wine Cellars and Wine Shops.

Villa Maria Sauvignon Blanc 1993　15　D
They always get enough lift from the fruit here to balance out the grassy acids. Superb.

PORTUGUESE WINE　RED

Altamesa Red Estremadura 1994　14　B
Simple, soft, ripe, very fruity, delicious chilled and poured over parched tongues.

Bright Brothers Douro Red 1994　14　C
Lush softness with a finish of ripe plum.

Grao Vasco, Dao, Sogrape 1990　13　C
Available from Victoria Wine Cellars and Wine Shops.

J. P. Vinhos Red 1994 `14` **B**

Soft fruit with a dry, savoury edge.

Leziria Adega Co-Operative de Almeirim `14` **B**

Touch drier than before but still excellent cherryish fruit and good value.

Ponte de Alcorce Ribatejo 1994 `15` **C**

Touches of true class here. Lovely rolling fruit and polished flavour. Could be chilled (lightly) for fat oily fish: salmon, sardines, mackerel.

Quinta da Pancas Cabernet Sauvignon
1992 `16` **D**

Impressively smooth and subtly chocolatey. Has wonderful fruity presumption which it carries off to a rich, dry finish.

Quinta de Camarate, Fonseca 1989 `15` **C**

Lots of ripe figs and black cherries. Delicious. Available from Victoria Wine Cellars and Wine Shops.

PORTUGUESE WINE WHITE

Altamesa Medium Dry White Estremadura
1994 `12` **B**

Altamesa White 1994 `14.5` **B**

Cheeky, chirpy white – flavour and style at a knock-down price.

Bright Brothers Fernao Pires/Chardonnay
1994 `13` **C**

Chello, Dry Vinho Verde 1994 `12` `C`

Douro White 1994 `12` `C`

Jose Neiva Aged White 1994 `12.5` `B`
Curious floral overtones. Selected stores.

Leziria Dry, Co-Operative de Almeirim 1993 `13` `B`
Always my favourite tasty, good value, Portuguese wine.

Leziria Medium Dry White, Almeirim `14` `B`

Moscatel de Setubal Fonseca 1989 `16.5` `D`
Bargain, deeply fruited pud wine with overtones of sweet ripe
melon and muscaty figs. Available from Victoria Wine Cellars.

Quinta de Azevedo Vinho Verde 1993 `14` `C`
Has a delicious prickle and acidic lift to the fruit which is
present if not clamorous. Available from Victoria Wine Cellars
and Wine Shops.

SOUTH AFRICAN WINE RED

Belvedere du Cap Syrah 1994 `14` `C`
Modern fruit-drop fruit surrounding a dry core. Good pizza
wine. Available from Victoria Wine Cellars and Wine Shops.

Cape View Cinsault/Shiraz, K Milne 1994 `15.5` `C`
Rich and soft yet has a serious side to its friendly gluggability.
Deep, flavourful, blackcurrant, I suppose – and wonder-
ful value.

Cape View Merlot, K. Milne 1994 `16.5` `C`
The people's Petrus of the Cape!! Simply, one of the best

merlots in the world for the money. It is typically leathery, giving, aromatic – but also lingering, gently tannic. A wine of massive charm and flavour. A bargain.

Clearsprings Cape Red 14 E

Good cheering glug: bright, breezy, bouncy.

Clos Malverne Pinotage 1994 13.5 D

This is a splendid little wine – but not the big one a £7 price tag demands. Soft, smoky, aromatic, juicy – it's a great glug. Victoria Wine Cellars only.

Fairview Cabernet Sauvignon 1994 14 D

The distant tannins only hit after the soft, ripe fruit has bludgeoned the tongue. Will develop well over a couple of years. Selected stores.

Fairview Shiraz/Merlot 1992 15.5 D

Delicious, rich-edged fruit with savouriness and sweet dryness.

Firgrove Ruby Cabernet/Cinsault, Bovlei 1995 15.5 B

Oh, the sunshine is crammed into every drop! Wonderful rolling fruit and polished plum flavours: dry, soft, smooth, aromatic, utterly beguiling. Selected stores.

Klein Constantia Shiraz 1992 14 C

Sweet/dry flow of flavour battles the tastebuds. Good fruit which is up-front rich, down-throat dry. Selected stores.

Overgaauw Tria Corda 1988 12 E

Too simple for the price. Victoria Wine Cellars only.

Stellenzicht Cabernet/Malbec 1992 16 C

Curious texture to this beast. almost feline, so the blackberry and plum fruit (which has a lovely weight to it) is well able to take care of itself with a variety of roast and grilled meat. A very good price for an individual, classy, well turned out wine.

Thelema Cabernet Sauvignon/Merlot 1991   13.5   E

A tenner's worth of fruit? Nope. But it's a lovely drinkable tannic-friendly wine for all that. Victoria Wine Cellars only.

Warwick Estate Cabernet Sauvignon 1991   13.5   E

Soft and juicy. Victoria Wine Cellars only.

SOUTH AFRICAN WINE   WHITE

Cape View Chardonnay Sur Lie, K. Milne 1994   15   C

Ripe pear and melon with a nuttiness on the finish. A good fish wine.

Cape View Chenin/Sauvignon 1995   15   C

Full of flavour, freshness, zip, fruit, modernity – and terrific old-fashioned value for money. Selected stores.

Cape White 1994   14   B

Soft fruit here. Terrific little glug.

Chenin Blanc Simonsvlei 1994   15   B

Full, rich, ripe pear and melon fruit. Satisfyingly gluggable by itself or with fish and chips.

Clearsprings Cape White   14   F

Rather a sweetish finish, off-dry I guess, to a pleasant quaffing wine of melony character (but little soul) for those wishing to move up from Lambrusco to drier and more complex fruit.

De Wetshof Lesca Chardonnay 1995

Pretty, delicate, engaging, finely tuned and deliciously understated. Will age interestingly in bottle for a couple of years, too. Selected stores.

Firgrove Colombard/Chenin Blanc, Bovlei 1995

Brilliant soft, peachy fruit and zingy pineapple acidity make for a lovely refreshing mouthful. Selected stores.

Graham Beck Lone Hill Chardonnay 1993

Available at Victoria Wine Cellars.

KWV Sauvignon Blanc 1995

Landema Falls Colombard/Chardonnay

Lovely, lushly fruity bargain with a crisp undertone and soft melon overtones. Brilliant buy.

Neethlingshof Gewurztraminer 1994

A pleasant rosy fruited aperitif. Available in Victoria Wine Cellars and Wine Shops.

Shiraz Blanc de Noirs, Van Loveren 1994

A subtle rose wine, dry and deliciously drinkable. An excellent aperitif. Available in Victoria Wine Cellars and Wine Shops.

Stellenzicht Sauvignon/Chardonnay 1992

Impressive. The chardonnay of the two takes the lead but it's an effective partnership, enriching all parties concerned. It's a bin end so by the time this book comes out there may only be the odd bottle left.

Stowells of Chelsea Chenin Blanc (3 litre)

Comes out bright and clean – here is fruit and zip and real style.

Table Bay Early Release

Very up-early fruit! Delicious, breezy, sunny, spring morning fruit.

White Ridge Riesling 1995

I would serve this with smoked fish, lemon and black pepper – and wait for the smile to spread to everyone's face. Selected stores.

White Ridge Sauvignon Blanc 1995

Plump gooseberry fruit with nettle-leaf acidity. Great refreshment with a touch of seriousness. Selected stores.

Yellowwood Ridge Sauvignon 1995

Rich and full without being cloying. Excellent with grilled mackerel or smoked fish. Selected stores.

SPANISH WINE RED

Campillo Rioja, Crianza 1989

Lovely vanilla edge to soft fruit which is plummy with subtle echoes of blackcurrant. Delicious.

Campo Viejo Rioja Gran Reserva 1982

Perfect weight of supple-limbed, ripe yet not heavy fruit. Available from Victoria Wine Shops.

Campo Viejo Rioja Reserva 1988

Casa Barco, Oaked Red, Vino de Mesa

Great value. Banana-soft, fresh fruit wine. Great for curry parties.

Castillo de Liria Valencia

An excellent mix of soft fruits at a bargain price.

Chivite Navarra Vina Marcos 1994

Dry-edged but plump and soupy up front. Terrific richness of fruit for the money. Selected stores.

Chivite Reserva Navarra 1990

Screamily high-pitched fruit which finishes long and vociferous. Must have food (roast pork would be good).

Contino Rioja Reserva 1989

CVNE Vina Real Rioja 1989 (half bottle)

Delicious half which delivers the whole dry rich fruit. Available from Victoria Wine Shops.

Don Darias

The Old Don seems a bit thinner than when I last encountered him but he's still hale and hearty and full of vanilla-ey fruit.

Ed's Red, Tempranillo La Mancha 1994

Stinks a bit on first opening, rhis wine, but the fruit is forceful and stylish with a texture for rich foods.

El Liso Tempranillo, La Mancha 1993

Imagine this wine with tarragon chicken! Halleluja!! Wonderful sweet edge, almost chocolate, to the deep, dry (and gently tannic) fruit which has cherries, plums and blackberries stitched on to a texture with the finish of rough velvet. Great character for the money. Sheer coconut on popping the cork – it assails the nostrils like a Bounty bar. Available at Victoria Wine Cellars and Wine Shops.

La Mancha Red

Light, warm, pretty good chilled.

Las Torres Merlot 1992

Expensive for the relative simplicity of the style. Available from Victoria Wine Cellars and Wine Shops.

Marques de Requena Reserva, Utiel Requena 1988

Puerta de la Villa Valdepenas 1994

Delicious: dry, plummy, subtle, rich. A bargain bundle of fruit.

Raimat Tempranillo 1990

The '89 vintage of this was pleasing but this newly released vintage is deeper and more complex and an altogether more charismatic bottle. It exhibits velvety berried fruits with a lovely balancing acidity and has delightfully soft fruit tannins and integrated wood tannins. This wine will age with great grace, and I see no reason, though it is delicious now, not to expect it to improve and lengthen its fruit over the next half decade and more – should anyone possess the saintly strength of will to keep from quaffing it. It rates 15 points now and with a few years' bottle age may well be knocking on 17's door.

Riazin Sin Crianza Rioja 1993

Think of it not as a rioja but as a simple, charming, uncomplicated, fresh, plum/cherry wine which is soft and highly quaffable.

Rivarey Red Rioja 1993

Torres Coronas 1991

Tres Ducados Rioja Reserva 1988 | 12 | C

Rather overripe.

SPANISH WINE   WHITE

La Mancha White 1994 | 14.5 | B

Fresh, very modern, highly gluggable. Has melon and pear-drop
flavours with a crisp yet giving finish. Bargain.

Marques de Vitoria | 8 | B

Monopole Barrel-fermented Rioja 1992 | 13 | D

If you like wood . . .

Rama Corta | 16.5 | C

Made by American Ed Flaherty in the Conca de Barbera region.
Baked plums (yet very dry to finish) on the palate with a hint of
licorice and blackcurrant richness. A terrific wine for the money
– quite terrific.

Rivarey Oaked Rioja | 12 | C

Good with spicy and/or creamy fish dishes.

Santara Chardonnay 1994 | 14 | C

Quirky rich edge to the fruit.

Torres Gran Vina Sol, Chardonnay 1992 | 14 | D

Well-constructed, naturally fruity and has a classy feel. Available
in Victoria Wine Cellars and Wine Shops.

Torres Sangredetoro 1991 | 15.5 | C

Licorice!? Very dry, starts well. Drink it in an hour – it fades.

USA WINE   RED

Atlas Peak Vineyards Sangiovese, Napa Valley 1991   `12` `F`

A truly delicious wine. Has class, style, fruit and flavour – but at £13 it is stunningly bad value except for sangiovese freaks. Only at Victoria Wine Cellars.

Beringer Cabernet Sauvignon 1991   `15` `F`

Expensive but packed with personality and flavour. Victoria Wine Cellars only.

Blossom Hill California   `12.5` `C`

Sweet and almost flowery.

Fetzer Valley Oaks Cabernet 1992   `14` `D`

Rich, characterful, classy, dry, very savoury.

Kenwood Mazzoni Geyserville Zinfandel 1993   `13.5` `E`

Beautiful, warm, sunny fruit. Selected stores.

Kenwood Sonoma Valley Nuns Canyon Zinfandel 1993   `14` `E`

More depth than the Geyserville zin and an extra edge of complexity. Selected stores.

Kenwood Zinfandel 1992   `14` `E`

Let this be your introduction to zin prior to moving on to heftier examples. Delicious but expensive. Soft, spicy, easygoing. Selected stores.

Mount Konocti Cabernet Sauvignon 1993   `15` `D`

Ripe and ready, well priced and most easy on the tastebuds.

Great to just glug and watch the sunset (or *Coronation Street*).
Floods the mouth with flavour. Selected stores.

Stratford Pinot Noir `13` `C`

Cherries, soft gamy cherries.

Stratford Zinfandel `13` `C`

Cinnamon and all-spice flavoured fruit.

USA WINE   WHITE

Blossom Hill `12` `C`

**Essensia Orange Muscat Halves 1992,
Andrew Quady (half bottle)** `14` `D`

Extraordinary stuff. Superbly rich and sweet and great with
strawberry tart.

Geyser Peak Chardonnay 1994   `E`

Delicate yet assertive – as long as you choose the food
carefully and it isn't overspiced. Sophisticated taste and style.
Selected stores.

Geyser Peak Sauvignon Blanc 1994 `15` `D`

Delicious richness with a subtle grassy undertone. Quite a class
act, this wine, and certainly better than many a sancerre at £3
more. Selected stores.

Sundial Chardonnay 1993 `13` `D`

Big sunny fruit – expressive.

FORTIFIED WINE RED

Cockburns Anno 1988 LBV 16 E

Resoundingly rich fruit with a chocolate and cherry liqueur ripeness to its edge. Lovely stuff for blue cheese.

Delaforce 1975 16 G

Great stuff: soft, plump, ripe, lingering, gorgeously velvet.

Dow's LBV 1988 in a Wooden Box 12 E

Dow's Ten Year Old Tawny Port (half bottle) 14 D

Perfect with the cheese or nuts. Rich, ripe, sweet fruit, fizzy edge.

Dows Crusted Port (bottled 1988) 14 G

Ripe, rich, ready, and rapidly happiness-inducing.

Fonseca Guimaraens 1967 15 H

Exclusive to Victoria Wine.

Garrafeira TE, Fonseca 1988 15 D

Blackberry crumble and strawberry jam. Available from Victoria Wine Shops and Off Licences.

Quinta de Vargellas 1982 16.5 G

A marvellous bottle of fruit so seductive (figs, creamy, nuts) that it defies description. Has a gorgeous lingering.

Quinta do Noval Colheita 1976 Tawny Port (half bottle) 15.5 E

Rich nuts, cream and myriad soft fruits. Delicious.

Taylors 1985 Vintage Port

Superb, rich, ripe fruit, beautifully balanced and softly insidious. Hedonistic tippling.

Warres Quinta de Cavadinha 1982

Prunes (armagnac flavoured) figs and cream. Rich, very rich, impossibly rich, smoky finish. Lovely port.

FORTIFIED WINE WHITE

Ole Manzanilla

Brilliant! Forget it's sherry. Grill loads of fresh prawns with chilli and garlic and invite the neighbours in.

Oloroso Seco (half bottle) `15.5` `C`

Bargain. Great with hard cheeses or soft TV melodramas. Victoria Wine Cellars only.

Palo Cortado (half bottle) `16` `C`

Remarkable wine. Nutty, very forceful and potently undercut by an exotic richness. Try it with nuts as an aperitif – well-chilled. Victoria Wine Cellars only.

Pedro Ximenez Superior Sherry (half bottle)

Rich, very sweet – strictly for fruitcakes.

Pellegrino Superiore Secco Marsala `14` `D`

An elegant, hugely original and sophisticated aperitif. Available from Victoria Wine Cellars.

SPARKLING WINE/CHAMPAGNE

Angas Brut Rose (Australian)   15 C

One of those New World sparklers which deliciously tickle the
nose and only lightly tickle the pocket but send shivers up the
spine of champagne makers.

Cava Brut, Victoria Wine   16.5 C

Delicious, classy, classic. Hint of fruit (perfect, just as it should
be) and great balancing acidity.

Cremant de Bourgogne, Blanc de Noirs,
Caves de Bailly (French)   15 D

Brilliant softish fruit with firm acids: excellent value. Available
from Victoria Wine Cellars and Wine Shops.

Croser Sparkling 1991 (Australian)   13 F

Available from Victoria Wine Cellars.

Cuvee Napa, Mumm, California   13.5 E

Cuvee Napa Rose, Mumm, California   14 E

Great stuff.

Deutz (New Zealand)   12 E

Just like Deutz champagne from the well-known Rheims
company.

Gallo California Brut   10 D

Light, soft – little personality. There's not sufficient acidity to
fine the fruit (what there is of it).

Giardino, Metodo Classico Pinot Noir/
Chardonnay (Italy)   12 C

Graham Beck Brut (South Africa) 11 D
Available at Victoria Wine Cellars and Wine Shops.

Green Point 1991 (Australia) 14 F

Green Point Rose 15 F
As good as many a pink bubbly at twice the price.

Jacques Monteau Brut 14 F
An exciting bottle of fruity champagne. Good enough to drink with smoked salmon.

Lindauer Brut 13.5 D
A delicious lemon sparkler.

Maison La Motte Sparkling Chardonnay 1992 (France) 12 E

Marques de Monistrol Brut Rose (Spanish) 14 E
This has some pleasant fruit but seems pricey for the experience.

Marquis de la Tour Brut, Ackerman 14 B
Brilliant apple-skin flavoured sparkler of dash and verve.

Marquis de la Tour Demi Sec (France) 11 C
For those with a sweetish tooth, this peachy bubbly is the business.

Mercier Brut Rose Champagne 11 G
Rather lean with the fruit and I think that rose, and especially that at £14 a bottle, should have more flavour and richness than white champagne. This example does not.

Moet et Chandon 1988 13 H
Frighteningly priced, but very posh.

Nautilus Cuvee Marlborough Brut (New Zealand) `14` `F`
Very limited stocks.

Pelorus 1989 (New Zealand) `13` `F`
Available from Victoria Wine Cellars.

Pierre Jourdan Cuvee Belle Rose `13` `F`
Victoria Wine Cellars only.

Pol Roger White Foil `12` `G`
Victoria Wine Cellars only.

Scharffenberger Brut (USA) `14.5` `E`
Limited stocks of this delicious wine.

Seppelt Great Western Brut `14` `C`
Light and breezy.

Seppelt Salinger Brut 1990 (Australia) `13` `E`
Has a subtle saline quality – almost like a sparkling fino. Good with smoked salmon.

Seppelts Salinger Sparkling Wine (Australia) `15` `F`
Mature yet fresh finishing. Some elegance. Dry.

Seppelts Sparkling Shiraz 1990 `16` `E`
Fabulous roaring fruit.

Simonsig Kaapse Vonkel Sparkling Brut 1992 (South Africa) `15` `E`
Delicious, classic bubbly. Terrific with smoked fish. Also great to lay down for AD 2000. Victoria Wine Cellars only.

Sparkling Chardonnay, Barbero (Italian) 13 C

Pleasant and inoffensive. Available from Victoria Wine Cellars and Wine Shops.

Torre del Gall Brut 1990 14 E

Excellent. Has an underlying richness of fruit class.

Veuve Clicquot Vintage Reserve 1988 12 H

Victoria Wine Cellars and selected Wine Shops.

Vintage Champagne 1989 (Victoria Wine) 12.5 G

A classic bottle of bubbles at a classic price (nearly £19). I'm not convinced it is quite worth this sum.

Yalumba Pinot Noir/Chardonnay 16 E

Elegant stylish fruit. Brilliant, balanced and fine.

WINE CELLAR

When I contemplate recent events at this wine retailer I am reminded of the time, well over twenty years ago now, when I met John Harvey-Jones in his office on the Embankment when he was a director of ICI. I had been expecting nothing more than the usual grey corporate personality in the usual grey striped suit. I was astonished to find a man with hair like a rock star (though not as Shakespearian as it is now) and a tie fluorescent enough to divert traffic. His mind was as original and lively as his garb.

Nowadays, of course, many is the executive who wears a bright tie and long hair – but is the mind original? Not in the least. He is a mere copycat – in uniform. Sir John still ploughs an original and lively furrow and he was ploughing it before most businessmen.

So it was with Oddbins. They were long-haired and brightly tied before anyone. It was an image which finally found its most faithful reflection in the company's wine list.

Which brings us to Wine Cellar. The name, I suppose, says it all. It is dull and cobwebbed, hand-me-down and trite. The wine list, on the other hand, is quite lively. The only thing is – it's someone else's idea. It is a copy of Oddbins' mould-breaking original.

The spring list this year tried to be witty. It showed corkscrews as springs on its front cover because it was The Spring List. Alas, few people made the connection due to the ineffectual typographical design which majored on the illustration rather than the words. Not a promising start (especially when the reader is already thinking 'where have I seen drawings done in this style before?' and, then, after a moment he says to himself, 'Oh yes, it's just like Ralph Steadman').

However, though the Wine Cellar wine list is inspired by Oddbins' visual and layout ideas, which have always been compatible, relevant and, most important of all, give the reader a comfortable time understanding what is written on the page, the designer (excuse me – I mean plagiariser) of this list makes a pig's ear of the silk purse of the original. The various type-faces in its pages fight like alley cats. Being sentenced to read this list from cover to cover would present a more awesome criminal deterrent than ten years in Wormwood Scrubs. Since the company has spent a fortune revamping itself and acquiring a pair of brave wine buyers who patently demonstrate more originality than their design department, this is a great pity.

Wine Cellar is the poshest subsidiary of Greenalls Cellars, which is based in Warrington in Cheshire. Greenalls also has two further wine shop brands: Cellar 5 and Berkeley Wines. The shops are mainly in the North and the Midlands; but the Wine Cellar shops are now creeping down south with an aim to make a national total, by the end of this year, of thirty branches. Cellar 5 has 300 branches and these are old-fashioned off-licences. Berkeley Wines is, so Greenalls tell me, a 'middle market wine retailer'. There are 150 of these. The wines in the section which follows this introduction are all Wine Cellar wines, though some may be available at the other subsidiaries.

The top three best-selling wines at Cellar 5 are Liebfraumilch, Lambrusco Bianco and Niersteiner Gutes Domtal. Three sweet cheapies and perfect street-corner off-licence wines. At Berkeley Wines the top three are Jacob's Creek Dry Red, Jacobs Creek Semillon/Chardonnay and Hardy's Stamp Series Shiraz/Cabernet. Three fruity, well-made, excellently priced Aussies (speaking volumes for the sophistication of this so-called 'middle market'). The top three best sellers at Wine Cellar are Hardy's Stamp Series Shiraz/Cabernet, Solana Red and Bulgarian Cabernet. Which leaves me totally confused. Isn't Wine Cellar supposed to be positioned above Berkeley Wines?

On the basis of customer preference there probably isn't much difference.

The difference is all in some marketing man's mind. (I say man because in my experience a woman would be much less keen to break things up into little bits – to fragmentise and keep spewing out subsidiaries. Could it be something to do with the fact that boys play with Lego and never grow out of it?) Nevertheless, what is certain is that the group as a whole is the third largest wine chain in the country.

Mr Nader Haghigi, the new broom in charge at Greenalls Cellars (he arrived in last May last year), will, I am sure, make clearer the distinctions between the disparate components of the group as time goes on. Or he may not. Nightvision, a video-drinks store concept, is being developed, as is something called a Greenalls Food Store. This latter has seen, or will see, the introduction of things like smoked salmon and fresh pasta into Wine Cellar shops. I must confess that I am extremely sceptical of that dreaded thing called 'consumer research', which tells companies that things like this are a good idea.

However, wine is my remit – so I'll mind my own business and say that as far as Wine Cellar and its wines are concerned I am absolutely clear in my mind. The new wine-buying team of Kevin Wilson (who baled out of William Low when it was absorbed by Tesco) and David Vaughan (who's knocked up more than two decades in the wine business) have put together an interesting group of wines. The total selection is over 650 different bottles. Says Mr Wilson:

'The days of pioneering areas of the world are over (unless somebody can find interesting wines in Mongolia). So it's now up to us as buyers to develop new wines and styles in combination with wine-makers. Being the new kids on the block, we are more flexible and responsive to the developing market and, therefore, will endeavour to continue to offer new and exciting wines to our customers.'

He expects to be introducing more wines from South Africa, Chile and Argentina as well as developing new wines in North

America and the south of France. This is heartening news to Wine Cellar customers. Who are they exactly? Mr Wilson again:

'What sort of person will buy their wine at Wine Cellar? Wine Cellar is targeted to satisfying the needs (both functional and emotional!) of high income families, stylish singles and those living in town houses and flats . . . whilst still offering a real welcome and choice to all other customer groups.'

Well now, Oddbins really do have something to keep them awake at night. Satisfying emotional needs, eh? This is an original stance for a wine retailer. If this is what that piece of expensive consumer research Greenalls doubtless commissioned came out and reported, then I take back everything I've ever said about the dangers of making marketing decisions based upon research. Emotional needs, eh! It's brilliant!

It's just so much of a pity this truly pioneering attitude is not reflected in the name of the place and not represented by the me-too design of the wine list. Is it too late to change the name of Wine Cellar to Jung & Freud Limited? Or how about The Absolutely Fabulous Wine Bottle Company? The possibilities are endless. And as for getting someone to design the wine list, may I suggest my ex-neighbour Mr David Hillman of Pentagram Design, London W11 (telephone: 0171 229 3477)?

Just a friendly suggestion. He'll know someone who'll come up with a great new name for you as well. The fees aren't high. (I'd be tempted to come up with a new name for your business myself in return for a case of your Novell Scala Dei Priorato 1993, the glorious red-bearded beast from Tarragona at £4.49 and 16 points, but, alas, it's not my place.

But do think about Jung & Freud as a new name, will you, Mr Haghigi? It has a ring . . . you've got to admit that . . . ?)

Wine Cellar
PO Box 476
Loushers Lane
Warrington
WA4 6RR

Tel 01925 444555
Fax 01925 415474
Special Wine availability telephone no.: 01925 602986

SEE STOP PRESS SECTION AT END OF BOOK FOR LAST-MINUTE ADDITIONS TO THIS RETAILER'S RANGE.

ARGENTINIAN WINE   RED

Cabernet Sauvignon Valle de Vistalba 1994   `14` `C`

Punk rock haircut fruit. Delicious with food!

Lurton Malbec/Tempranillo 1995   `14` `C`

Forgive the pong, concentrate on the sweet fruit.

**Viejo Surco Sangiovese/Cabernet
1995**   `12` `C`

Tannin overpowering what fruit there is. Needs time to develop
– and it should do this over 6 months to a year rather well. Also
at Cellar 5 stores.

ARGENTINIAN WINE   WHITE

Viejo Surco Chardonnay/Chenin 1995   `13.5` `C`

Viejo Surco Torrontes/Chenin 1995   `15` `C`

A kind of exotic fruitiness here, fresh but not overplayed or too
rude, and it is delicious. Also at Cellar 5 stores.

AUSTRALIAN WINE   RED

Bucklow Hill Dry Red 1994   `13` `C`

Bucklow Hill Shiraz/Cabernet 1994   `12` `C`

Church Road Cabernet Sauvignon 1992 ⟨14⟩ ⟨E⟩

Old-style, tannic bourgeois bordeaux copy. I'd prefer this wine to be a 100 per cent NZ wine, not a poor relative.

Hardys Bankside Shiraz 1992 ⟨15⟩ ⟨D⟩

Soft and appealing. Great with fancy chicken ensembles.

Ironstone Cabernet/Shiraz 1992 ⟨16⟩ ⟨D⟩

Something interesting to get your teeth into for not a lot of money. Rich tannins, gravy-edged fruit, and a deep delivery of flavour.

Lindemans Limestone Ridge Coonawarra Shiraz/Cabernet 1991 ⟨16⟩ ⟨E⟩

Save it for Christmas lunch – gorgeous velvet fruit of effortless charm.

Lindemans Pyrus Coonawarra 1991 ⟨15.5⟩ ⟨E⟩

Swirling fruit, coated in dry, subtle tannin. Great roast meat wine.

Penfolds Bin 2 Shiraz/Mourvedre 1993 ⟨15.5⟩

One of the most successful two-grape blends from Oz on sale. A rich, satisfying wine of serious style yet quaffable disposition. Will age well and develop in bottle, perhaps for a couple of years?

Peter Lehmann Grenache, Barossa Valley 1994 ⟨15⟩

Rich, structured, deep, dry, flavoursome – terrific rich drinking for under £4.

Peter Lehmann Shiraz 1991 ⟨16⟩ ⟨D⟩

Wonderful, rich, complex gravy.

AUSTRALIAN WINE

Bucklow Hill Dry White 1994 `12` `C`

Bucklow Hill Semillon/Chardonnay 1994 `13` `C`

Goundrey Estate Chardonnay Mount Barker 1993 `15` `D`

Severely delicious. Grilled chicken cries out for it.

Hardys Padthaway Chardonnay 1993 `16` `D`

Oily fruit bursting with flavour, dry rich fruit and rolling texture.

Ironstone Semillon Chardonnay, W Australia 1994 `15` `D`

Delightful citric and subtle tropical fruit acids undercutting the richness of the frontal attack.

Lindeman's Semillon Botrytis 1987 (half bottle) `16` `D`

Extraordinary, medicinally-edged fruit. Quite wonderful with fruit and cheese.

Margaret River Semillon, Amberley 1993 `12` `E`

Curious cosmetic (powdery) edged fruit of some richness.

Peter Lehmann Chenin Blanc, Barossa Valley 1994 `15` `C`

Delicious. Or should I say delishlush? After a bottle of this wine you may have no choice.

**Rothbury Trident Chardonnay/Semillon/
Sauvignon Blanc 1994** | 14 | C |

Rich, soft and good with smoked fish.

CHILEAN WINE

Villard Cabernet Sauvignon 1992 | 13 | D |

Andes Peaks Cabernet/Merlot 1993 | 14 | C |

Rich fruit, dry, smooth, subtle tannins.

Andes Peaks Cabernet/Merlot 1994 | 14 | C |

Cherries and ripe plums. Good news for pasta eaters. Also at
Cellar 5 stores.

Carmen Cabernet Sauvignon 1993 | 13 | C |

Some distant richness and flavour but a touch overpriced.

Carmen Reserve Merlot 1993 | 14.5 | D |

Rich, ripe, savoury, full – lots of flavour. Not a big, bruising
wine but authoritative.

Errazuriz Cabernet Sauvignon 1990 | 16 | D |

Subtle hints of mint to the full-blooded beauty which is never
blowsy or overripe.

**Hedges Cabernet/Merlot, Washington
State 1993** | 16 | D |

Rather distinguished. Not cheap but then it couldn't be for it
has a luxurious structure, lovely fruit, lingering finish and terrific
style. Delicious.

Villard Cabernet Sauvignon 1992 | 13 | D |

Villard Merlot 1992 `13` `D`

CHILEAN WINE   WHITE

Andes Peaks Chardonnay 1995 `15` `C`
Good price for the rich smoothness of the fruit on offer.

Andes Peaks Sauvignon Blanc 1995 `13.5` `C`
Pear-drop undertones to the fresh fruit. Good refreshing glug.

Carmen Sauvignon Blanc 1994 `15` `C`
Lovely calm fruit, insistent but not strident, harmoniously close to the acidity which gives the wine a delicious fresh style with flavour.

Villard Sauvignon Blanc, Aconcagua 1994 `14` `C`
Suppressed gorgeosity.

Vina Casablanca Sauvignon, White Label 1994 `13.5` `C`

FRENCH WINE   RED

Abbaye de Rignac Buzet 1993 `12` `C`
Rather light.

Bourgogne Hautes Cotes de Beaune, Les Caves des Hautes Cotes 1992 `10` `D`

Brouilly Domaine les Nazins, Duboeuf 1994 `10` `D`

Chateau Brulescaille, Cotes de Bourg 1992 | 13.5 | D

Chateau des Mattes, Corbieres Rocobere 1991 | 14 | C

Rich, deep, satisfyingly drily conceived and wrily expressed.

Chateau Haut Lagrange, Pessac Leognan 1992 | 13 | E

Some lovely potential in the tannins here – or drink now with pink kidneys in red wine sauce.

Chateau l'Etoile, Graves 1993 | 13 | D

Healthy armpit aroma. Good fruit, not exciting as it might be with age, but good with food (roast lamb).

Chateau Monbrison, Cru Bourgeois, Margaux 1992 | 11 | F

Good start but the rest doesn't add up to £13's worth of wine. Only at Wine Cellar.

Chateau Moulin Pey-Labrie, Canon Fronsac 1992 | 12 | E

Rather a touch expensive for the lack of flourish on the fruit. Only at Wine Cellar.

Chateau Peyrou, Cotes de Castillon 1990 | 16 | D

Wonderful, no-nonsense, tannicky shaped fruit. Brilliant flavour, depth, structure and weight. Superb with all sorts of meat and cheese dishes.

Chateau Thieuley, Bordeaux Rouge 1993 | 12 | D

Wine Cellar only.

Chatellinie de Lastours Corbieres 1990 | 15 | C

Lovely licorice and soft berried fruit flavours. Subdued earthiness. Smashing tipple.

Chinon Domaine de la Diligence, Couly Dutheuil 1992

11   D

Light, very light.

Claret Calvet 1994

12   C

Also at Cellar 5 stores.

Domaine d'Estradelle Fitou 1992

14.5   C

How elegant and sprightly some of these burgundies have become! Terrific fruit here.

Domaine de la Baume VdP d'Oc 1991

13   D

Elegant. Touch subdued.

Domaine de la Giraudier Chinon 1993

13.5   C

Good subdued dried raspberry fruit and soft tannins.

Domaine les Pascales Coteaux du Languedoc 1994

16.5   C

Lovely tannins, polished yet spicy, which snag food, like hooks in fish, and permit the deep, deep fruit to work with all manner of rich, savoury dishes.

Domaine Pierre Gauthier Bourgeuil 1992

12   D

Gigondas, les Vins du Troubadour 1993

12   D

Les Terres Noires Merlot/Cabernet Sauvignon 1994

14   C

Lovely savoury fruit. Great with grilled sausages.

Medoc Barrel Aged, Calvet 1990

10   E

Mercurey La Morandine, Domaine Sounit 1992   10 E

Dull and expensive. Wine Cellar only.

Merlot VdP d'Oc Lurton 1994   14 C

Very, very pleasant, almost too pleasant for a peasant. I'd have liked a little more dirt under the fingernails. But it's a lovely soft wine with aroma and flavour. Delicious to drink chilled, by itself or with simple foods. Also at Cellar 5 stores.

Moulin a Vent, Domaine des Rosiers, Duboeuf 1993   10 E

Rasteau, Cotes de Rhone Villages 1993   13 D

Only fails to convince more persuasively because of the price set against the aroma and the juicy fruit.

Saint-Joseph Les Larmes, Alain Paret 1990   11 D

Savigny les Beaune Fourneaux, Domaine Chandon de Briailles 1992   11 F

Some signs of life.

Volnay, Domaine Marquis d'Angerville 1992   10 G

FRENCH WINE   WHITE

Angelico, Bordeaux Blanc 1994   12.5 C

Soft and fruity.

Baudin Chardonnay VdP d'Oc 1993   16 C

Coolly classy fruit, handsomely joined to beautifully balanced acid. Lovely.

Bergerac Blanc Sec, Domaine de Pigeonnier 1994
14 C

Good comforting fruit and a good-edged finish. Tasty.

Chardonnay Lurton VdP d'Oc 1994
15 C

Softly expressive fruit, finely crafted. Classy.

Chateau Ducla, Entre Deux Mers 1994
14 D

Flavour and style.

Chateau Haut Lagrange, Pessac Leognan 1992
14 E

Great with oysters and prawns and the suchlike. Expensive but impressive. Only at Wine Cellar.

Chateau la Tuilerie, Entre Deux Mers 1994
12.5 C

Chateau Thieuley, Bordeaux Blanc 1994
14 D

Classy, quite classy.

Chateau Thieuley, Bordeaux Clairet 1994
13.5 D

A dry, classy rose.

Chateau Vigne Lourac, Gaillac Blanc 1993
12 C

Possibly a shellfish contender.

Domaine de la Tour Signy, Haut Poitou 1994
13.5 C

Hint of melon but mostly clean and fresh fruit which goes with shellfish.

Domaine la Galaoubis, VdP des Cotes de Gascogne, Ryman 1994
13.5 C

Good attack at the front.

Domaine Pillot Bourgogne Aligote 1993 `12` `D`

Laforet Bourgogne Chardonnay, Drouhin 1994 `11` `D`

Les Fumees Blanches Sauvignon Blanc, VdP d'Oc 1994 `15.5` `C`

Absolutely delicious, lively acid balance counterpointing deep melony fruit. Excellent style.

Les Terres Noires, Marsanne sur Lie, VdP de l'Herault 1994 `13` `C`

Oddly untypical. Fails to convince on the finish.

Lurton Chenin Blanc 1995 `13` `C`

Hints at stylishness without quite convincingly demonstrating it.

Lurton Chenin/Chardonnay 1995 `13.5` `C`

Has bite and flavour.

Macon Vire, Domaine Emile Gillet, Thevenet 1992 `13` `F`

Delicious. Very pricey.

Menetou Salon, Leon Vatan 1994 `14` `E`

Is it worth £7.50? It is a touch overpriced but it is as near a sancerre as you can get (but better than most). Only at Wine Cellar.

Meursault, Domaine Matrot 1990 `10` `G`

Pinot Blanc, Woelflin 1993 `12` `D`

Rully, Premier Cru, Meix Cadot 1993 `12.5` `E`

Only at Wine Cellar.

Sainte Foy Moelleux, Bordeaux 1994

Might be great with a mild blue cheese.

Sancerre Vieilles Vignes, Fournier 1993

Overpriced. The Menetou Salon is better at £2.50 less. Only at Wine Cellar.

Viognier Domaine St Victor, VdP de l'Herault 1994

Expensive curiosity: banana/peachy fruit, soft, flowing, delicious.

Vouvray Demi Sec Domaine Bourillon, Dorleans 1993

Unusual restrained honey fruit. Great aperitif or with Thai food.

White Burgundy, Chardonnay Cave de Vire 1993

GERMAN WINE   RED

Siegendorf Rot 1993

Hints of opulence and quiet discipline.

GERMAN WINE   WHITE

Dr Loosen Riesling 1992

Keep for 3/4 years but if you must drink it now, chill it and serve with smoked salmon.

Erdener Treppchen Riesling Spatlese 1988 `11` `C`

Graacher Himmelreich Riesling Kabinett, Dr Loosen 1989 `14` `E`

Lovely aperitif wine of distinction.

Hochheimer Konigin Victoriaberg Riesling Kabinett 1991 `13.5` `C`

Nice petrol tones forming here.

Riesling Classic, Moselland 1993 `13` `C`

Pleasant aperitif – nothing more.

Riesling Kabinett, Gunderloch 1993 `11` `D`

Riesling Kabinett Rheinpfalz, Lingenfelder 1992 `13` `D`

Weissburgunder Pinot Blanc Kabinett Siegendorf 1994 `10` `D`

HUNGARIAN WINE   WHITE

Chapel Hill Chardonnay, Balaton Boglar 1993 `15` `B`

Has flavour, fruit and good acid balance. Good woody touches too. Also at Cellar 5 stores.

Dry Muscat, Nagyrede Region 1994 `13.5` `B`

Easy-drinking aperitif. Too light for food. Also at Cellar 5 stores.

Pinot Gris, Nagyrede 1994   `13` `B`

Aperitif – a light glug. Also available at Cellar 5 stores.

Sauvignon Blanc Gyongyos Estate 1994   `12` `C`

Feeblest vintage yet? Not as exciting as it once was, for sure.

Tokaji Furmont, Chateau Megyer 1993   `10` `C`

Dull. So dull it is hard to credit why anyone would bottle it, let alone ship it, shelve it, and pay £4.99 to let it slip down the throat.

ITALIAN WINE   RED

Bardolino Arvedi d'Emilei 1994   `14` `C`

Light, dry and fruity. Too simplistic a description? Well, it's warm, too, and gently brambly. Good with risotto.

Dolcetto d'Asti, Araldica 1994   `11.5` `C`

Juicy, very simple.

Gasparini Venegazza 1991   `13` `E`

Some grip here and flavour.

Merlot Trentino Ca'Vit 1993   `13` `C`

Dark cherry fruit.

Montepulciano d'Abruzzo, Umani Ronchi 1993   `15` `C`

Brilliant value for such flavour and depth. Great with casseroles.

Sangiovese di Toscano, Rocca delle Macie 1993   `13.5` `C`

Villa di Bossi, Chianti Rufina Riserva, Marchesi Gondi 1988

`10` `E`

Yes, it's got fruit, yes, it's got flavour, yes, it's got tannins and acids. It all adds up to a drinkable wine – but a tenner is not a comfortable swap for all this.

ITALIAN WINE WHITE

Bianco di Custoza Arvedi d'Emilei 1994

`11` `C`

Chardonnay del Piemonte, Alasia 1994

`13.5` `C`

Good fruit and flavour.

Cortese del Piemonte, Alasia 1994

`13` `C`

Aperitif.

Galestro Gazebo, Marchesi de Frescobaldi 1994

`12` `C`

A £2.99 wine at best.

'I Capitelli' Recioto di Soave, Anselmi 1992 (half bottle)

`13` `E`

Try it with Dolce Latte.

La Prendina Bianco 1993

`14.5` `D`

Apples, currants and melons with a fruit finish which recalls no fruit on earth. Interesting wine for smoked fish (eel especially).

Moscato di Pantelleria, Pellegrino 1994 (half bottle)

`15` `C`

Soft yet ripe, very sweet but complex and has a wonderful prolonged waxy fruit finish.

Passito di Pantelleria, Pellegrino 1993 `15` `E`

Wonderful with lemon tart – utterly hedonistic.

San Vincenzo Soave Classico, Anselmi 1994 `10` `E`

LEBANESE WINE RED

Domaine de Kefraya 1992 `13.5` `C`

Handsome and fruity.

NEW ZEALAND WINE RED

Villa Maria Cabernet Sauvignon 1992 `13` `E`

Soft, fresh, easy.

NEW ZEALAND WINE WHITE

Brancott Estate 'B' Sauvignon Blanc 1993 `11` `F`

Overpriced and gawky fruit/acid balance. Takes it out on the pocket but doesn't quite put it back on the palate.

Church Road Chardonnay 1993 `16` `E`

Very elegant, stylish and satisfyingly fruity, adult drinking.

Cloudy Bay Sauvignon Blanc 1994 `17` `E`

Intense gooseberry and subtle grapefruit/asparagus fruitiness.

Superb wine of huge class. Brilliant fruit. Polished wine-making.

Grove Mill Sauvignon Blanc, Marlborough 1994 `13` `E`

Nettley, floral, quirky. Rates 14 at Sainsbury's, where it costs about £1.00 less. Only at Wine Cellar.

Lincoln Estate Chenin Blanc 1994 `12` `D`

Lincoln Vineyards Chardonnay 1994 `13.5` `D`

Proper and polished.

Lincoln Vineyards Chardonnay, Parklands 1994 `15` `E`

Firm and controlled.

Neudorf Nelson, Sauvignon Blanc 1993 `13.5` `E`

A wonderfully civilised, delicate wine of immense presence and wit. Not a bruiser, it almost shuns food to demand only music or conversation as company. It is an expensive wine but it is beautifully crafted. Only at Wine Cellar.

Renwick Estate 'R' Chardonnay 1991 `13` `F`

Delicious, elegant, but what a price!

Rothbury Estate Chardonnay, Marlborough 1994 `13.5` `E`

Impressive but not at nine quid. Only at Wine Cellar.

Villa Maria Chenin/Chardonnay 1993 `14` `D`

Delicious, rich-edged, sour melon fruit.

PORTUGUESE WINE RED

Casa de Santar Dao, Reserva 1992   `13` `C`

Brisk yet juicy. Curious.

Pedras do Monte, Terras do Sado 1994   `15.5` `C`

Light but very effectively fruited and well shaped. Plum and
cherry flavours – good lightly chilled. Also at Cellar 5 stores.

Quinta da Foz de Arouce, Beiras 1990   `13.5` `E`

Sweetly fruity yet dry with excellent tannins.

Quinta da Lagoalva Ribatejo 1992   `13.5` `C`

Touch pricey and ever so slightly off balance. But not un-
deliciously so.

Quinta da Pancas Cabernet Sauvignon
1992   `16` `D`

Delightful personality: giving, dry, fruity – not a harsh edge in
sight.

Terras de Xisto Alentejo 1993   `14.5` `C`

Lots of soft, gently gripping fruit which is full, but not overfull,
of savoury flavour. Has character, too. Also at Cellar 5 stores.

Tinto da Talha Alentejo 1993   `13.5` `C`

PORTUGUESE WINE WHITE

Estramadura Branco Jose Neiva 1994   `14` `C`

Good basic glug which has a richness of finish which will work
with grilled chicken as well as grilled salmon.

Jose Neiva Aged White 1994 `12.5` `B`

Curious floral overtones. Selected stores.

Rueda Hermanos Lurton 1993 `13` `C`

SOUTH AFRICAN WINE   RED

Kanonkop Pinotage 1993 `14` `E`

Soft and simple style here – unusually.

Neil Ellis Cabernet Sauvignon 1992 `13.5` `D`

Tannins and acid driving the fruit. Wait a year for the fruit to climb out of the back seat.

Paarl Ridge Red 1994 `14` `C`

Great pasta and pizza wine. Might work with mild vegetable curries.

Welmoed Winery Pinotage 1993 `13.5` `C`

Interesting baked apple tone to the rich, tannic fruit. Great with roast meats.

SOUTH AFRICAN WINE   WHITE

KWV Sauvignon Blanc 1995 `13.5` `C`

Namaqua Colombard 1994 `14` `C`

Delicious aroma and plump fruit – finish not as rich as it might be.

Paarl Ridge Chenin Blanc 1994

SPANISH WINE RED

Baso Garnacho, Navarra 1994

Chocolate, spice, plums and blackberries with a long finish which turns cherryish after several seconds, this garnacha's fruit is earthily and spicily served up in a rich broth of extreme savoury depth. An individual may discover a star or ski down Everest naked without oxygen or he may make this wine, and I have no doubt which is the greater achievement and the one capable of providing humankind with the most joy. Its depth of flavour requires a strong stomach, it is true, but not a concomitant depth of pocket.

Berceo Rioja Crianza 1992

Casa de la Vina Valdepenas Cencibel 1994

Soft, simple, easy-drinking pleasure.

Contino Rioja Reserva 1986

Highly drinkable except for its sinking effect on the pocket.

Guelbenzu Navarra Crianza 1991

Richness and flavour here.

Hermanos Tempranillo, Lurton 1994

Ringing fruit, good tannins, strikingly well-formed acid balance. Superb with roast and grilled meat and veg.

Las Campanas Navarra Crianza 1991

Drink it with roast chicken and tarragon. Sublime!

Ochoa Navarra Tinto 1992

Lovely richness of fruit with complexity, flavour and vivid depth.

Priorato Novell Scala Dei 1993 16 C

Real depth of flavour with rustic tannins smiting the teeth. Terrific wine for spicy meat dishes and other pleasant fare. Great with turkey on Christmas Day.

Priorato Novell Scala Dei 1994 14 C

Just about makes 14. It is not, yet, as potent on the tastebuds as the '93 vintage but it will get there – and though it won't possess the earlier vintage's huge fruity clout it will be a handsome, brushed velvet wine with patches of wool and leather.

Santara Merlot 1993

Rich, easy drinking.

Solana Tempranillo 1994

Vega Cubillas, Ribera del Duero 1990

Quirky quality, quaintly querulous.

Vina Olabarri Rioja Reserva 1989

Lush vanilla edge of subtle deliciousness in this wine.

SPANISH WINE WHITE

Solana Blanco 1994

Delightful little thing. Pity it's not £3.99 but life's never perfect.

URUGUAY WINE   RED

Castol Pujol Tannat 1991   `14.5` `C`

Great value.

USA WINE   RED

**Benziger Cabernet Sauvignon, Sonoma
1992**   `13.5` `E`

**Fetzer Vineyards Pinot Noir, Santa
Barbara 1993**   `13.5` `D`

Deliciously inviting, classic aroma of pinot – truffley and
mature. Fruit rather basic with only an echo of the classic
touch of wild strawberry and farmyard compost.

Firesteed Pinot Noir 1993   `12` `E`

Garnet Pinot Noir, Saintsbury 1993 `13` `E`

Sweet, friendly pinot.

Madrona Cabernet Sauvignon 1993 `14.5` `D`

Big and rich.

Madrona Zinfandel 1993   `13` `D`

Soft, sweet, easy-going.

**Terra Rosa Cabernet Sauvignon, Laurel
Glen 1992**   `15` `D`

Tannins and acid. Lovely! But don't drink it for at least
2/3 years.

USA WINE — WHITE

Chardonnay Carneros Benziger 1993 14.5 E
Almost as rich as the Sultan of Brunei.

Dry Creek Vineyards Chenin Blanc 1994 15.5 D
Delicious, absolutely tongue-teasingly delicious.

Hedges Fume Chardonnay, Washington State 1993 13 D

Madrona Late Harvest Riesling 1993 (half bottle) 13.5 C
Weeps with sweet fruit.

Murphy-Goode Fume Blanc Dry Sauvignon Blanc 1993 15 E
Lush hints of bruising fruitiness which feels elegant on the finish.

FORTIFIED WINE

Quinta do Crasto 1985 17.5 G
Beautiful, with a stunning finish. Quite exceptional.

Quinta do Crasto Late Bottled Vintage 1988 16 E
Gorgeous ripe fruit – like figs baked in the sun and overflowing with flavour.

Quinta do Noval 1970 16 H
Chocolate fruit of great richness.

Sandemans 1970   15   H
Wallow in it.

SPARKLING WINE/CHAMPAGNE

Ariston Brut Champagne   14   G
Pleasant.

Champagne Henriot Blanc de Blancs   14   G
Palatial.

Champagne Le Brun de Neville Brut   14   G
Polished.

Chardonnay Vin Mousseux (France)   13   D
Peachy.

Dom Ruinart 'R' Champagne Brut   12   H
Pale.

Eliseo Chardonnay, Chiarli (Italy)   10   B

Gloria Ferrer Brut (California)   12   F
Pooh.

Henri Macquart Champagne Brut   15   F
Positive.

Henriot Brut Champagne   10   G
Pallid.

Nicholas Feuillate Champagne Blanc de Blancs `14` `G`

Potent.

Quartet, Roederer Estate California `10` `F`

Pricey.

Ruggeri Prosecco, Spago Frizzante (Italy) `13` `D`

Seaview Brut (Australian) `14` `D`

Prim.

STOP PRESS

MAJESTIC

AUSTRALIAN WINE   RED

Tasmania Wine Company Pinot Noir 1991
Certainly gamier in the fruit department and more attractive
aromatically than many a red burgundy.

AUSTRALIAN WINE   WHITE

Seaview McLaren Vale Chardonnay 1994
Fruity and full but not overripe. Delicious with fish and
chicken dishes.

FRENCH WINE   RED

**Baron Philippe de Rothschild Cabernet
Sauvignon VdP d'Oc 1994**
Words fail me as inspiration failed the wine-maker.

**Baron Philippe de Rothschild Merlot VdP
d'Oc 1994**
What really gets my goat about a wine like this is that some poor
sap will see the name on the label and be impressed. Overpriced
ordinaire.

Chateau Teyssier St Emilion 1993   13   E

Dry, and needs 3 years more to soften and develop.

Chenas Domaine des Pierres 1994   10   D

Cotes du Rhone Rose Levallin 1994   12   C

Domaine de Montauberon Syrah 1994   11   C

Hairy beast.

FRENCH WINE   WHITE

Baron Philippe de Rothschild Chardonnay VdP d'Oc 1994   11   C

Faint glimmerings of varietal interest but they flicker rather than flame. Absurd price.

Baron Philippe de Rothschild Sauvignon VdP d'Oc 1994   10   C

It insults ditchwater to categorise this wine as so dull.

Chardonnay de Bourgogne Dufouleur Pere et Fils 1993   11   D

Chateau de Chamirey Mercurey 1992   10   E

Barely rates 10, so dull is it. And it costs a tenner! Scandalous!

Chateau de Montfort Vouvray 1992   11   C

Macon Davaye Domaine de la Croix Senailles 1994   13   D

Not bad, but what a price to pay for a not bad wine when terrific £2.99 chardonnays exist.

Saint-Veran Jacques Depargneux 1994

Struggles at this price to dazzle the wine rater with drinkers' interest at heart.

Tete de Cuvee Blanche de Bosredon
Bergerac Blanc Sec 1993

Starts well, but finishes not so gamely.

GERMAN WINE WHITE

Niersteiner Brudersberg Riesling Spatlese,
Heyl zu Herrnsheim 1993 (half bottle)

Ravishing fruit which is outside my catalogue of fruit analogies. Coffee and walnuts? Something like this haunts the finish of this beautifully poised and crafted wine. It will reach 20 points by AD 2000.

Niersteiner Brudersberg Riesling Spatlese
Trocken, Heyl zu Herrnsheim 1993
(half bottle)

Not as effective as the conventional spatlese version above.

Rudesheimer Drachenstein Riesling
Halbtrocken Georg Breuer 1993

Will time make it better value? Sharpen the fruit? Vivify the style? I have no idea.

Scharzhof Riesling, Egon-Muller Scharzhof
1994

Schlossbockelheimer Kupfergruber
Riesling Kabinett 1994

Fruit and acid still arguing the toss but they will be perfectly married in 5 years or so.

Silvaner Trocken Niersteiner Rosenberg, Heyl zu Herrnstein 1994

I suspect this may be a little corker in some years time. But it's a faint suspicion.

Wachenheimer Schenkenbohl Riesling Kabinett 1989

Petrol tones from under the rich blanket of fruit and acid. A lovely complex aperitif.

Wiltinger Braune Kupp Kabinett, Egon-Muller Scharzhof 1994

13 E

Delicate and an expensive delicacy at that – but wait 7/8 years and 17 points will emerge.

ITALIAN WINE   RED

Clemente VII Chianti Classico 1991
10 C

Dull.

Negroamaro de Salento, 'Le Trulle' 1994
14 C

Such soft fruit with a concentrated finish. Excellent balance, style, flavour and price.

ITALIAN WINE   WHITE

Chardonnay del Salento Vigneto di Caramia 1994

Rich and ready for anything: salmon, grilled chicken, noodles, duck. It has elegance and subdued power. Classy.

Frascati Superiore 1994

Simple clean fun – like badminton. Not quite as lively but reasonably fresh and fruity.

Soave Cantina delle Terre 1994

Good nutty fruit here. Good with grilled sardines.

PORTUGUESE WINE RED

Bright Brothers Estremadura 1994

Soft, savoury, enticing – but a little lacking for a four-quid wine.

PORTUGUESE WINE WHITE

Joao Pires Muscat 1994

Delicious, musky, sensual aperitif. Or drink it with scallops served with a puree of minted peas.

SOUTH AFRICAN WINE RED

Backsberg Klein Babylonstoren 1992

Good soft tannins to rich-edged soft fruit.

Backsberg Shiraz 1991

Finishing sweet.

SPANISH WINE RED

Principe de Viana Cabernet Sauvignon 1991 `14` `C`

Solid, impactful, savoury and serious. Good with roast meat, vegetables and cheese dishes.

Ribera del Duero Balbas 1994 `13` `D`

Pleasant enough but not at seven quid.

Torres Gran Sangredetoro 1989 `14.5` `D`

Has aplomb and class, good balance and texture. Deliciously thought-provoking, complex, subtle. Has greatly improved since first tasted.

Vina Azabache Garnacha 1994 `13.5` `C`

Juicy, fruity, soft, gluggable, hearty, friendly – but it's a £2.99 wine!

Vinas de Vero Pinot Noir 1991 `10` `D`

Six quid for such loose pinot? Outrageous.

SPANISH WINE WHITE

Principe de Viana Chardonnay 1994 `13` `C`

The fruit isn't quite up to the wood.

Vinas del Vero Chardonnay Barrel Fermented, 1993 `13.5` `D`

Good with rich fish, I guess.

USA WINE — RED

Creston Vineyard Zinandel, Paso Robles 1991 | 12.5 | C

Simple black cherry fruit. A most curiously unambitious zin, but good for beginners.

Napa North Mourvedre 1994 | 14 | D

Chocolate coating to the rich dark savoury fruit. Delicious.

ZIMBABWEAN WINE — RED

Mukuya Estate Merlot 1995 | 12.5 | C

Soft dark fruit of minor interest to merlot lovers but the rest of us might find the wine amusing to drink with pasta.

ZIMBABWEAN WINE — WHITE

Mukuya Estate Chenin Blanc 1995 | 14 | B

Brisk, modern and fruity with a crisp finish to the soft fruit. A thoroughly gluggable wine.

SPARKLING WINE/CHAMPAGNE

Gloria Ferrer Brut, Sonoma County (USA) | 13 | E

A cava house makes this in California but charges a lot more than cava and doesn't get quite so much attractive fruit.

Quartet, Anderson Valley (USA) [13.5] [F]

A hint of a meaty edge gives this rather expensive wine great smoked fish compatibility.

Rosemount Brut (Australia) [15] [E]

Delicious gentle bubbly with a classy structure and real poise: the supple fruit and gentle acid are nigh perfect.

ODDBINS

Baileys Shiraz 1993

It's like a quirky, soupier Cotes du Rhone but wilder. Blackberries, plums and violets with a dry edge of savoury fruitiness make this a marvellous, big wine to enjoy with heavy food.

Coldstream Hills Pinot Noir   14   E

Good warmth of attack on the nose (you wrinkle in pleasure at the gaminess of the smell) and the fruit is pleasantly wild strawberry/raspberry tinged. Expensive treat for pinot freaks.

Coldstream Hills Reserve Pinot Noir 1993   12   F

Deeper bouquet than the non-reserve and richer fruit but the finish is not, sadly, as positive. It's wishy-washy. Not then a better wine for more money. Thus, it rates less.

Lenswood St George Vineyard Coonawarra
Cabernet Sauvignon 1991

A soft, rich cabernet of cushy leather texture and bright brambly fruit. Undoubtedly classy, it will improve for several years.

Lindemans Limestone Ridge Vineyards
Coonawarra Shiraz/Cabernet 1991   16   F

Screamingly rich, high-pitched finish of a concentration the years can only thicken. Certainly a wine for AD 2000 but also for now: it's velvet cassis with hardly a harsh tannic note anywhere.

Lindemans Pyrus Coonawarra 1991 `15.5` `F`

A cabernet sauvignon, merlot, malbec, cabernet franc ensemble which is typical Lindemans at this level: ripe, rich and very pushy on the finish. A touch too self-consciously ripe? I'd like to see how it tastes in 2/3 years.

On flavour alone the two wines above rate high. But their gloss and polish mask a contempt for real character. The nigh on £12 price tags for each are seriously absurd and they will not improve massively with age. They are *too* smooth to offer a fit for food. To hike them to the table is to wear silk to mine coal.

AUSTRALIAN WINE   WHITE

Lenswood Chardonnay 1993 `14` `E`

High price but it's a crafted chardonnay of old world temperament and New World ripe fruit. Has a feel of a quirky high class montrachet but then wallops you with Oz flavour.

Mitchelton Goulburn Valley Riesling 1994 `14` `C`

Muted in its final flourish of rich fruit and quiet acidity, but a delicious aperitif wine.

W. W. McLaren Vale Chardonnay 1994 `15` `C`

A delicate shell of flavour under a rich, enveloping middle of ripe melony fruit which finishes firmly. In the modern mould with classic hints.

CHILEAN WINE RED

Concha y Toro Syrah 1995

Oh you beauty! Raven-haired and pouting, full of fire and unabashed fruit, this is a velvet-textured wine of inimitable immediacy.

Santa Carolina Red Wine 1994

Simple, fruity, even a touch elegant. But good glugging at what must be the lowest level, pricewise, Chile reds reach.

CHILEAN WINE WHITE

Concha y Toro Sauvignon Blanc 1995

Complex, vivid, vibrant, exotic (but not weird), this is a stunning wine which makes the tastebuds ache with pleasure.

Santa Carolina Chardonnay 1995

Melon (ogen), fresh lemon peel and a hint of pineapple all knitted into a rich, textured wine of such deliciousness it soothes the most savage breast.

Santa Carolina Sauvignon Blanc 1995

Good fruit and balance, not as crisp or concentrated as some past vintages, but superbly likable.

FRENCH WINE   WHITE

J & F Lurton Domaine des Salices
Sauvignon 1994   `13.5` `C`

Fails to rate 14 because of the price not the fruit. It really is a
simply delicious £2.99 wine.

ITALIAN WINE   RED

Lamaoine, Tenuta di Castelgiocondo
Montalcino Merlot 1992   `13.5` `E`

Difficult to dislike (price apart) for it is a rich merlot of soft
concentrated savouriness and depth of fruit. But it is at least
twice the price it should be.

SOUTH AFRICAN WINE   RED

Woodlands Pinot Noir 1994   `11` `D`

Feeble and even a touch coarse.

THRESHER
UNWINS
WINE CELLAR

SPANISH WINE
RED

Torres Gran Sangredetoro 1989

Has aplomb and class, good balance and texture. Deliciously thought-provoking, complex, subtle. Has greatly improved since first tasted.

VICTORIA WINE

FRENCH WINE WHITE

Chateau Terres Douces Oak Aged
Bordeaux Blanc

Very classy Fruit, beautifully balanced in really classy Bordeaux
style.